ST. MARY'S COLLEGE OF MARYLAND LIBRARY
ST. MARY'S CITY, MARYLAND

THE GREAT POETS OF ITALY

LORENZO DE MEDICI

THE GREAT POETS OF ITALY

TOGETHER WITH
A BRIEF CONNECTING SKETCH
OF ITALIAN LITERATURE

BY

OSCAR KUHNS

WITH PORTRAITS

Essay Index Reprint Series

BOOKS FOR LIBRARIES PRESS
FREEPORT, NEW YORK

First Published 1903
Reprinted 1969

STANDARD BOOK NUMBER:
8369-1146-6

LIBRARY OF CONGRESS CATALOG CARD NUMBER:
75-86767

PRINTED IN THE UNITED STATES OF AMERICA

To the Memory of my Brother

HENRY CLARENCE KUHNS

whose unfailing kindness alone made possible for me an academic career. His heart was gentle and filled with unselfish love for others; and the conduct of his life was such that those who knew him best, know of a surety that he is now among those blessed dead who have died in the Lord.

με μάλιστα καθίκετο πένθος ἄλαστον.   ODYSSEY I., 342.

PREFACE

THE body of this book formed the second part of a volume on the Latin and Italian poets, prepared, in collaboration with Professor F. J. Miller, of Chicago University, for the Chautauqua Literary and Scientific Circle (1901-1902). In rearranging this material for a wider public, two new chapters have been added, while extensive changes have been made in the rest of the book. Being in Italy when the chapters on Dante were written, I found myself unable to procure a copy of Rossetti's or Norton's translation of the "New Life," and was thus obliged to make my own version of the passages quoted from that work.

I desire to thank the following publishers for their courtesy in allowing me to use the various translations quoted in this book: Houghton, Mifflin & Co. (Longfellow's translation of the "Divine Comedy"), D. Appleton & Co., Dodd, Mead & Co., John Lane, F. A. Stokes Co., Harper & Brothers.

OSCAR KUHNS.

MIDDLETOWN, CONN., *October* 28, 1903.

CONTENTS

CHAPTER		PAGE
I.	The Origins of Italian Literature	1
II.	Dante: His Life and Minor Works	27
III.	The Divine Comedy	54
IV.	Petrarch and Boccaccio	117
V.	The Renaissance	157
VI.	Ariosto	188
VII.	Tasso	215
VIII.	The Period of Decadence and the Revival	251
IX.	The Nineteenth Century	284

LIST OF ILLUSTRATIONS

	PAGE
LORENZO DE MEDICI (page 179) . . Frontispiece	
From the painting by Giorgio Vasari in Uffizi Gallery, Florence.	
DANTE	28
From the death mask in "The Original Portraits of Dante," by Charles Eliot Norton.	
PETRARCH	120
From the fresco by Andrea Castagno.	
BOCCACCIO	146
From the fresco by Andrea Castagno.	
POLITIAN	174
From the engraving by P. Caronni.	
MICHELANGELO	186
From the painting (attributed to Bugiardini) in the Uffizi Gallery, Florence.	
ARIOSTO	188
From the engraving by Enea Vico.	
TASSO	216
After the painting by Pietro Ermini.	
ALFIERI	264
After the painting by V. Gozzini.	
LEOPARDI	290
After the drawing by G. Turchi.	
CARDUCCI	310
From a photograph.	
FOGAZZARO	340
From a photograph.	

THE GREAT POETS OF ITALY

I

THE ORIGINS OF ITALIAN LITERATURE

Perhaps the first phenomenon that strikes the attention of the student of Italian literature is its comparatively recent origin. In the north and south of France the Old French and Provençal languages had, before the tenth century, begun to develop a literature, which by the end of the twelfth had risen to a high degree of cultivation; indeed, by that time Provençal had attained its highest point, and had already begun to decline. In Italy, however, we cannot trace the beginning of a literature, properly so-called, further back than the thirteenth century.

Among the various causes which may be assigned for this phenomenon, the most important undoubtedly is the fact that the Italians have always looked on themselves as of one race with the ancient

THE GREAT POETS OF ITALY

Romans, and the heirs of all the glorious traditions attached to the names of the heroes, poets, and artists of the Eternal City. In similar manner they regarded Latin as their true mother-tongue, of which the vernacular was a mere corruption. Hence it came to pass that all the literature which we find in Italy before the thirteenth century, and a large proportion of that written in the fourteenth, fifteenth, and sixteenth centuries, was in Latin and not in Italian, which seemed to the writers of those days unworthy of forming the medium of expression in poetry and learning.

This feeling of kinship was a natural one for those who lived in the same cities in which the Romans had lived, surrounded by the imposing ruins of the ancient world, speaking a language which, although essentially a modern one, was still nearer to Latin than French, Provençal or Spanish. For these men the irruptions of the Northern barbarians, — the Goths, the Lombards, and later the Normans, — were only a break in the continuity of the historical development of the Latin race in Italy. This spirit — which explains the popularity and temporary success of Arnold of Brescia, in the twelfth century, and of Cola di Rienzi, in the fourteenth, in their efforts to restore the old forms

ORIGINS OF ITALIAN LITERATURE

of the Roman republic — must be kept constantly in mind, by the student, not only of the political history of Italy, but of its literature and art as well.

Yet this natural feeling does not rest altogether on fact. The Italians of to-day are not the pure descendants of the ancient Romans, but, like the other so-called Latin races, are of mixed origin, more nearly related, it is true, to the Romans, yet in general formed by the same ethnical process as their neighbors.

With the downfall of Rome, Italy, like France and Spain, was overrun by the hordes of German tribes, which, leaving the cold and inhospitable regions of the North, sought for more congenial climes in the sunny South. As the Franks in France, the Visigoths and Vandals in Spain, so the Ostrogoths in Italy, toward the end of the fifth century, conquered and colonized the country, and under Theodoric restored for a brief time an appearance of prosperity. In the sixth century came the Lombards, and after destroying and devastating city and country as far south as Rome, and even beyond, finally settled in upper Italy, now known from them as Lombardy. Several centuries later came the Normans from France and conquered Sicily and the southern extremity of the peninsula. All these peoples were of German origin, and being gradually merged with the conquered race, formed what we now call the Italian people.[1]

It goes without saying that the Latin language was profoundly affected by all these changes. Although the German invaders gradually adopted the civilization of the conquered land, including the language, yet they could not help influencing this civilization and impressing it with their own individual stamp.

With regard to the language, we must bear in mind that even in the time of Vergil and Cicero, Latin had two forms, one the elegant and artificial language of literature, and the other the idiom of the common people, or the vernacular. Many of the peculiar phonetic, grammatical, and syntactical phenomena which characterize the modern Romance languages existed in this so-called " vulgar Latin," long before the fall of Rome, the irruption of the Northern barbarians, and the consequent formation of new nations and new tongues.

All the Romance languages have been derived from this " vulgar Latin," each one being specially

---

[1] In Southern Italy, especially in Sicily, there is a large infusion of Greek and Saracen blood.

ORIGINS OF ITALIAN LITERATURE

influenced by its peculiar environments, and by the various German, Celtic, and other dialects to which it was subjected. Thus the "vulgar Latin" imported by Roman colonists into Gaul, and influenced by the Franks, produced the French language; in the same way "vulgar Latin," plus the various local and foreign influences to which it was subjected in Italy, produced the various dialects of that country, Venetian, Tuscan, Neapolitan, and Sicilian. While literary Latin, although becoming more and more corrupt as the years went by, continued in Italy to be the language of the church, of the courts of law, and of what literature there was, the vernacular — i. e., the various dialects — was used in all the operations of daily life.

We have evidence that this popular tongue must have been in existence as far back as the seventh century, for in Latin public documents dating from that period on, we find occasional words and fragments of phrases, — especially the names of persons and places, — which are marked by the special characteristics of the Italian language. These expressions, embedded in the Latin documents, like pebbles in sand, become more and more numerous as we approach the tenth century, until finally, in the year 960, we meet for the first time

THE GREAT POETS OF ITALY

with a complete Italian sentence, in a legal document concerning the boundaries of a certain piece of property in Capua; four years later we find almost the same formula in a similar document. Toward the end of the eleventh century certain frescoes were painted in the lower church of Saint Clement in Rome, where they may still be seen, and among them is one beneath which is found an explanation in Italian.

In spite of the fact, however, that these monuments of early Italian increase from year to year, they were not numerous before the thirteenth century. The very scarcity of them shows the tenacity with which the people clung to the traditions of Rome, for not only literature, but even public and private documents were written in Latin. This literary tradition never wholly died out in Italy, even in the darkest days of her history. It is true that in the terrible disorders that accompanied the slow agony of dying Rome, a long period of darkness and ignorance set in. The empire was split into two parts and the seat of the emperor was transferred to Constantinople; the Goths and Lombards conquered the north of Italy, the Saracens and Normans the south. All through the Dark Ages Italy was the prey of foreign marauders; the Huns —

ORIGINS OF ITALIAN LITERATURE

those scourges of the nations — came as far as Rome; the Arabs obtained foothold in Sicily, scoured the seas, and even ravaged the Campagna up to the very walls of the Eternal City.

Not only did devoted Italy suffer from outsiders, but discord and civil conflicts rent her very entrails. When Charlemagne was crowned emperor in 800 by Pope Leo III., as a reward for having defended Rome against the incursions of the Lombards, it was thought that the reëstablishment of the Roman empire would bring in a new era of peace and glory. With the death of the great king, however, anarchy once more reigned supreme. His successors in the empire (for the most part weaklings) were kept busy with the affairs of Germany and regarded Italy, "the garden of the empire," as Dante calls it, with indifference. In Italy itself there was no such thing as patriotism or feeling of national unity. The people were oppressed by the nobles, who themselves were in a continual state of warfare with each other. In the eleventh century a new power arose in the form of free cities, chief among them being Venice, Genoa, Pisa, and Florence. These, however, only increased the disorder which already existed; city fought with city, and even within the same walls the various families formed parties and feuds, which led to incessant strife, of which murder, rapine, and arson were the usual concomitants.

No wonder, then, that in the midst of all this anarchy and confusion, Roman civilization almost died out. What the barbarians had spared, the church itself tried to destroy. Having finally triumphed over pagan Rome, it fought pagan civilization; the early Christian fathers looked on art and literature as the work of demons; the clergy were forbidden to read the classic writers except for grammatical purposes, the subject matter being deemed poisonous to the souls of Christians. Even so great a man as Pope Gregory despised classical antiquity. During the long period when Italy was the prey of Saracen and Hun, when pestilence and famine stalked gauntly through the desolated land, civilization sank to its lowest point. Superstition and asceticism held full sway in religion; men sought relief from the sufferings of the life that now is in the contemplation of a new and happier state in the life to come. Hence arose the widespread conviction that God is best pleased with those who despise this life, with all its beauty and pleasure, pride and glory, pomp and power.

In spite of this apparent death, however, a spark of life still existed. Through all this dolorous period, schools could be found, in which a half-barbarous Latin was rudely taught, as being the language of the church. There never was a time when Latin authors were not read to some extent in school and monastery.

With the eleventh century a change for the better began in the intellectual, as well as in the political life of Italy. The rise of cities, the crusades, even the unholy contest between pope and emperor gave new stimulus to the minds of all, and led to the beginning of a new era. The defeat of the German emperors through papal intrigue increased the power of the free cities, which were thus made independent of trans-Alpine over-lordship, and which now began to enter upon that long career of prosperity and intellectual conquest which is the wonder of the student of the mediæval history of Italy.

This intellectual movement of the eleventh century, which gave a new and strong impulse to the study of philosophy and theology, resulted in a rich literature in these departments of learning. Peter Damian, who was of great service to Gregory VII. in his war with the German emperors, became a leader in the study of philosophy and wrote many celebrated works. Other Italian philosophers and theologians, Lanfranc, Anselm, and Peter Lombard, taught in foreign schools. In the thirteenth century Italy produced two of the greatest of the mediæval philosophers, St. Thomas Aquinas and St. Bonaventura. Later the newly founded University of Bologna became the centre of an eager study of law, which resulted in the writing of many books on jurisprudence.

This late and artificial bloom of Latin literature in theology and philosophy brought the necessity of a more satisfactory study of the Latin language itself. Hence many new grammars, rhetorics, and texts were written. In a similar manner the newly awakened interest in science (such as it was) brought in a new class of books, corresponding to our modern encyclopædias. From the twelfth century on, all over Europe, a large number of these compendiums were compiled, containing a summary of all the knowledge of the times; chief among these encyclopædias was the vast Speculum Majus (the Greater Mirror) of Vincent of Beauvais, containing 82 books and 9905 chapters. Very popular, also, were the moral and didactic treatises. Symbolism took possession of all literature. The phenomena of nature became types of religious life — even the writings of pagan antiquity were treated symbolically and made to reveal prophecies of Chris-

ORIGINS OF ITALIAN LITERATURE

tian doctrine; Vergil, in a famous passage, was supposed to have foretold the coming of the Saviour, and even the "Ars Amatoria" of Ovid, "of the earth earthy," if ever poem was, was interpreted in terms of Christian mysticism.

All the above-mentioned literature, however, so far as it existed in Italy before the thirteenth century, was written in Latin; we must dismiss it, therefore, with this brief mention, and pass on to the true subject of this book, Italian literature properly so-called, which, as we have already seen, cannot be said to have existed before the thirteenth century.

One feature which is largely characteristic of all subsequent periods of Italian literature, marks the formative period thereof, that is, a comparative lack of invention and originality, and a spirit of imitation of other literatures, distant either in time or space. In order to trace its early beginnings to their sources, we must go outside the borders of Italy. For nearly two hundred years the south of France had been the home of a large number of elegant lyrical poets, whose fame and influence had spread over all Europe. These troubadours, as they were called, were welcomed not only at the courts of the princes and nobles of Provence, but were

THE GREAT POETS OF ITALY

likewise honored guests in Northern France, Spain, and Italy. The latter country had long been closely connected with the south of France by means of commerce and politics. Hence it was natural for the troubadours to seek the rewards of their art in the brilliant courts of Italy. Toward the end of the twelfth century some of the best known of them, among them the famous Pierre Vidal and Rambaud de Vaqueiras, made their way thither. After the terrible crusade against the Albigenses, — which not only cruelly slaughtered tens of thousands of earnest Christians, but likewise destroyed forever the independence and prosperity of Provence, and thus, by destroying the courts of noble families, put a sudden stop to the flourishing literature, — large numbers of the wandering minstrels came to Northern Italy.

It was not long before their influence began to manifest itself here, first in the north, and later in the south and centre. The North Italian poets began to imitate the troubadours, and soon a considerable body of poetry had been composed by native poets, in the manner and — a phenomenon worthy of note — in the language itself of their Provençal models. This is due to the relationship between the dialects of Northern Italy and Provençal, and also

ORIGINS OF ITALIAN LITERATURE

to the fact that at that time the latter tongue was far more elegant and cultivated than the other Romance languages. This North Italian poetry is always included in the Provençal collections, and the writers are known as troubadours in spite of their Italian nationality. Among the most famous are Bartolomeo Zorzi of Venice, Bonifaccio Calvo of Genoa, and especially Sordello of Mantua, praised by Dante in a famous passage of the Purgatory, and the subject of Browning's well-known poem of the same name.

We see, then, that the above poets belong to the history of Provençal literature, rather than to that of Italian literature. To find the first springs of national poetry in Italy, we must traverse the whole length of the peninsula and arrive at the court of Frederick II. (1194–1250) in Sicily, which at this time was far ahead of the rest of the country in civilization, art, and literature. Frederick himself was a many-sided man, warrior, statesman, lawyer, and scholar, and stands out among his contemporaries, especially in matters of religious tolerance. He welcomed to his court not only the scholars, poets, and artists of Europe, but likewise Arabs, who were at that time in possession of a high degree of culture. He caused many Greek and Arab authors to be translated into Latin, among them Aristotle; he founded the University of Naples; above all, by his own mighty personality, he made a deep impression on the times.

Frederick's ministers were, like himself, men of culture and learning. Chief among them was Pier delle Vigne, statesman and poet, the cause of whose tragic death by his own hand is told by Dante in the "Inferno."[1]

The influence of the troubadours made itself felt in Sicily, about the same time as in Northern Italy, only here the imitation was in the Italian language and not in Provençal. Among the early Sicilian poets who wrote after the manner of the troubadours, was the Emperor Frederick II. himself, his son, Enzo, and Pier delle Vigne. From an æsthetic point of view, this early indigenous poetry is of little interest, but as the beginning of a movement which culminated in the "New Life" and "Divine Comedy" of Dante, it is of very great importance.

It had no originality or freshness, but was a slavish imitation of Provençal models, the conventionalities of which were transported bodily, without any change, except that they were poorer. Love is the only theme, and the type always remains the same.

[1] Canto xiii.

ORIGINS OF ITALIAN LITERATURE

The lover is humble, a feudal vassal of his lady who stands far above him, all beauty and virtue, but a cold and lifeless abstraction. She usually treats her lover with disdain or indifference, while he pours forth the protestations of his love, extols her beauty, and laments her hardness of heart. All these things, repeated countless times, in almost the same language, became monotonous in the Provençal poets, and naturally much more so in their Italian imitators.

This Sicilian school of poetry did not last long; it perished with the downfall of the Hohenstaufens. It found a continuation, however, in middle Italy, especially in the province of Tuscany, which, from this time on, becomes the centre of the literary and artistic life of Italy. The poetry of the court of Frederick had not been written in the Sicilian dialect, but in a sort of court language not very dissimilar to the Tuscan. It is probable that among the poets of the Sicilian school some were Tuscans, and that after the death of Frederick, they returned home, bringing with them the poetical doctrines which they had learned.

However this may be, we find a direct continuation of the movement in Tuscany. We see the same slavish imitation of the troubadours, the same ideas, and the same poetical language and tricks of style. In addition to the influence of the Sicilian school, there was a direct imitation of the Provençal poets; thus Guittone d' Arezzo, the leader of the early Tuscan school, wrote and spoke Provençal, and Dante, in his "Purgatory," introduces the troubadour Arnaut Daniel, as speaking in his native tongue.

One phase of Provençal poetry, the political, had — strangely enough considering the stormy times — not been imitated by the poets at the court of Frederick II. From the first, however, the Tuscans included politics in their poetry, and one of the strongest of Guittone's poems is a song on the battle of Montaperti (1260).

Guittone d' Arezzo is the direct literary ancestor of Dante, and the first original Italian poet. Hence he deserves a word or two even in this brief sketch. He was born in 1230 near Arezzo in Tuscany, hence his name. After a youth spent in the pursuit of pleasure, he was converted, and looking on all things earthly as mere vanities, he left his wife and family and joined the recently founded military-religious order of the Knights of St. Mary. He died at Florence in 1294. In early life he had been gay and dissipated; his last years he spent in the exercises of religious asceticism. These two parts cor-

ORIGINS OF ITALIAN LITERATURE

respond to two phases of his poetry. In the first he was a follower of the Sicilian school and wrote love poetry; in the second he discarded this "foolishness" and wrote political, moral, and theological discussions in verse. His poetry has little æsthetic value, but is important as forming a transition between the early Sicilian school and the group of poets, the greatest member of which was Dante. His writing against earthly love and his praise of heavenly love marks an important change in the development of Italian poetry and opens the path which leads up to "Beatrice" and the "Divine Comedy." The following sonnet to the Virgin Mary gives a good idea of the religious poetry of Guittone.

> Lady of Heaven, the mother glorified
>   Of glory, which is Jesus, — He whose death
>   Us from the gates of Hell delivereth
> And our first parents' error sets aside : —
> Behold this earthly Love, how his darts glide —
>   How sharpened — to what fate — throughout this earth!
>   Pitiful mother, partner of our birth,
> Win these from following where his flight doth guide.
> And O, inspire in me that holy love
>   Which leads the soul back to its origin,
>   Till of all other love the link do fail.
> This water only can this fire reprove, —
>   Only such cure suffice for suchlike sin;
>   As nail from out a plank is struck by nail.[1]

[1] Translated by Rossetti.

THE GREAT POETS OF ITALY

The next important step in this progress is marked by Guido Guinicelli, a learned lawyer and judge of Bologna (situated in the province of Romagna and separated from Tuscany by the Apennines), a city which at that time was the seat of a flourishing university and the centre of a keen intellectual life.

Guinicelli was born about 1220, was prominent in political as well as in literary circles, was banished in 1274, and died in 1276. He was a follower of Guittone, and like him his first poetry was in the manner of the Sicilian school. He changed later and began a new school, the *dolce stil nuovo*, as Dante calls it. The change shows itself especially in the new conception of love, and of its origin, growth, and effects.

The troubadours and their Sicilian imitators declared that love came from seeing, that it entered through the eyes of the beholder, and thence descended to the heart. Guinicelli says, on the contrary, that love does not come from without, but dwells, " as a bird in its nest," in the heart and is an attribute thereof. This is not true, however, of all men, but only of those who are virtuous and good. Only the gentle heart can love, and a noble character is not the effect of love, but its cause.

ORIGINS OF ITALIAN LITERATURE

These sentiments are expressed in the following lines, translated by Rossetti:

>Within the gentle breast Love shelters him,
>   As birds within the green shade of the grove.
>Before the gentle heart, in Nature's scheme,
>   Love was not, or the gentle heart ere Love.
>   For with the sun at once,
>   So sprang the light immediately; nor was
>   Its birth before the sun's.
>   And Love hath its effect in gentleness
>   Of very self; even as
>   Within the middle fire the heat's excess.
>
>The fire of love comes to the gentle heart
>   Like as its virtue to a precious stone;
>To which no star its influence can impart
>   Till it is made a pure thing by the sun:
>   For when the sun hath smit
>   From out its essence that which there was vile,
>   The star endoweth it.
>   And so the heart created by God's breath
>   Pure, true, and clean from guile,
>   A woman, like a star, enamoureth.
>
>In gentle heart Love for like reason is
>   For which the lamp's high flame is fanned and bow'd;
>Clear, piercing bright, it shines for its own bliss;
>   Nor would it burn there else, it is so proud.
>   For evil natures meet
>   With Love as it were water met with fire,
>   As cold abhorring heat.
>   Through gentle heart Love doth a track divine,—
>   Like knowing like; the same
>   As diamond runs through iron in the mine.

THE GREAT POETS OF ITALY

The sun strikes full upon the mud all day:
  It remains vile, nor the sun's worth is less.
" By race I am gentle," the proud man doth say:
  He is the mud, the sun is gentleness.
    Let no man predicate
That aught the name of gentleness should have,
    Even in a king's estate,
Except the heart there be a gentle man's.
    The star-beam lights the wave,—
Heaven holds the star and the star's radiance.

God, in the understanding of high Heaven,
  Burns more than in our sight the living sun:
There to behold His Face unveiled is given;
  And Heaven, whose will is homage paid to One,
    Fulfils the things which live
In God, from the beginning excellent.
    So should my lady give
That truth which in her eyes is glorified.
    On which her heart is bent,
To me whose service waiteth at her side.

My lady, God shall ask, " What daredst thou?
  (When my soul stands with all her acts review'd;)
Thou passedst Heaven, into My sight, as now,
  To make Me of vain love similitude.
    To me doth praise belong,
And to the Queen of all the realm of grace
    Who slayeth fraud and wrong."
Then may I plead : " As though from Thee he came,
    Love wore an angel's face:
Lord, if I loved her, count it not my shame."

ORIGINS OF ITALIAN LITERATURE

Whereas, the love of the troubadours was romantic and chivalrous, the love of Guinicelli was intellectual and philosophical. With him earthly affections become purified and spiritualized. The old repertory of conventional expressions are gradually discarded, and new forms take their place, soon to become conventional in their turn. Love and the poet's Lady remain abstract, but have now a different signification. The Lady is still treated as a perfect being, but she becomes now a symbol of something higher. Love for her leads to virtue and to God; poetry receives an allegorical character, and its real end becomes the inculcation of philosophical truth under the veil of earthly love. The importance of Guinicelli for us is his influence on Dante, for the new school was not continued in Bologna, but found its chief followers in Florence. We are thus led naturally up to the works of the great Florentine poet whom we shall study in the next two chapters.

In the meantime, however, we must cast a brief glance at certain other early phases of Italian literature, which later developed into important branches of poetry and prose.

Northern Italy, as we have seen, had no share in beginning an indigenous lyrical poetry. It did, however, have an early literature of its own, in the form of religious and didactic poetry, for the most part translations from Latin and French originals. In Umbria, the home of St. Francis, and the centre of those waves of religious excitement, which so profoundly affected Italy in the thirteenth century, a popular religious lyric arose. St. Francis himself deserves some mention in literary history, if only, on account of his famous song of praise, which he instructed his followers to sing as they wandered, like spiritual troubadours, through the land. He was no mere ascetic, but loved the beauty of nature and had a tender love for all creatures. Quaintly enough, he was wont to call birds and animals, and even inanimate objects, such as the sun and moon, by the name of brother and sister.[1] Among his followers was Thomas of Celano, who wrote that most solemn and majestic of all Latin hymns, " Dies Irae."

The astonishing popularity and spread of the new order founded by St. Francis can only be explained by the terrible sufferings of the times. All Italy was stirred by deep religious excitement. In 1233, the movement reached its high-water mark. Old and young, high and low, leaving their ordinary

[1] His last words were, " Welcome, sister death."

ORIGINS OF ITALIAN LITERATURE

occupations and business, marched in processions through the land singing pious songs; the country folk streamed to the cities to hear the sermons which were given morning, noon, and night.

About the year 1260, a similar movement started, that of the Flagellants, so-called from their custom of carrying whips with which they lashed themselves in token of repentance. The times were dark and stormy, the never-ending feuds between the papal and imperial parties brought in their train murder and rapine, while famine and pestilence stalked through the land. Suddenly a priest, named Fasani, appeared in Perugia, who said that he had been sent by heaven to prophesy terrible punishments on a sinful world. Once more the processions began, and the aroused and penitent multitudes moved through the land, lashing themselves with whips and singing pious songs.

The literary effect of all this religious excitement was far-reaching, especially important for us in that it prepared the way for Dante, not only by creating the proper atmosphere, but by the production of hymns and visionary journeys into the unseen world. The religious lyrics or hymns, which the multitudes sang, were known as *Laudi*, or songs of praise. They were not the artificial imitation of foreign

THE GREAT POETS OF ITALY

poets, like the early Sicilian and Tuscan poetry, but the genuine product of the soil. They were composed for and sung by the great mass of the people who could not understand Latin. They were spread far and wide and made popular by the Flagellants, and thus became true folk-songs.

The most famous of the writers of these *Laudi* in the thirteenth century was Jacopone da Todi, the story of whose conversion is extremely touching. He was a rich young lawyer of Florence, full of the pride of life. At a certain festivity his wife was killed by an accident, and under her costly garments was found, next to her skin, a hair-shirt, such as was worn by penitents. The tragic death of his wife and this evidence of her religious feelings converted the once proud Jacopone, who joined a religious order and devoted the rest of his life to the service of God.[1] Besides being the author of a

---

[1] Matthew Arnold makes a beautiful application of this story in his sonnet *Austerity of Poetry* —

> That son of Italy who tried to blow,
> Ere Dante came, the trump of sacred song,
> In his light youth amid a festal throng
> Sate with his bride to see a public show.
>
> Fair was the bride, and on her front did glow
> Youth like a star; and what to youth belong —
> Gay raiment, sparkling gauds, elation strong.
> A prop gave way! crash fell a platform! lo,

ORIGINS OF ITALIAN LITERATURE

number of *Laudi* and religious poems, he probably wrote the famous Latin hymn, *Stabat Mater*.

Before we close this chapter we must say a word or two concerning another branch of early literature whose influence is not great on Dante or his immediate successors, but which was destined to bloom forth later in a new kind of poetry, which has become the peculiar glory of Italy. The introduction into Italy of the French national heroic epic (the *chansons de geste*) began about the same time as the introduction of the Provençal lyric. In Northern Italy these romances were not only read but imitated, and about the second half of the thirteenth century, arose a mongrel sort of literature, written in a language half French, half Italian. The most popular of these poems were those dealing with Charlemagne, who, as the protector of the pope and the restorer of the Roman empire, was looked upon by the Italians as one of their own race. These old *chansons de geste*, however, in coming to Italy, lost much of their original signifi-

> 'Mid struggling sufferers, hurt to death, she lay;
> Shuddering they drew her garments off — and found
> A robe of sackcloth next the smooth white skin.
> Such, poets, is your bride, the Muse! young, gay,
> Radiant, adorn'd outside; a hidden ground
> Of thought and of austerity within.

THE GREAT POETS OF ITALY

cance. The spirit and ideals could scarcely be understood by the Italians, to whom feudal society was largely unknown. What they liked in the French romances was not religious or patriotic sentiments, but adventures and the wonderful deeds of the heroes. The object, then, of the rude early writers of the Franco-Italian epic was to interest their hearers and arouse curiosity. Hence they became monopolized by wandering minstrels, who sang in the streets and public squares to the people who gathered about them, much as their descendants gather about the Punch and Judy shows and the wandering musicians of to-day. For nearly two hundred years the French romances existed in Italy in this humble state, until, as we shall see later, they were incorporated into regular literature by Pulci, Boiardo, and Ariosto.[1]

[1] For the early period of Italian literature, the best authority is Gaspary, who wrote in German, but the first volume of whose work has just been translated into English, and published in the Bohn Library. An indispensable book is Rossetti's *Dante and his Circle*, which contains many excellent translations from the early poets of Italy.

II

DANTE: HIS LIFE AND MINOR WORKS

IN the preceding chapter we have outlined the development of early Italian poetry, endeavoring to show how from the Sicilian school it was carried over to Central Italy; how Guido Guinicelli, in Bologna, had transformed it from a slavish imitation of the troubadours into a new school of symbolical philosophical poetry, and finally, how from Bologna the new doctrines spread to Tuscany.

There were a number of early poets of Florence and other Tuscan cities who wrote in the manner of Guido Guinicelli, among the best known being Cino da Pistoia, Lapo Gianni, Dante da Majano, and, especially worthy of note, Guido Cavalcanti. The latter, who was the intimate friend of Dante, was a member of a noble family, and was prominent in all the intellectual and poetical life of Florence. He was among those who were exiled from the city in 1300, and died soon after his re-

THE GREAT POETS OF ITALY

turn in the same year. Dante refers to him in the "New Life" as the "first of his friends," and records in the Inferno a pathetic interview with his father in the city of Dis. To him and a mutual friend Lapo, he addressed the following beautiful sonnet, so well translated by Shelley:—

> Guido, I would that Lapo, thou and I,
> Led by some strong enchantment, might ascend
> A magic ship, whose charmèd sails should fly,
> With winds at will where'er our thoughts might wend,
> And that no change, nor any evil chance
> Should mar our joyous voyage; but it might be,
> That even satiety should still enhance
> Between our hearts their strict community;
> And that the bounteous wizard then would place
> Vanna and Bice and my gentle love,
> Companions of our wandering, and would grace
> With passionate talk, wherever we might rove,
> Our time, and each were as content and free
> As I believe that thou and I should be.

As a sample of Guido Cavalcanti's own poetical skill we may take the following sonnet, translated by Cary:—

> Whatso is fair in lady's face or mind,
>   And gentle knights caparison'd and gay,
> Singing of sweet birds unto love inclined,
>   And gallant barks that cut the watery way;
> The white snow falling without any wind,
>   The cloudless sky at break of early day

DANTE

DANTE: LIFE AND MINOR WORKS

> The crystal stream, with flowers the meadow lined,
>   Silver, and gold, and azure for array;
> To him that sees the beauty and the worth
>   Whose power doth meet and in my lady dwell,
>   All seem as vile, their price and lustre gone.
> And, as the heaven is higher than the earth,
>   So she in knowledge doth each one excel,
>   Not slow to good in nature like her own.

It is with Dante alone, however, that we can busy ourselves here, for in him are summed up all the various tendencies and characteristics of his predecessors and contemporaries.

The figure of Dante Alighieri is one of the saddest in literary history; his life seemed to contain all the sorrow that can fall to the lot of humankind. An exile from his native city, separated from family and friends, deprived of his property, and thus forced to live in poverty or become the recipient of charity, disappointed in his patriotic hopes, the only thing left him to do was to turn his eyes inward and to build up out of his very sufferings and sorrow, his immortal poem: —

> Ah! from what agony of heart and brain,
>   What exultations trampling on despair,
>   What tenderness, what tears, what hate of wrong,
>   What passionate outcry of a soul in pain,
>   Uprose this poem of the earth and air, —
>   This mediæval miracle of song.

THE GREAT POETS OF ITALY

We see, then, that even more important than in the case of other poets is some knowledge of the life of the great Florentine.

Unfortunately we have not a reliable and complete record of that life. Legend and fancy have been interwoven with facts so closely that often it is hard to separate one from the other. The following data, however, are well-established. Dante Alighieri was born in Florence in the year 1265, the day and month being uncertain, but probably falling between May 18th and June 17th. He belonged to a family which was counted among the lesser nobility. Dante himself does not seem to have been able to trace his ancestry further back than four generations. In the fifteenth Canto of " Paradiso " there is a famous passage where the poet tells how he meets in Mars his great-great-grandfather, Cacciaguida, who gives him certain autobiographical details: that he was baptized at the church of San Giovanni in Florence; that he had two brothers; that his wife (from whom the family drew the name of Alighieri) came from the Po Valley; that he had gone on the crusades with the Emperor Conrad, by whom he had been dubbed knight; and finally, that he had been killed by the Arabs. This is as far back as Dante could trace

DANTE: LIFE AND MINOR WORKS

his ancestry, as is evident from the words of Cacciaguida: —

> My ancestors and I our birthplace had
> > Where first is found the last ward of the city
> > By him who runneth in your annual game.[1]
> Suffice it of my elders to hear this;
> > But who they were, and whence they thither came,
> > Silence is more considerate than speech.

Of Dante's immediate family we know little, for, strangely enough in one who reveals himself so completely in his poetry, he says nothing of either father or mother. As to his education, we can only infer it from his works and the condition of the times. The statements made by Boccaccio and Villani concerning his early school life are fables. He did not go to school under Brunetto Latini, for the latter had no school; although Dante was undoubtedly influenced by Latini's "Tresor" (a vast encyclopedical compilation of contemporary knowledge) which laid the foundations of the poet's learning. Moreover, it may well be that the distinguished statesman, judge, and writer directed by his personal counsel the studies of the bright young scholar, for whom he prophesied a brilliant career.

[1] The house in which Cacciaguida was born stood in the Mercato Vecchio, or Old Market, at the beginning of the last ward or *sesto* of Florence toward the east, called the Porta San Pietro.

THE GREAT POETS OF ITALY

Hence Dante's joy and gratitude at meeting in the "Inferno" the "dear paternal image of him who had taught him how man becomes eternal."

It is certain that Dante studied the regular curriculum of mediæval education, the so-called seven liberal arts, consisting of the Quadrivium and the Trivium.[1] He knew Latin, but no Greek — he quotes frequently Vergil, Horace, Statius, and others. He was a profound student of philosophy and theology; loved art, music, and poetry. In the "Divine Comedy" he shows a wide knowledge, embracing practically all the science and learning of the times. All this he largely taught himself, especially in his early life. Later he visited the universities of Padua and Bologna, and probably Paris. It is quite unlikely, however, that he got as far as Oxford, as Mr. Gladstone endeavored to prove some years ago. He was not unacquainted with military life, having been present at the battle of Campaldino and at the surrender of Caprona.

He was married before 1298 to Gemma Donati, and thus became related to one of the most powerful families in Florence. Here again he shows a

---

[1] The Quadrivium included arithmetic, geometry, astronomy, and music; the Trivium, grammar (i. e., Latin), dialectics and rhetoric.

strange reticence, never mentioning his wife or children. We have no reason, however, to believe his marriage unhappy, or that he lacked affection for his children.

It is true that his wife did not follow him in exile, but there was reason enough for this in his poverty and wandering life. The apotheosis of Beatrice need not presuppose lack of conjugal affection, for his love for her was entirely Platonic and became later a mere symbol of the spiritual life. He had by Gemma several children, two sons, Pietro and Jacopo, and one daughter, Beatrice; that he had another daughter, named Antonia, is probable, but not certain. His children joined him later in life in Ravenna.

Of the greatest importance for the understanding of the "Divine Comedy" is a knowledge of the political doctrines and of the public life of Dante. Tuscany at that time was in a wild and stormy condition. It shared in the terrible disorders of the struggle between the Guelphs and Ghibellines (the former supporting the pope, the latter the emperor). It likewise had private quarrels of its own. The old feudal nobility had been repressed by the rise of the cities, into which the nobles themselves had migrated, and where they kept up an incessant series of quarrels among themselves or with the free citizens. Yet, in spite of this constant state of warfare, the cities of Tuscany increased in power and prosperity, especially Florence. We need only remember that at the time Dante entered public life (1300) an extraordinary activity manifested itself in all branches of public works; new streets, squares, and bridges were laid out and built; the foundations of the cathedral had been laid, and Santa Croce and the Palazzo Vecchio had been begun. Such extensive works of public improvement presuppose a high degree of prosperity and culture. The political condition of Florence itself at this time was something as follows: In 1265 (to go back a few years in order to get the proper perspective), Charles of Anjou, brother of the king of France, had been called by Pope Urban IV. to Italy to aid him in his war against the house of Swabia; and through him the mighty imperial family of the Hohenstaufens, which had counted among its members Frederick Barbarossa and Frederick II., was destroyed. Manfred, the natural son of Frederick II., was killed at the battle of Beneventum (1266), and his nephew, the sixteen-year-old Conradin, the last member of the family, was betrayed into the hands of Charles after the battle of Tagliacozza and

DANTE: LIFE AND MINOR WORKS

brutally beheaded in the public square of Naples (1268). It was through Charles of Anjou that the Ghibellines, who, having been banished from Florence in 1258, had returned after the battle of Montaperti in 1260, were once more driven from the city, and that the Guelphs, that is, the supporters of the pope, were restored to power.

The government was subject to frequent changes, becoming, however, more and more democratic in character. The decree of Gian della Bella had declared all nobles ineligible to public office, and had granted the right to govern to those only who belonged to a guild or who exercised a profession. It was undoubtedly to render himself eligible to office that Dante joined the guild of physicians. In 1300 he was elected one of the six priors who ruled the city for a period of two months only. From this brief term of office Dante himself dates all his later misfortunes.

At this time, in addition to the two great parties of Guelphs and Ghibellines, which existed in Florence as in the rest of Italy, there were in the city two minor parties, which at first had nothing to do with papal or imperial politics. These parties, known as Whites and Blacks, came from Pistoia, over which Florence exercised a sort of protectorate. The rulers of the latter city tried to smooth out the quarrels of the above local factions of Pistoia, by taking the chiefs of both parties to themselves; but the quarrels continued in Florence, and soon the whole city was drawn into the contest, the Blacks being led by Corso Donati, and the Whites by the family of the Cerchi.

Pope Boniface VIII., who claimed Tuscany as the heir of the Countess Matilda, endeavored to take advantage of the state of discord in order to further his own selfish plans. For this purpose he sent the Cardinal Acquasparta to Florence, who, failing to accomplish his mission, excommunicated the recalcitrant city and left it in a rage. At this juncture the Priors, of whom, as we have seen, Dante was one, thought to still the discord by banishing the leaders of the Whites and Blacks, — an act, however, which only served to bring the hatred of both parties on the heads of the magistrates.

In 1301 Charles of Valois was called to Florence, ostensibly to pacify the divided city; he favored the party of the Blacks, however, and let in Corso Donati, who had been exiled the year before, and for five days murder, fire, and rapine raged through the streets of the devoted city. All the Whites who

DANTE: LIFE AND MINOR WORKS

were not slain were exiled and their property confiscated or destroyed. Among the exiled was Dante. There are several decrees against him still extant in the archives of Florence. The first is dated January 27, 1302, and accuses him, with several others, of extortion, bribery, defalcation of public money, and hostility to the pope and the church. We need not say that of all these accusations the latter alone was true. In case the accused did not appear before the court to answer the charges, they were condemned, in contumacy, to pay a fine of five hundred gold florins; if this was not paid within three days, their property should be confiscated. This decree was followed by another, on March 10, 1302, in which the same charges were repeated, and in which Dante, as a delinquent, was declared an outlaw, and condemned to be burned alive if ever caught within Florentine territory.

Thus begins the poignant story of Dante's exile. We know but few definite details of that long period of wandering. He himself says, in his "Banquet," that he traveled all over Italy, "a pilgrim, almost a beggar."

In the seventeenth Canto of "Paradise," already mentioned, Cacciaguida gives a brief summary of Dante's exile in the form of a prophecy: —

THE GREAT POETS OF ITALY

As forth from Athens went Hippolytus,
    By reason of his step-dame false and cruel,
    So thou from Florence must perforce depart.
Already this is willed, and this is sought for;
    And soon it shall be done by him who thinks it,[1]
    Where every day the Christ is bought and sold.
The blame shall follow the offended party
    In outcry as is usual; but the vengeance
    Shall witness to the truth that doth dispense it.
Thou shalt abandon everything beloved
    Most tenderly, and this the arrow is
    Which first the bow of banishment shoots forth.
Thou shalt have proof how savoureth of salt
    The bread of others, and how hard a road
    The going down and up another's stairs.
And that which most shall weigh upon thy shoulders
    Will be the bad and foolish company
    With which into this valley thou shalt fall;
For all ingrate, all mad and impious
    Will they become against thee; but soon after
    They, and not thou, shall have the forehead scarlet.
Of their bestiality, their own proceedings
    Shall furnish proof: so 't will be well for thee
    A party to have made thee by thyself.
Thine earliest refuge and thine earliest inn
    Shall be the mighty Lombard's courtesy,
    Who on the Ladder bears the holy bird,
Who such benign regard shall have for thee
    That 'twixt you twain, in doing and in asking,
    That shall be first which is with others last.

[1] Pope Boniface VIII. in Rome.

DANTE: LIFE AND MINOR WORKS

We see from these lines that Dante first went to Verona, the seat of Bartolommeo della Scala (the " great Lombard," whose coat of arms was a ladder (" scala ") with an eagle perched upon it. From there he went to Bologna, thence to Padua, and thence to the Lunigiana. It is about this time that he is said to have gone to Paris (this is probable), and to Germany, Flanders, and England; it is not at all probable that he ever saw the last-mentioned place.

Dante never gave up altogether the hope that he might one day return to Florence. He yearned all his life for the " beautiful sheep-fold " where he had lived as a lamb. Yet even this happiness he would not accept at the price of dishonor. When, in 1312, a general amnesty was proclaimed by Florence, and he might have returned if he would consent to certain humiliating conditions, he wrote the following noble words to a friend in Florence: —

This is not the way of coming home, my father! Yet, if you or other find one not beneath the fame of Dante and his honor, that will I gladly pursue. But if by no such way can I enter Florence, then Florence shall I never enter. And what then! Can I not behold the sun and the stars from every spot of earth ? Shall I not be able to meditate on the sweetest truths in every place beneath the sky, unless I make myself ignoble, yea, ignominious to the people and state of Florence ? Nor shall bread be wanting.

THE GREAT POETS OF ITALY

A great hope rose above the horizon of his life when Henry VII., of Luxemburg, came to Italy to restore the ancient power of the empire. Dante's letters written at this time are couchéd in exultant, almost extravagant, language: "Rejoice, O Italy," he cried, "for thy bridegroom, the comfort of the world, and the glory of the people, the most merciful Henry, the divine Augustus and Cæsar is hastening hither to the wedding feast." His joy and exultation, alas! were doomed to a speedy end.

In 1312 Henry, who, after the murder of Albert, had been crowned emperor (in 1309), came to Pisa, thence to Rome. Then, after having in vain besieged Florence, which had become the leader of the anti-imperial movement, he retired to Buonconvento, where he died (probably from poison) August 24, 1313.

With the tragic death of Henry, Dante seems to have given up all hope of earthly happiness and from now on turned his eyes to heaven, from which alone he could hope for justice to himself and peace and righteousness for unhappy Italy. The composition of the "Divine Comedy" dates from this period. His final refuge and place of rest was at Ravenna, at the court of Guido da Polenta, uncle of Francesca da Rimini, whose pathetic story is quoted in the next chapter. Here, in comparative comfort and peace, he spent the evening of his life, occupying his time in writing the " Divine Comedy " and in occasional journeys, in the interest of his patron. In 1321, while on one of these journeys to Venice, he caught fever and died on the 13th of September of that year.

Many anecdotes and legends are told of these years of exile. Thus it is said that while in Verona, as he was walking one day through the streets, some women saw him and said: " Behold, there is the man who has been in hell." A beautiful story is told in a letter, doubtful, however, written by Fra Ilario of the Monastery of Santa Croce on Monte Corvo, to the effect that one day a dust-stained, travel-worn man, carrying a roll of manuscript under his arm, knocked at the door of the monastery, and on being asked what he wanted, answered " pace, pace " (peace, peace). This legend has been beautifully rendered by Longfellow in the following lines: —

> Methinks I see thee stand with pallid cheeks
> By Fra Ilario in his diocese,
> As on the convent walls in golden streaks
> The ascending sunbeams mark the day's decrease.

THE GREAT POETS OF ITALY

And as he asks what there the stranger seeks
Thy voice along the cloisters whispers " peace."

Dante's character reveals itself in all its phases in his works. His youth as represented in the "New Life" was a happy one, filled with ardor for study, with affection for friends, and with the ecstasy of a pure and virtuous love. He needed, however, the death of Beatrice, the long years of exile, and the disappointment of all his hopes to develop that strong and noble character which the world admires almost as much as his poetry. He was an enthusiastic student, yet mingled with the affairs of men; never willingly doing wrong himself, he was unyielding in what he conceived to be right, and consecrated his consummate powers to the cause of the noble and the good. His own conscience was clear, and under this "breastplate," as he called it, he went steadily on his way. He was proud of his learning, strong in his opinions, and does not hesitate to constitute himself the stern judge of all his contemporaries; this in a lesser man would have seemed presumptuous; in Dante it was only the prosecution of a solemn and, as he thought, a God-given duty. Yet in spite of this sternness his heart was soft and tender. Like Tennyson's poet, Dante was "dowered with love of

DANTE: LIFE AND MINOR WORKS

love," as well as with " hate of hate and scorn of scorn."

Those who read only the " Inferno " may get the impression of a savage, revengeful spirit; but the " Purgatorio " and " Paradiso " are full of tenderest poetry, of sublimest imagination, and show their author to have had a heart full of love and gentleness, sweetness and light. A deep melancholy weighed over the whole later life of Dante; his heart never ceased to long for home and friends. Yet this melancholy is not pessimism; he never lost his confidence in God, never doubted right would win.

It is this inspiring combination of noble qualities in Dante's reflected character, on every page of the " Divine Comedy,"which makes the study of the latter not merely an æsthetic pleasure, but a spiritual exercise, ennobling and uplifting the minds of those who read it with the " spirit and with the understanding also."

The works of Dante are not many. They consist of prose and poetry, the former comprising the so-called " Banquet " (Convivio) and the essay on " Universal Monarchy " (De Monarchia). The " Banquet " was to have been finished in fifteen books or chapters, but is only a fragment of four. It is a sort of encyclopædia of knowledge, such as were so popular in the Middle Ages, but written in Italian, in order to bring it within the reach of the unlearned reader. It is full of the scholastic learning of the times, and while not attractive to the ordinary reader, is of great importance for a complete understanding of the "Divine Comedy." Likewise important in this respect is the political treatise on the "Monarchy," in which Dante sums up his theory of world-politics. This book, written in Latin, is divided into three parts: in Book I., the author shows the necessity of a universal empire; in Book II., he shows the right of Rome to be the seat of this empire; in Book III., he shows the independence of the emperor in his relations to the pope. This theory of the separation of the church and state runs like a thread through the whole of the "Divine Comedy," in which Dante constantly attributes the sufferings of Italy to the lust for temporal power on the part of the pope and clergy.

For the general reader, however, the most interesting of Dante's writings, after the "Divine Comedy," is the "New Life," a strange and beautiful little book which serves as a prologue to the "Divine Comedy." It is the story of Dante's love for Beatrice Portinari, the daughter of Folco, a neighbor and friend of the poet's father. It is a simple story, containing but few actual events, the details consisting for the most part of repetitions of the theory of love propounded by Guido Guinicelli, of analyses of Dante's own state of mind, and of mystical visions. The form of the book is peculiar, part prose, part poetry, the latter being accompanied by a brief commentary. Yet there is a truth and sincerity in the book which proves that it is no mere allegory or symbol, but the record of an actual love on the part of Dante for the fair young Florentine girl who is its heroine.

Dante tells us in quaint and scholastic language how he first saw Beatrice at a May festival, when she was at the beginning of her ninth year and he was at the end of his. She was dressed in red, with ornaments suited to her youthful age, and was so beautiful "that surely one could say of her the words of the poet, Homer: 'She seemed not the daughter of mortal man but of God.'" He tells us, further, how he felt the spirit of love awaken within him and how, after that first meeting, he sought every opportunity of seeing her again.

Nine years later, again in May, he records another occasion when he met Beatrice; this time dressed in white and accompanied by two ladies, "and passing along the street she turned her eyes toward the place where I stood, very timid, and through her ineffable courtesy she gently saluted me, so that it seemed to me that I experienced all the depths of bliss. The hour was precisely the ninth of that day, and inasmuch as it was the first time that her words reached my ears, such sweetness came upon me that, intoxicated, as it were, with joy, I left the people and went to my solitary chamber, and began to muse upon this most courteous lady." This love, accompanied as it was with violent alternations of joy and sorrow, produced a strong effect on Dante; his health suffered, his nerves were shattered, and he became frail and weak. Yet he refused to tell her name, although he confessed that love was the cause of his sufferings. "And when they ask me by means of whom love brought me to this wretched state, I looked at them with a smile, but said nothing."

In order, however, to put people on the wrong track, he pretended to love another lady, and so successful was this subterfuge, that even Beatrice herself was deceived by it, so that one day, meeting Dante, she refused to salute him, an act which filled him with deepest affliction. "Now after my happiness was denied me, there came upon me so much grief that leaving all people I went my way to a solitary place to bathe the earth with bitterest tears; and when I was somewhat relieved by this weeping, I entered my chamber where I could lament without being heard, and there I began to call on my lady for mercy, and saying: 'Love, help thy faithful one,' I fell asleep in tears like a little, beaten child."

As we have already said, there is little action in this book, only a few meetings in the street, in church, or at funerals; even the death of Beatrice's father is spoken of vaguely and allusively. The importance of all lies in the psychological analysis of feelings and thoughts of the poet. The descriptions of Beatrice are vague, and her figure is wrapped in an atmosphere of " vaporous twilight." Her beauty is not presented to us by means of word-painting, but rather by its effect on all who beheld her. This is illustrated in the following sonnet, which is justly considered the most beautiful not only of Dante's poetry but of all Italian literature: —

> So gentle and so noble doth appear
> My lady when she passes through the street,
> That none her salutation dare repeat
> And all eyes turn from her as if in fear.
> She goes her way, and cannot help but hear
> The praise of all, — yet modest still and sweet;

> Something she seems come down from heaven, — her seat,
> To earth a miracle to show men here.
> So pleasing doth she seem unto the eye,
>   That to the heart a sweetness seems to move,
> A sweetness only known to those who feel;
> And from her lips a spirit seems to steal, —
>   A gentle spirit soft and full of love, —
> That whispers to the souls of all men, — "sigh."

The effect of all these conflicting sentiments which agitated Dante's bosom was to throw him into a serious illness, in the course of which he had a terrible vision of the approaching death of Beatrice. " Now a few days after this, it happened that there came upon me a dolorous infirmity, whence for nine days I suffered most bitter pain; this led me to such weakness that I was not able to move from my bed. I say, then, that on the ninth day, feeling my pain almost intolerable, there came to me a thought concerning my lady. And when I had thought somewhat of her, and turned again in thought to my own weakened life, and considered how fragile is its duration, even though it be in health, I began to weep to myself over so much misery. Whence I said to myself with sighs: verily the most gentle Beatrice must sometime die. Wherefore there came upon me so great a depression that I closed my eyes and began to wander in mind, so that there appeared to me certain faces of ladies with disheveled hair, who said to me, 'Thou also shalt die.' And after these ladies certain other faces, horribly distorted, appeared and said: 'Thou art dead.' Then I seemed to see ladies with disheveled hair going along the street weeping, and wondrous sad; and the sun grew dark, so that the stars showed themselves, of such color that methought they wept; and the birds as they flew fell dead; and there were mighty earthquakes; and as I wondered and was smitten with terror in such fancies, methought I saw a friend come to me and say: 'Dost thou not know? Thy peerless lady has departed this life.' Then I began to weep very piteously, and not only in dream, but bathing my cheeks in real tears. And I dreamed that I looked skyward and saw a multitude of angels flying upwards, and they had before them a small cloud, exceedingly white.[1] And the angels seemed to be singing gloriously, and the words which I seemed to hear were these: 'Hosanna in the Highest,' and naught else could I hear. Then it seemed to me that my heart, which was so full of love, said to me: 'It is true, indeed, that our lady lies dead.' And so strong was my wandering fancy that it

[1] The soul of Beatrice.

showed me this lady dead; and I seemed to see ladies covering her head with a very white veil, and her face had so great an aspect of humility that she seemed to say: 'I have gone to behold the beginning of peace.' And then I seemed to have returned to my own room, and there I looked toward heaven and began to cry out in tears: 'O, soul most beautiful, how blessed is he who beholds thee.' And as I said these words with sobs and tears, and called on death to come to me, a young and gentle lady who was at my bedside, thinking that my tears and cries were for grief on account of my infirmity began also to weep in great fear. Whereupon other ladies who were in the room, noticed that I wept, and leading away from my bedside her who was joined to me by close ties of blood,[1] they came to me to wake me from my dream, and saying: 'Weep no more,' and again: 'Be not so discomforted.' And as they thus spoke, my strong fancy ceased, and just as I was about to say: 'O, Beatrice, blessed art thou,' and I had already said, 'O Beatrice —' giving a start I opened my eyes and saw that I had been dreaming."

The presentiment of Dante in the above exquisite passage came true. Beatrice, too fair and good

---

[1] Dante's sister.

DANTE: LIFE AND MINOR WORKS

for earth, was called by God to himself. One day the poet sat down to write a poem in praise of her, and had finished one stanza when the news came that Beatrice was dead. At first he seemed too benumbed even for tears, and after a quotation from Jeremiah — " How doth the city sit solitary that was full of people! How is she become a widow! she that was great among the nations," he gives a fantastic discussion of the symbolical figure nine and its connection with the life and death of Beatrice. Then the tears began to flow, and unutterable sadness took possession of his heart. A whole year after he tells us how one day he sat thinking of her and drawing the picture of an angel, a picture, alas! which was never finished as he was interrupted by visitors.[1] At another time he tells how one day he saw a number of pilgrims passing through Florence on their way to Rome, and to them he addressed one of the most beautiful of his sonnets : —

> Oh, pilgrims who move on with steps so slow,
> Musing perchance of friends now far away;

[1] You and I would rather see that angel,
Painted by the tenderness of Dante,
Would we not? than read a fresh " Inferno."
BROWNING (One Word More).

THE GREAT POETS OF ITALY

So distant is your native land, oh say!
As by your actions ye do seem to show?
For lo! you weep and mourn not when you go,
   Through these our city streets, so sad to-day;
   Nor unto us your meed of pity pay,
Bowed as we are 'neath heavy weight of woe.

If while I speak you will but wait and hear, —
Surely, — my heart in sighing whispers me, —
That then you shall go on with sorrow deep.
Florence has lost its Beatrice dear;
And words that tell what she was wont to be,
Are potent to make all that hear them weep.

With these lines the "New Life" practically ends. After one more sonnet, in which he tells how he was lifted in spirit and had a vision of Beatrice in Paradise, he concludes the book with the following paragraph, in which we first see a definite purpose on the part of Dante to write a long poem in praise of Beatrice: "After this sonnet there appeared to me a wonderful vision, in which I saw things which made me resolve to say no more of this blessed one until I should be able to treat more worthily of her, and to come to that I study as much as I can, as she truly knows. So that if it shall be the pleasure of Him in whom all things live that my life endure for some years more, I hope to say of her that which has never yet been said of mortal woman. And then may it please Him who is Lord of Courtesy, that my soul may go to see the glory of its lady, that is, the blessed Beatrice who gloriously looks on the face of Him 'qui est per cuncta sæcula benedictus in sæcula sæculorum.'" (Who is blessed throughout all the ages.)

III

THE DIVINE COMEDY

We have seen, at the end of the last chapter, how Dante had made a vow to glorify Beatrice, as no other woman had ever been glorified, and how he studied and labored to prepare himself for the lofty task. The "Divine Comedy" is the fulfillment of this "immense promise." Although it is probable that Dante did not begin to write this poem till after the death of Henry VII. (1313), yet there can be no doubt that it was slowly developing in his mind during all the years of his exile.

The "Divine Comedy" is divided into three parts or books, *canticas*, as they are called by Dante: "Inferno," "Purgatorio," and "Paradiso," each one containing thirty-three cantos, with one additional introductory canto prefixed to the "Inferno." Even the number of lines in the three *canticas* is approximately the same.[1] Dante's love for number

---

[1] *Inferno*, 4720; *Purgatorio*, 4755; *Paradiso*, 4758.

THE DIVINE COMEDY

symbols was shown in the "New Life," hence we are justified in accepting the theory that the threefold division of the poem is symbolical of the Trinity, and that the thirty-three cantos of each *cantica* represent the years of the Saviour's life. It is worthy of note that the last word in each of the three books is " stars."

The allegory of the "Divine Comedy" has been the subject of countless discussions. The consensus of the best modern commentators seems to be, however, that although the allegory is more or less political, it is chiefly religious. The great theme is the salvation of the human soul, represented by Dante himself, who is the protagonist of the poem. As he wanders first through Hell, he sees in all its loathly horrors the " exceeding sinfulness of sin," and realizes its inevitable punishment; as he climbs the steep slopes of Purgatory, at first with infinite difficulty, but with ever-increasing ease as he approaches the summit, he learns by his own experience how hard it is to root out the natural tendencies to sin that pull the soul downward ; and finally, as he mounts from heaven to heaven, till he arrives in the very presence of God himself, he experiences the joy unspeakable that comes to him who, having purged himself of sin, is found worthy to join "the innumerable company of saints and the spirits of just men made perfect."

The "Divine Comedy" is a visionary journey through the three supernatural worlds, Hell, Purgatory, and Paradise. Such visions were by no means infrequent in the Middle Ages, and Dante had many predecessors. He simply adopted a poetical device well known to his contemporaries. What differentiated him from others is the dramatic and intensely personal character of his vision; the consummate skill with which he interwove into this one poem all the science, learning, philosophy, and history of the times; and the lovely poetry in which all these things are embalmed. To appreciate the vast difference between the "Divine Comedy" and previous works of a similar nature, we need only to read a few pages of such crude books as the "Visions of Alberico," "Tugdale" and "Saint Brandon."

To Dante and his contemporaries the supernatural world was not what it is to us to-day, a vast, unbounded space filled with star-systems like our own; the topography of Hell, Purgatory, and Paradise seemed to them as definite as that of our own planet. The Ptolemaic system of astronomy (overthrown by Copernicus, yet still form-

THE DIVINE COMEDY

ing the framework of Milton's "Paradise Lost") was accepted with implicit confidence. According to this system the universe consisted of ten heavens or concentric spheres, in the centre of which was our earth, immovable itself, while around it revolved the heavenly spheres. The earth was surrounded by an atmosphere of air, then one of fire, and then came in order the heavens of the moon, Mercury, Venus, the sun; Mars, Jupiter, Saturn, the fixed stars, and the Primum Mobile (the source of the motion of the spheres) beyond which stretched out to infinity the Empyrean, the heaven of light and love, the seat of God and the angels.

According to Dante, Hell is situated in the interior of the earth, being in shape a sort of funnel with the point downward, and reaching to the centre of the earth, which is also the centre of the universe. Purgatory rises in the form of a truncated cone on the surface of the southern hemisphere, having, in solid form, the same shape as the hollow funnel of Hell. It was formed of the earth which fled before Lucifer, and splashed up behind him like water, when, after his revolt against the Almighty he was flung headlong from heaven and became fixed in the centre of the earth, as far as

THE GREAT POETS OF ITALY

possible, according to the Ptolemaic system, from the Empyrean and from God.

Hell is formed of nine concentric, ever-narrowing terraces, or circles, exhibiting a great variety of landscapes, rivers, and lakes, gloomy forests and sandy deserts, all shrouded in utter darkness except where flickering flames tear the thick pall of night or the red-hot walls of Dis gleam balefully over the waters of the Stygian marsh. Here are punished the various groups of sinners, whom Dante sees, whose suffering he describes, and with whom he converses, as he makes his way downward from circle to circle.

It was in the year 1300, at Easter time, when Dante began his strange and eventful pilgrimage, "midway in this our mortal life," he says in the first line of the poem, that is when he himself was thirty-five years old. He finds himself lost in a dense forest, not knowing how he came there, and after wandering for some time, reaches the foot of a lofty mountain, whose top is lighted by the rays of the morning sun. He is about to make his way thither, when he is stopped by the appearance, one after the other, of three terrible beasts, a leopard, a lion, and a wolf. He falls back in terror to the forest, when suddenly he sees a figure advancing

THE DIVINE COMEDY

toward him and learns that this is Vergil, who has been sent by Beatrice (now in heaven) to lead her lover from the wood of sin to salvation. To do this it will be necessary for Dante to pass through the infernal world, then up the craggy heights of Purgatory to the Earthly Paradise, where Beatrice herself will take charge of him and lead him from heaven to heaven, even to the presence of God himself. Dante's courage and confidence fail at this prospect, he is not Æneas or St. Paul, he says, to undertake such supernatural journeys, but when Vergil tells him that Beatrice herself has sent him, Dante expresses his willingness to undertake the difficult and awe-inspiring task.

It is night-fall when they reach the gate of Hell, over which is written the dread inscription: —

>Through me the way is to the city dolent;
>>Through me the way is to eternal dole;
>>Through me the way among the people lost.
>Justice incited my sublime Creator;
>>Created me divine Omnipotence,
>>The highest Wisdom and the primal Love.
>Before me there were no created things,
>>Only eterne, and I eternal last.
>>All hope abandon, ye who enter in!'

Entering in they are met with the sound of sighs, moans, and lamentations, mingled with curses hoarse

THE GREAT POETS OF ITALY

and deep, and the beating of hands, all making a hideous din in the starless air, in which a long train of spirits are whirled about hither and thither, stung by wasps and hornets. These spirits are the souls of those ignoble ones who were neither for God nor against him.

> This miserable mode
> Maintain the melancholy souls of those
> Who lived withouten infamy or praise.
> Commingled are they with that caitiff choir
> Of Angels, who have not rebellious been,
> Nor faithful were to God, but were for self.
> The heavens expelled them, not to be less fair;
> Nor them the nethermore abyss receives,
> For glory none the damned would have from them.

Here Dante recognizes the soul of him who made the " great refusal," recalling thus the strange story of the aged hermit, Peter Murrone, who after fifty-five years and more of solitary life in a cave high up among the Abruzzi Mountains, was forced to ascend the papal throne, and who after a short period of ineffectual reign under the name of Celestine V., resigned, thus making way for Boniface VIII., Dante's bitter enemy. Vergil's contemptuous remark concerning these souls —

> " Let us not speak of them, but look and pass " —

has become proverbial.

THE DIVINE COMEDY

Soon after this the two poets reach the shores of the Acheron, where Charon, the infernal boatman, is busy ferrying the souls of the damned across the river. He refuses to take Dante in his boat, and the latter falls into a swoon, from which he is aroused by a clap of thunder, and finds himself on the other side. How he was carried over we are not told. The wanderers are now in Limbo or the first circle of Hell, in which are contained the souls of unbaptized children and of the great and good of the pagan world, especially the poets and philosophers of ancient Greece and Rome, who, having lived before the coming of Christ, had, through no fault of their own, died without faith in Him who alone can save. These souls are not punished by physical pain, as is the case with those in the following circles, but nourishing forever a desire which they have no hope of ever having satisfied, they pass the endless years of eternity in gentle melancholy. Here Dante meets the spirits of Homer, Ovid, Horace, and Lucan, who treat him kindly and make him one of the band, thus consecrating him as a great poet.

> When they together had discoursed somewhat,
> They turned to me with signs of salutation,
> And on beholding this, my Master smiled;

THE GREAT POETS OF ITALY

And more of honour still, much more, they did me,
  In that they made me one of their own band;
  So that the sixth was I, 'mid so much wit.
Thus we went on as far as to the light,
  Things saying 't is becoming to keep silent,
  As was the saying of them where I was.
We came unto a noble castle's foot,
  Seven times encompassëd with lofty walls,
  Defended round by a fair rivulet;
This we passed over even as firm ground;
  Through portals seven I entered with these Sages;
  We came into a meadow of fresh verdure.
People were there with solemn eyes and slow,
  Of great authority in their countenance;
  They spake but seldom, and with gentle voices.
Thus we withdrew ourselves upon one side
  Into an opening luminous and lofty,
  So that they all of them were visible.
There opposite, upon the green enamel,
  Were pointed out to me the mighty spirits,
  Whom to have seen I feel myself exalted.
I saw Electra with companions many,
  'Mongst whom I knew both Hector and Æneas,
  Cæsar in armour with gerfalcon eyes;
I saw Camilla and Penthesilea
  On the other side, and saw the King Latinus,
  Who with Lavinia his daughter sat;
I saw that Brutus who drove Tarquin forth,
  Lucretia, Julia, Marcia, and Cornelia,
  And saw alone, apart, the Saladin.

Leaving this beautiful oasis in the infernal desert, the poets enter the second circle, where Hell

THE DIVINE COMEDY

may be said really to begin. Here Dante sees the monster Minos, the judge of the infernal regions, who assigns to each soul its proper circle, indicating the number thereof by winding his tail about his body a corresponding number of times. In Circle II. are the souls of the licentious, blown about forever by a violent wind. Among them Dante recognizes the famous lovers of antiquity, Dido, Helen, Cleopatra. His attention is especially attracted toward two spirits, who, locked closely in each other's arms, are blown hither and thither like chaff before the wind. Calling upon them to tell him who they are, he hears the pathetic story of Francesca da Rimini, perhaps the most famous and beautiful passage in all poetry : —

>   After that I had listened to my Teacher,
>   Naming the dames of eld and cavaliers,
>   Pity prevailed, and I was nigh bewildered.
>   And I began : " O poet, willingly
>   Speak would I to those two, who go together
>   And seem upon the wind to be so light."
>   And he to me : " Thou 'lt mark, when they shall be
>   Nearer to us ; and then do thou implore them
>   By love which leadeth them, and they will come."
>   Soon as the wind in our direction sways them,
>   My voice uplift I : " O ye weary souls !
>   Come speak to us, if no one interdicts it."
>   As turtle-doves, called onward by desire,

THE GREAT POETS OF ITALY

With open and steady wings to the sweet nest
Fly through the air by their volition borne,
So came they from the band where Dido is,
Approaching us athwart the air malign,
So strong was the affectionate appeal.
"O living creature gracious and benignant,
Who visiting goest through the purple air
Us, who have stained the world incarnadine,
If were the King of the Universe our friend,
We would pray unto him to give thee peace,
Since thou hast pity on our woe perverse.
Of what it pleases thee to hear and speak,
That will we hear, and we will speak to you,
While silent is the wind, as it is now.
Sitteth the city, wherein I was born,
Upon the sea-shore where the Po descends
To rest in peace with all his retinue.
Love, that on gentle heart doth swiftly seize,
Seized this man for the person beautiful
That was ta'en from me, and still the mode offends me.
Love, that exempts no one beloved from loving,
Seized me with pleasure of this man so strongly,
That, as thou seest, it doth not yet desert me;
Love has conducted us unto one death;
Caïna [1] waiteth him who quenched our life!"
These words were borne along from them to us.
As soon as I had heard those souls tormented,
I bowed my face, and so long held it down
Until the poet said to me: "What thinkest?"
When I made answer, I began: "Alas!
How many pleasant thoughts, how much desire,
Conducted these unto the dolorous pass!"

[1] A division of the lowest circle of Hell, where fratricides are punished.

THE DIVINE COMEDY

Then unto them I turned me, and I spake,
    And I began : " Thine agonies, Francesca,
    Sad and compassionate to weeping make me.
But tell me, at the time of those sweet sighs,
    By what and in what manner Love conceded,
    That you should know your dubious desires ? "
And she to ask me : " There is no greater sorrow
    Than to be mindful of the happy time
    In misery, and that thy Teacher [1] knows.
But, if to recognise the earliest root
    Of love in us thou hast so great desire,
    I will do even as he who weeps and speaks.
One day we reading were for our delight
    Of Launcelot, how Love did him enthral.
    Alone we were and without any fear.
Full many a time our eyes together drew
    That reading, and drove the colour from our faces;
    But one point only was it that o'ercame us.
When as we read of the much-longed-for smile
    Being by such a noble lover kissed,
    This one who ne'er from me shall be divided,
Kissed me upon the mouth all palpitating.
    Galeotto [2] was the book and he who wrote it.
    That day no farther did we read therein."
And all the while one spirit uttered this,
    The other one did weep so, that, for pity,
    I swooned away as if I had been dying,
And fell, even as a dead body falls.

Passing rapidly over Circle III., in which the

---

[1] Boethius, from whom Dante quotes this sentence.

[2] Sir Galahad, who had brought Launcelot and Queen Guinevere together. The book did the same thing for Paolo and Francesca.

THE GREAT POETS OF ITALY

gluttons lie in mire under a pelting storm of hail, snow, and rain, torn to pieces by the three-throated Cerberus; and Circle IV., where misers and spendthrifts roll great weights against each other and upbraid each the other with his besetting sin; we come to Circle V., where in the dark and dismal waters of the Styx, the wrathful and the melancholy are plunged. It is worthy of note that Dante makes low spirits or mental depression as much a sin as violence and lack of self-control: —

> Said the good Master: " Son, thou now beholdest
> The souls of those whom anger overcame;
> And likewise I would have thee know for certain
> Beneath the water people are who sigh
> And make this water bubble at the surface,
> As the eye tells thee wheresoe'er it turns.
> Fixed in the mire they say, ' We sullen were
> In the sweet air, which by the sun is gladdened,
> Bearing within ourselves the sluggish reek;
> Now we are sullen in this sable mire.'
> This hymn do they keep gurgling in their throats,
> For with unbroken words they cannot say it."
> Thus we went circling round the filthy fen
> A great arc 'twixt the dry bank and the swamp,
> With eyes turned unto those who gorge the mire;
> Unto the foot of a tower we came at last.

As they stand at the foot of this dark tower, a light flashes from its top, and another light, far off above the waters, sends back an answer through the

THE DIVINE COMEDY

murky air. Dante, full of curiosity, turns to Vergil for explanation : —

> I say, continuing, that long before
>   We to the foot of that high tower had come,
>   Our eyes went upward to the summit of it,
> By reason of two flamelets we saw placed there,
>   And from afar another answer them,
>   So far, that hardly could the eye attain it.
> And, to the sea of all discernment turned.[1]
>   I said : "What sayeth this and what respondeth
>   That other fire? and who are they that made it?"
> And he to me : "Across the turbid waves
>   What is expected thou canst now discern,
>   If reek of the morass conceal it not."
> Cord never shot an arrow from itself
>   That sped away athwart the air so swift
>   As I beheld a very little boat
> Come o'er the water tow'rds us at that moment,
>   Under the guidance of a single pilot,
>   Who shouted, "Now art thou arrived, fell soul?"

Entering into this boat, they cross the Styx, and soon approach the other shore, where luridly picturesque in the ink-black atmosphere rise the red-hot walls and towers of the city of Dis : —

> And the good Master said : "Even now, my Son,
>   The city draweth near whose name is Dis,
>   With the grave citizens, with the great throng."
> And I : "Its mosques already, Master, clearly

---

[1] Vergil.

THE GREAT POETS OF ITALY

    Within there in the valley I discern
    Vermilion, as if issuing from the fire
They were." And he to me: "The fire eternal
    That kindles them within makes them look red,
    As thou beholdest in this nether Hell."
Then we arrived within the moats profound,
    That circumvallate that disconsolate city;
    The walls appeared to me to be of iron.
Not without making first a circuit wide,
    We came unto a place where loud the pilot
    Cried out to us, "Debark, here is the entrance."
More than a thousand at the gates I saw
    Out of the Heavens rained down, who angrily
    Were saying, "Who is this that without death
Goes through the kingdom of the people dead?"
    And my sagacious Master made a sign
    Of wishing secretly to speak with them.
A little then they quelled their great disdain,
    And said: "Come thou alone, and he begone
    Who has so boldly entered these dominions.
Let him return alone by his mad road;
    Try, if he can; for thou shalt here remain,
    Who hast escorted him through such dark regions."
Think, Reader, if I was discomforted
    At utterance of the accursed words;
    For never to return here I believed.

While not only Dante but Vergil himself stand in dismay before the closed gates of the city, and the threatening devils on the walls, they hear a roar like that of a mighty wind, and behold! over the waters of the Styx a celestial messenger comes dryshod, puts to flight the recalcitrant devils, and open-

THE DIVINE COMEDY

ing the gates with a touch of his wand, departs without having uttered a word.

Entering the city, Dante sees a vast cemetery covered with tombs, whence issue flames, and in which are shut up the souls of those who denied the immortality of the soul. Here occurs the celebrated scene between Dante and Farinata degli Uberti, who alone, after the battle of Montaperti, in 1260, when the victorious Ghibellines seriously contemplated razing Florence to the ground, opposed the proposition and thus saved his native city from destruction. Here also Dante sees the father of his friend, Guido Cavalcanti.

In the centre of the cemetery yawns a tremendous abyss, which leads to the lower regions of Hell. Before they descend this, however, Vergil explains to Dante the various kinds of sins which are punished in Hell. Those he has seen hitherto (gluttony, licentiousness, avarice, wrath, and melancholy) all belong to the category of incontinence; those which are to come are due to malice, and harm not only oneself but others. The sixth circle, that of the heretics, in which they now are, forms a transition between the above two general divisions. In Circle VII., the next one below them, are punished the violent, subdivided into three classes:

1, those who were violent against their fellow-men, — tyrants, murderers, and robbers; 2, those who were violent against themselves, — suicides and gamblers; 3, those who were violent against God, nature, and art, — blasphemers, sodomites, and usurers. In Circles VIII. and IX. are the fraudulent and traitors, the various classes of which are given later.

After this explanation, the two poets descend the rocky cliff, and find at the bottom a blood-red river, where, guarded by centaurs, are plunged the souls of murderers and robbers, in various depths according to the heinousness of their cruelty and crimes. Crossing this stream they come to a dark and gloomy wood, composed of trees gnarled and twisted into all sorts of fantastic shapes, grimly recalling the contortions of a human body in pain, and covered with poisonous thorns. On the branches sit hideous harpies, half woman, half bird. Each of these trees contains the soul of a suicide. Dante, breaking off a small branch, is horrified to see human blood slowly ooze from the break, while a hissing noise is heard, like that of escaping steam, which resolves itself finally into words. From these words he learns that the soul contained in this tree is that of Pier delle Vigne, prime minister of Frederick II., who

THE DIVINE COMEDY

tells his sad and pathetic story, how he became the victim of slander and court-intrigue, and how, being unjustly imprisoned by his master, he committed suicide.

Beyond this gruesome forest the wanderers come out upon a vast, sandy desert, utterly treeless, where they see many wretched souls, some lying supine, some crouching down in a sitting posture, some walking incessantly about, but all forever trying, though in vain, to ward off from their naked bodies countless flakes of flame which fall slowly and steadily like snow

"Among the Alps when the wind is still."

Here are punished the blasphemers, violent against God; usurers, violent against art; and sodomites, violent against nature. Among the latter Dante recognizes and converses with his old friend, Brunetto Latini, who prophesies to him his future fame and his exile from Florence, —

> And he to me: "If thou thy star do follow,
>   Thou canst not fail thee of a glorious port,
>   If well I judged in the life beautiful.
> And if I had not died so prematurely,
>   Seeing Heaven thus benignant unto thee,
>   I would have given thee comfort in the work.
> But that ungrateful and malignant people,[1]

[1] The Florentines.

THE GREAT POETS OF ITALY

>   Which of old time from Fesole descended,
>   And smacks still of the mountain and the granite,
> Will make itself, for thy good deeds, thy foe;
>   And it is right; for among crabbed sorbs
>   It ill befits the sweet fig to bear fruit."

To this Dante answers, —

> "If my entreaty wholly were fulfilled,"
>   Replied I to him, " not yet would you be
>   In banishment from human nature placed;
> For in my mind is fixed, and touches now
>   My heart the dear and good paternal image
>   Of you, when in the world from hour to hour
> You taught me how a man becomes eternal;
>   And how much I am grateful, while I live
>   Behooves that in my language be discerned.
> What you narrate of my career I write,
>   And keep it to be glossed with other text
>   By a Lady [1] who can do it, if I reach her.
> This much will I have manifest to you;
>   Provided that my conscience do not chide me,
>   For whatsoever Fortune I am ready.
> Such handsel is not new unto mine ears;
>   Therefore let Fortune turn her wheel around
>   As it may please her, and the churl his mattock."

The poets then descend the tremendous cliff leading to Circle VIII. on the back of Geryon, a fantastic monster, with face of a good man, but body of a beast, many-colored and covered over with complicated figures, being a symbol of the fraud

[1] Beatrice.

THE DIVINE COMEDY

punished in the next circle. This Circle (VIII.) is subdivided into ten concentric rings, or ditches, with the floor gradually descending to a well in the centre, thus resembling the circular rows of seats in an amphitheatre, converging to the arena. In these ten *male-bolge*, as Dante calls them, *i. e.*, evil pits, are ten different kinds of fraudulent, panderers, flatterers, those guilty of simony, false prophets, magicians, thieves, barterers (those who sell public offices), evil counselors, schismatics, and hypocrites, all punished with diabolic ingenuity, hewn asunder by the sword, boiled in lakes of burning pitch, bitten by poisonous snakes, wasted by dire and hideous disease. As an example of the horrors seen in these evil pits we give one vivid picture, that of the famous Troubadour Bertrand de Born, who, having incited the young son of Henry II. of England to rebel against his father, is punished in Hell by having his head cut off and carrying it in his hand: —

> But I remained to look upon the crowd;
> And saw a thing which I should be afraid,
> Without some further proof, even to recount,
> If it were not that conscience reassures me,
> That good companion which emboldens man
> Beneath the hauberk of its feeling pure.
> I truly saw, and still I seem to see it,
> A trunk without a head walk in like manner
> As walked the others of the mournful herd.

THE GREAT POETS OF ITALY

And by the hair it held the head dissevered,
　Hung from the hand in fashion of a lantern,
　And that upon us gazed and said: "O me!"
It of itself made to itself a lamp,
　And they were two in one and one in two;
　How that can be, He knows who so ordains it.
When it was come close to the bridge's foot,
　It lifted high its arm with all the head,
　To bring more closely unto us its words,
Which were: "Behold now the sore penalty,
　Thou, who dost breathing go the dead beholding;
　Behold if any be as great as this.
And so that thou may carry news of me,
　Know that Bertram de Born am I, the same
　Who gave to the Young King the evil comfort.
I made the father and the son rebellious;
　Achitophel not more with Absalom
　And David did with his accursed goadings.
Because I parted persons so united,
　Parted do I now bear my brain, alas!
　From its beginning, which is in this trunk.
Thus is observed in me the counterpoise."

In the eighth pit are the souls of evil counselors, so completely swathed in flames that their forms cannot be seen. Dante's attention is especially attracted to one of these moving flames, with a double-tipped point, which proves to contain the souls of Diomede and Ulysses, who, as they had once been together in fraud, are now inseparable in punishment. This story of his last voyage and final ship-

THE DIVINE COMEDY

wreck, told by Ulysses, how in his old age, weary of the monotony of home life and longing to know the secret of the great Western ocean, he set sail with his old companions, is full of imaginative grandeur, —

> When now the flame had come unto that point,
>   Where to my leader it seemed time and place,
>   After this fashion did I hear him speak:
> "O ye, who are twofold within one fire,
>   If I deserved of you, while I was living,
>   If I deserved of you or much or little
> When in the world I wrote the lofty verses,
>   Do not move on, but one of you declare
>   Whither, being lost, he went away to die."
> Then of the antique flame the greater horn,
>   Murmuring, began to wave itself about
>   Even as a flame doth which the wind fatigues.
> Thereafterward, the summit to and fro
>   Moving as if it were the tongue that spake,
>   It uttered forth a voice, and said: "When I
> From Circe had departed, who concealed me
>   More than a year there near unto Gaëta,
>   Or ever yet Æneas named it so,
> Nor fondness for my son, nor reverence
>   For my old father, nor the due affection
>   Which joyous should have made Penelope,
> Could overcome within me the desire
>   I had to be experienced of the world,
>   And of the vice and virtue of mankind;
> But I put forth on the high open sea
>   With one sole ship, and that small company
>   By which I never had deserted been.

THE GREAT POETS OF ITALY

Both of the shores I saw as far as Spain,
    Far as Morocco, and the isle of Sardes,
    And the others which that sea bathes round about.
I and my company were old and slow
    When at that narrow passage we arrived
    Where Hercules his landmarks set as signals,[1]
That man no farther onward should adventure.
    On the right hand behind me left I Seville,
    And on the other already had left Ceuta.
'O brothers, who amid a hundred thousand
    Perils,' I said, 'have come unto the West,
    To this so inconsiderable vigil
Which is remaining of your senses still
    Be ye unwilling to deny the knowledge,
    Following the sun, of the unpeopled world.
Consider ye the seed from which ye sprang;
    Ye were not made to live like unto brutes,
    But for pursuit of virtue and of knowledge.'
So eager did I render my companions,
    With this brief exhortation, for the voyage,
    That then I hardly could have held them back.
And having turned our stern unto the morning,
    We of the oars made wings for our mad flight,
    Evermore gaining on the larboard side.
Already all the stars of the other pole
    The night beheld, and ours so very low
    It did not rise above the ocean floor.
Five times rekindled and as many quenched
    Had been the splendour underneath the moon,
    Since we had entered into the deep pass,
When there appeared to us a mountain, dim

[1] The Straits of Gibraltar.

THE DIVINE COMEDY

>   From distance, and it seemed to me so high
>   As I had never any one beheld.
>   Joyful were we, and soon it turned to weeping;
>   For out of the new land a whirlwind rose,
>   And smote upon the fore part of the ship.
>   Three times it made her whirl with all the waters,
>   At the fourth time it made the stern uplift,
>   And the prow downward go, as pleased Another,
>   Until the sea above us closed again."

In the centre of the amphitheatre of Male-bolge is a deep and vast well, guarded by giants, one of whom takes the poets in his arms and deposits them at the bottom. Here they find the ninth and last circle, where in four divisions the traitors against relatives, friends, country, and benefactors, are fixed (like flies in amber) in a solid lake of ice, swept by bitter, cold winds. Among the traitors to their country Dante sees one man who is gnawing in relentless rage at the head of another fixed in the ice in front of him. Inquiring the cause of this terrible cruelty, Dante hears the following story, couched in language which Goethe has declared to be without an equal in all poetry: —

>   His mouth uplifted from his grim repast,
>   That sinner, wiping it upon the hair
>   Of the same head that he behind had wasted.
>   Then he began: " Thou wilt that I renew
>   The desperate grief, which wrings my heart already
>   To think of only, ere I speak of it;

THE GREAT POETS OF ITALY

But if my words be seed that may bear fruit
    Of infamy to the traitor whom I gnaw,
    Speaking and weeping shalt thou see together.
I know not who thou art, nor by what mode
    Thou hast come down here; but a Florentine
    Thou seemest to me truly, when I hear thee.
Thou hast to know I was Count Ugolino,[1]
    And this one was Ruggieri the Archbishop;
    Now I will tell thee why I am such a neighbor.
That, by effect of his malicious thoughts,
    Trusting in him I was made prisoner,
    And after put to death, I need not say;
But ne'ertheless what thou canst not have heard,
    That is to say, how cruel was my death,
    Hear shalt thou, and shalt know if he has wronged me.
A narrow perforation in the mew,
    Which bears because of me the title of Famine,
    And in which others still must be locked up,
Had shown me through its opening many moons
    Already, when I dreamed the evil dream
    Which of the future rent for me the veil.
This one appeared to me as lord and master,
    Hunting the wolf and whelps upon the mountain
    For which the Pisans cannot Lucca see.
With sleuth-hounds gaunt, and eager, and well trained,
    Gualandi with Sismondi and Lanfranchi
    He had sent out before him to the front.
After brief course seemed unto me forespent
    The father and the sons, and with sharp tushes
    It seemed to me I saw their flanks ripped open.

---

[1] Count Ugolino della Gherardesca was Podestà of Pisa. With his two sons and grandsons he was thrown into a tower and starved to death.

THE DIVINE COMEDY

When I before the morrow was awake,
    Moaning amid their sleep I heard my sons
    Who with me were, and asking after bread.
Cruel indeed art thou, if yet thou grieve not,
    Thinking of what my heart foreboded me,
    And weep'st thou not, what art thou wont to weep at?
They were awake now, and the hour drew nigh
    At which our food used to be brought to us,
    And through his dream was each one apprehensive;
And I heard locking up the under door
    Of the horrible tower; whereat without a word
    I gazed into the faces of my sons.
I wept not, I within so turned to stone;
    They wept; and darling little Anselm mine
    Said: 'Thou dost gaze so, father, what doth ail thee?'
Still not a tear I shed, nor answer made
    All of that day, nor yet the night thereafter,
    Until another sun rose on the world.
As now a little glimmer made its way
    Into the dolorous prison, and I saw
    Upon four faces my own very aspect,
Both of my hands in agony I bit;
    And, thinking that I did it from desire
    Of eating, on a sudden they uprose,
And said they: 'Father, much less pain 't will give us
    If thou do eat of us; thyself didst clothe us
    With this poor flesh, and do thou strip it off.'
I calmed me then, not to make them more sad.
    That day we all were silent, and the next.
    Ah! obdurate earth, wherefore didst thou not open?
When we had come unto the fourth day, Gaddo
    Threw himself down outstretched before my feet,
    Saying, 'My father, why dost thou not help me?'
And there he died; and, as thou seest me,

THE GREAT POETS OF ITALY

> I saw the three fall, one by one, between
> The fifth day and the sixth; whence I betook me,
> Already blind, to groping over each,
> And three days called them after they were dead;
> Then hunger did what sorrow could not do."
> When he had said this, with his eyes distorted,
> The wretched skull resumed he with his teeth,
> Which, as a dog's, upon the bone were strong.

Arriving at the very bottom of Hell, the poets see the body of Lucifer fixed in the centre thereof (which is at the same time the centre of the earth and of the universe), with its upper part projecting into the freezing air. This monstrous figure, as hideous now as it had been beautiful before his revolt against God, has three pair of wings and three heads, in the mouths of which he tears to pieces the three arch-traitors, Judas, Brutus, and Cassius.

The wanderers climb along the hairy sides of Lucifer and finally reach a cavity which corresponds to the lowest part of Hell, and up into which are thrust the legs of the monster. They have thus passed the centre of earth and are now in the other or southern hemisphere. Making their way upward along the course of a stream they finally come out into the open air, where the mount of Purgatory rises sheer up from the surface of the great southern sea.

THE DIVINE COMEDY

The first cantos of the "Purgatorio" are of wonderful beauty, and their loveliness is heightened by contrast, coming as it does after the darkness, filth, and horrors of Hell. Issuing from the subterranean passage just before sunrise, the poets see before them a vast expanse of sea, lighted up by the soft rays of Venus, the morning star, and gradually becoming brighter as the dawn advances: —

> Sweet colour of the oriental sapphire,
>   That was upgathered in the cloudless aspect
>   Of the pure air, as far as the first circle,
> Unto mine eyes did recommence delight
>   Soon as I issued forth from the dead air,
>   Which had with sadness filled mine eyes and breast.
> The beauteous planet, that to love incites,
>   Was making all the orient to laugh,
>   Veiling the Fishes that were in her escort.
> To the right hand I turned, and fixed my mind
>   Upon the other pole, and saw four stars
>   Ne'er seen before save by the primal people.
> Rejoicing in their flamelets seemed the heaven.
>   O thou septentrional and widowed site,
>   Because thou art deprived of seeing these!

As they stand watching this scene, a venerable old man (Cato, the guardian of the island) approaches and tells them to go to the seashore and wipe off the stains of Hell with the reeds that grow there: —

THE GREAT POETS OF ITALY

    The dawn was vanquishing the matin hour
        Which fled before it, so that from afar
        I recognised the trembling of the sea.
    Along the solitary plain we went
        As one who unto the lost road returns,
        And till he finds it seems to go in vain.
    As soon as we were come to where the dew
        Fights with the sun, and, being in a part
        Where shadow falls, little evaporates,
    Both of his hands upon the grass outspread
        In gentle manner did my Master place;
        Whence I, who of his action was aware,
    Extended unto him my tearful cheeks;
        There did he make in me uncovered wholly
        That hue which Hell had covered up in me.
    Then came we down upon the desert shore
        Which never yet saw navigate its waters
        Any that afterward had known return.
    There he begirt me as the other pleased;
        O marvellous! for even as he culled
        The humble plant, such it sprang up again
    Suddenly there where he uprooted it.

As they linger by the seaside, they see a bright light far off over the waters, which, as it approaches, turns out to be a boat wafted by angelic wings and bearing to Purgatory the souls of the saved, among them a musician, a friend of Dante's, who at his request sings one of the poet's own songs: —

    Already had the sun the horizon reached
        Whose circle of meridian covers o'er
        Jerusalem with its most lofty point,

THE DIVINE COMEDY

And night that opposite to him revolves
    Was issuing forth from Ganges with the Scales
    That fall from out her hand when she exceedeth;
So that the white and the vermilion cheeks
    Of beautiful Aurora, where I was,
    By too great age were changing into orange.
We still were on the border of the sea,
    Like people who are thinking of their road,
    Who go in heart, and with the body stay;
And lo! as when, upon the approach of morning,
    Through the gross vapours Mars grows fiery red
    Down in the West upon the ocean floor,
Appeared to me — may I again behold it! —
    A light along the sea so swiftly coming,
    Its motion by no flight of wing is equalled;
From which when I a little had withdrawn
    Mine eyes, that I might question my Conductor,
    Again I saw it brighter grown and larger.
Then on each side of it appeared to me
    I knew not what of white, and underneath it
    Little by little there came forth another.
My Master yet had uttered not a word
    While the first whiteness into wings unfolded;
    But when he clearly recognised the pilot,
He cried: "Make haste, make haste, to bow the knee!
    Behold the Angel of God! fold thou thy hands!
    Henceforward shalt thou see such officers!
See how he scorneth human arguments,
    So that nor oar he wants, nor other sail
    Than his own wings, between so distant shores.
See how he holds them pointed up to heaven,
    Fanning the air with the eternal pinions,
    That do not moult themselves like mortal hair!"

THE GREAT POETS OF ITALY

Then as still nearer and more near us came
    The Bird Divine, more radiant he appeared,
    So that near by the eye could not endure him,
But down I cast it ; and he came to shore
    With a small vessel, very swift and light,
    So that the water swallowed naught thereof.
Upon the stern stood the Celestial Pilot;
    Beatitude seemed written in his face,
    And more than a hundred spirits sat within.
" *In exitu Israel de Ægypto!* "
    They chanted all together in one voice,
    With whatso in that psalm is after written.
Then made he sign of holy rood upon them,
    Whereat all cast themselves upon the shore,
    And he departed swiftly as he came.
The throng which still remained there unfamiliar
    Seemed with the place, all round about them gazing,
    As one who in new matters makes essay.
On every side was darting forth the day
    The sun who had with his resplendent shafts
    From the mid-heaven chased forth the Capricorn,
When the new people lifted up their faces
    Towards us, saying to us : " If ye know,
    Show us the way to go unto the mountain."
And answer made Virgilius : " Ye believe
    Perchance that we have knowledge of this place,
    But we are strangers even as yourselves.
Just now we came, a little while before you,
    Another way, which was so rough and steep,
    That mounting will henceforth seem sport to us."
The souls who had, from seeing me draw breath,
    Become aware that I was still alive,
    Pallid in their astonishment became ;
And as to messenger who bears the olive

THE DIVINE COMEDY

The people throng to listen to the news,
And no one shows himself afraid of crowding,
So at the sight of me stood motionless
Those fortunate spirits, all of them, as if
Oblivious to go and make them fair.
One from among them saw I coming forward,
As to embrace me, with such great affection,
That it incited me to do the like.
O empty shadows, save in aspect only!
Three times behind it did I clasp my hands,
As oft returned with them to my own breast!
I think with wonder I depicted me;
Whereat the shadow smiled and backward drew;
And I, pursuing it, pressed farther forward.
Gently it said that I should stay my steps;
Then knew I who it was, and I entreated
That it would stop awhile to speak with me.
It made reply to me: "Even as I loved thee
In mortal body, so I love thee free;
Therefore I stop; but wherefore goest thou?"
"My own Casella! to return once more
There where I am, I make this journey," said I;
"But how from thee has so much time been taken?"
And he to me: "No outrage has been done me,
If he who takes both when and whom he pleases
Has many times denied to me this passage,
For of a righteous will his own is made.
He, sooth to say, for three months past has taken
Whoever wished to enter with all peace;
Whence I, who now had turned unto that shore
Where salt the waters of the Tiber grow,
Benignantly by him have been received.
Unto that outlet now his wing is pointed,

THE GREAT POETS OF ITALY

    Because for evermore assemble there
        Those who tow'rds Acheron do not descend."
And I: "If some new law take not from thee
        Memory or practice of the song of love,
        Which used to quiet in me all my longings,
Thee may it please to comfort therewithal
        Somewhat this soul of mine, that with its body
        Hitherward coming is so much distressed."
"*Love, that within my mind discourses with me,*"[1]
        Forthwith began he so melodiously,
        The melody within me still is sounding.
My Master, and myself, and all that people
        Which with him were, appeared as satisfied
        As if naught else might touch the mind of any.
We all of us were moveless and attentive
        Unto his notes; and lo! the grave old man,
        Exclaiming: "What is this, ye laggard spirits?
What negligence, what standing still is this?
        Run to the mountain to strip off the slough,
        That lets not God be manifest to you."
Even as when, collecting grain or tares,
        The doves, together at their pasture met,
        Quiet, nor showing their accustomed pride,
If aught appear of which they are afraid,
        Upon a sudden leave their food alone,
        Because they are assailed by greater care;
So that fresh company did I behold
        The song relinquish, and go tow'rds the hill,
        As one who goes, and knows not whitherward;
Nor was our own departure less in haste.

Thus rebuked by Cato for delaying, even thus

---

[1] This is the first line of the second *canzone* of Dante's *Banquet*.

THE DIVINE COMEDY

innocently, their first duty, which is to purge away their sins, the company of spirits breaks up, and Dante and Vergil make their way to the mountain of Purgatory, which lifts its seven terraces almost perpendicularly from the sea.

Before reaching the first of these terraces, however, they pass over a steep and rocky slope, Ante-purgatory, as it may be called, where linger the souls of those who, although saved, neglected their repentance till late in life, or who died in contumacy with Holy Church. Among the latter Dante sees Manfred, the unfortunate son of Frederick II.,

"Beautiful and of noble aspect,"

who was slain at Benevento, in 1266, and likewise Buonconte da Montefeltro, who was killed in the battle of Campaldino (1289), and whose account of the post-mortem fate of his body is singularly impressive: "There is nothing like it in literature," says Ruskin: —

>And I to him: "What violence or what chance
>Led thee astray so far from Campaldino,
>That never has thy sepulture been known?"
>"Oh," he replied, "at Casentino's foot
>A river crosses named Archiano, born
>Above the Hermitage in Apennine.
>There where the name thereof becometh void [1]

[1] Where the Archiano loses its name by flowing into the Arno.

THE GREAT POETS OF ITALY

> Did I arrive, pierced through and through the throat,
>   Fleeing on foot, and bloodying the plain;
> There my sight lost I, and my utterance
>   Ceased in the name of Mary, and thereat
>   I fell, and tenantless my flesh remained.
> Truth will I speak, repeat it to the living;
>   God's Angel took me up, and he of hell
>   Shouted: 'O thou from heaven, why dost thou rob me?
> Thou bearest away the eternal part of him,
>   For one poor little tear, that takes him from me;
>   But with the rest I'll deal in other fashion!'
> Well knowest thou how in the air is gathered
>   That humid vapour which to water turns,
>   Soon as it rises where the cold doth grasp it.
> He joined that evil will, which aye seeks evil,
>   To intellect, and moved the mist and wind
>   By means of power, which his own nature gave;
> Thereafter, when the day was spent, the valley
>   From Pratomagno to the great yoke [1] covered
>   With fog, and made the heaven above intent,
> So that the pregnant air to water changed;
>   Down fell the rain, and to the gullies came
>   Whate'er of it earth tolerated not;
> And as it mingled with the mighty torrents,
>   Towards the royal river with such speed
>   It headlong rushed, that nothing held it back.
> My frozen body near unto its outlet
>   The robust Archian found, and into Arno
>   Thrust it, and loosened from my breast the cross
> I made of me, when agony o'ercame me;
>   It rolled me on the banks and on the bottom,
>   Then with its booty covered and begirt me."

[1] Ridge of the Apennines.

THE DIVINE COMEDY

After leaving Buonconte, Dante and Vergil make their way upward and finally come across the spirit of Sordello, the famous troubadour, a native of Mantua and thus a fellow-citizen of Vergil. The cordiality with which they greet each other gives Dante an opportunity to vent his indignation at the discord existing in Italy: —

> Ah! servile Italy, grief's hostelry!
>   A ship without a pilot in great tempest!
>   No Lady thou of Provinces, but brothel!
> That noble soul was so impatient, only
>   At the sweet sound of his own native land,
>   To make its citizen glad welcome there;
> And now within thee are not without war
>   Thy living ones, and one doth gnaw the other
>   Of those whom one wall and one fosse shut in!
> Search, wretched one, all round about the shores
>   Thy seaboard, and then look within thy bosom,
>   If any part of thee enjoyeth peace!

As night is coming on, during which upward progress cannot be made, Sordello conducts Dante and Vergil to a pleasant valley: —

> Little had we withdrawn us from that place,
>   When I perceived the mount was hollowed out
>   In fashion as the valleys here are hollowed.
> "Thitherward," said that shade, "will we repair,
>   Where of itself the hill-side makes a lap,
>   And there for the new day will we await."
> 'T wixt hill and plain there was a winding path

THE GREAT POETS OF ITALY

>   Which led us to the margin of that dell,
>   Where dies the border more than half away.
> Gold and fine silver, and scarlet and pearl-white,
>   The Indian wood resplendent and serene,
>   Fresh emerald the moment it is broken,
> By herbage and by flowers within that hollow
>   Planted, each one in colour would be vanquished,
>   As by its greater vanquished is the less.
> Nor in that place had nature painted only,
>   But of the sweetness of a thousand odours
>   Made there a mingled fragrance and unknown.
> "*Salve Regina*," on the green and flowers
>   There seated, singing, spirits I beheld,
>   Which were not visible outside the valley.

Here Sordello points out the souls of mighty princes who left deep traces in the history of the times, among them the Emperor Rudolph of Germany, Peter of Aragon, Philip III. of France, and

>   "The monarch of the simple life,"

Henry III. of England. The scene that follows is one of the most celebrated as well as one of the most beautiful passages in the "Divine Comedy":—

>   'T was now the hour that turneth back desire
>   In those who sail the sea, and melts the heart,
>   The day they 've said to their sweet friends farewell,
>   And the new pilgrim penetrates with love,
>   If he doth hear from far away a bell
>   That seemeth to deplore the dying day,
>   When I began to make of no avail

THE DIVINE COMEDY

    My hearing, and to watch one of the souls
        Uprisen, that begged attention with its hand.
It joined and lifted upward both its palms,
        Fixing its eyes upon the orient,
        As if it said to God, " Naught else I care for."
" *Te lucis ante* " so devoutly issued
        Forth from its mouth, and with such dulcet notes,
        It made me issue forth from my own mind.
And then the others, sweetly and devoutly,
        Accompanied it through all the hymn entire,
        Having their eyes on the supernal wheels.
Here, Reader, fix thine eyes well on the truth,
        For now indeed so subtile is the veil,
        Surely to penetrate within is easy.
I saw that army of the gentle-born
        Thereafterward in silence upward gaze,
        As if in expectation, pale and humble;
And from on high come forth and down descend,
        I saw two Angels with two flaming swords,
        Truncated and deprivëd of their points.
Green as the little leaflets just now born
        Their garments were, which, by their verdant pinions
        Beaten and blown abroad, they trailed behind.
One just above us came to take his station,
        And one descended to the opposite bank,
        So that the people were contained between them.
Clearly in them discerned I the blond head;
        But in their faces was the eye bewildered,
        As faculty confounded by excess.
" From Mary's bosom both of them have come,"
        Sordello said, " as guardians of the valley
        Against the serpent, that will come anon."
Whereupon I, who knew not by what road,

THE GREAT POETS OF ITALY

    Turned round about, and closely drew myself,
    Utterly frozen, to the faithful shoulders.
    . . . .

My greedy eyes still wandered up to heaven,
    Still to that point where slowest are the stars,
    Even as a wheel the nearest to its axle.
And my Conductor: "Son, what dost thou gaze at
    Up there?" And I to him: "At those three torches
    With which this hither pole is all on fire."
And he to me: "The four resplendent stars
    Thou sawest this morning are down yonder low,
    And these have mounted up to where those were."
As he was speaking, to himself Sordello
    Drew him, and said, "Lo there our Adversary!"
    And pointed with his finger to look thither.
Upon the side on which the little valley
    No barrier hath, a serpent was; perchance
    The same which gave to Eve the bitter food.
'Twixt grass and flowers came on the evil streak,
    Turning at times its head about, and licking
    Its back like to a beast that smoothes itself.
I did not see, and therefore cannot say
    How the celestial falcons 'gan to move,
    But well I saw that they were both in motion.
Hearing the air cleft by their verdant wings,
    The serpent fled, and round the Angels wheeled,
    Up to their stations flying back alike.

After conversing with several friends whom he meets here, Dante falls asleep and is carried, thus unconscious, by Lucia (symbol of divine grace) to the gate of Purgatory proper. When he awakes the sun is two hours high. Three steps lead to the

THE DIVINE COMEDY

gate, one dark and broken, symbol of a "broken and a contrite heart"; one of smooth, white marble (confession), and one purple (repentance). On the threshold of diamond (the immovable foundation of Holy Church) sits an angel with a sword and two keys; with the former he cuts seven P's on Dante's forehead (alluding to the Latin word for sin, *peccatum*), and with the latter he opens the gate, which as it swings open sends forth a sound of heavenly music: —

>   Then pushed the portals of the sacred door,
>   Exclaiming: "Enter; but I give you warning
>   That forth returns whoever looks behind."
>   And when upon their hinges were turned round
>   The swivels of that consecrated gate,
>   Which are of metal, massive and sonorous,
>   Roared not so loud, nor so discordant seemed
>   Tarpeia, when was ta'en from it the good
>   Metellus, wherefore meagre it remained.[1]
>   At the first thunder-peal I turned attentive,
>   And "*Te Deum laudamus*" seemed to hear
>   In voices mingled with sweet melody.
>   Exactly such an image rendered me
>   That which I heard, as we are wont to catch,
>   When people singing with the organ stand;
>   For now we hear, and now hear not, the words.

[1] Allusion to the defense by Metellus of the Roman treasury on the Tarpeian hill, when Cæsar robbed it.

THE GREAT POETS OF ITALY

In Terrace I. are punished the proud, crushed beneath enormous weights. On the side of the mountain wall are sculptured wonderful bas-reliefs, representing examples of humility; especially famous is the one which tells the story of Trajan's justice, a story which led Pope Gregory to make a prayer to God, who granted it, for the release of the pagan emperor's soul from hell: —

> There the high glory of the Roman Prince
>   Was chronicled, whose great beneficence
>   Moved Gregory to his great victory;
> 'T is of the Emperor Trajan I am speaking;
>   And a poor widow at his bridle stood,
>   In attitude of weeping and of grief.
> Around about him seemed it thronged and full
>   Of cavaliers, and the eagles in the gold
>   Above them visibly in the wind were moving.
> The wretched woman in the midst of these
>   Seemed to be saying: "Give me vengeance, Lord,
>   For my dead son, for whom my heart is breaking."
> And he to answer her: "Now wait until
>   I shall return." And she: "My Lord," like one
>   In whom grief is impatient, "shouldst thou not
> Return?" And he: "Who shall be where I am
>   Will give it thee." And she: "Good deed of others
>   What boots it thee, if thou neglect thine own?"
> Whence he: "Now comfort thee, for it behoves me
>   That I discharge my duty ere I move;
>   Justice so wills, and pity doth retain me."

THE DIVINE COMEDY

> He who on no new thing has ever looked
>   Was the creator of this visible language,
>   Novel to us, for here it is not found.

Further on in the same terrace they see similar sculptures representing examples of punished pride, such as the fall of Lucifer, and the destruction of Niobe. In each of the following terraces these examples of sin and the opposite virtue are given, represented, however, by various means.

Among the proud, Dante sees the miniature-painter, Oderisi of Adubbio, who pronounces those words on the vanity of earthly fame, which have been proverbial: —

> O thou vain glory of the human powers,
>   How little green upon thy summit lingers,
>   If 't be not followed by an age of grossness!
> In painting Cimabue thought that he
>   Should hold the field, now Giotto has the cry,
>   So that the other's fame is growing dim.
> So has one Guido from the other taken
>   The glory of our tongue, and he perchance
>   Is born, who from the nest shall chase them both.
> Naught is this mundane rumour but a breath
>   Of wind, that comes now this way and now that,
>   And changes name, because it changes side.

Passing through Terrace II., where the envious sit sadly against the rocky wall, with their eye-lids sewn together, and Terrace III., where the wrathful are shrouded in a black, stifling mist, the poets reach Terrace IV., where the slothful are punished. Here Vergil explains the apparent paradox that love is the root of all evil as well as good. Love, he says, is the desire for something; desire for those things which harm others; *i. e.*, love for evil produces pride, envy, and wrath. These are punished in the first three terraces. Insufficient desire or love for that which is good, *i. e.*, God, is punished in Terrace IV., that of the " slothful in well-doing"; excessive desire for merely earthly things, which are not evil in themselves, but only in their excess, produces avarice, gluttony and licentiousness; these are punished in the last three terraces.

Ascending now to Terrace V., Dante sees the souls of Pope Adrian and Hugh Capet, founder of the long dynasty of the kings of France, who gives a brief but admirable summary of the development of the monarchy in France. As they are walking along this terrace, suddenly a mighty earthquake shakes the whole mountain, and while Dante is still filled with amazement and dread at this strange phenomenon, they are overtaken by the spirit of Statius, who explains the cause of the earthquake, telling how, when a soul has been completely purged

THE DIVINE COMEDY

of its sins, and the time of its redemption has arrived, it rises spontaneously from its place, and joyfully makes its way toward the heavens above, while the whole mountain rejoices with him, and the spirits along the slope above and below cry out: "Glory to God in the highest!"

Statius now accompanies Dante and Vergil and all three mount to Terrace VI., where the gluttons are punished, being worn to skin and bone by hunger and thirst, which are only increased by the sight of waterfalls and trees laden with fruit. The last terrace is swathed in flames of fire, within which move about the licentious. Here Dante sees many famous poets, and greets with especial joy Guido Guinicelli of Bologna, who, he says, was

> The father
> Of me and of my betters, who had ever
> Practised the sweet and gracious rhymes of love.

Through this wall of living flame, Dante, too, must pass before he can reach the summit of Purgatory. His spirit, indeed, is willing, but his flesh is weak; he hesitates long before daring to enter the fiery furnace. Vergil urges him on in the tenderest manner —

> "My son,
> Here may indeed be torment, but not death,

THE GREAT POETS OF ITALY

Remember thee, remember! and if I
    On Geryon have safely guided thee
    What shall I do now I am nearer God?
Believe for certain, shouldst thou stand a full
    Millennium in the bosom of this flame,
    It could not make thee bald a single hair.
And if perchance thou think that I deceive thee,
    Draw near to it, and put it to the proof
    With thine own hands upon thy garment's hem.
Now lay aside, now lay aside all fear,
    Turn hitherward, and onward come securely;"
    And I still motionless, and 'gainst my conscience!
Seeing me stand still motionless and stubborn,
    Somewhat disturbed he said: "Now look thou, Son,
    'Twixt Beatrice and thee there is this wall."
As at the name of Thisbe oped his lids
    The dying Pyramus, and gazed upon her,
    What time the mulberry became vermilion,
Even thus, my obduracy being softened,
    I turned to my wise Guide, hearing the name
    That in my memory evermore is welling.
Whereat he wagged his head, and said: "How now?
    Shall we stay on this side?" then smiled as one
    Does at a child who's vanquished by an apple.
Then into the fire in front of me he entered,
    Beseeching Statius to come after me,
    Who a long way before divided us.
When I was in it, into molten glass
    I would have cast me to refresh myself,
    So without measure was the burning there!
And my sweet Father, to encourage me,
    Discoursing still of Beatrice went on,
    Saying: "Her eyes I seem to see already!"

THE DIVINE COMEDY

>A voice, that on the other side was singing,
>>Directed us, and we, attent alone
>>On that, came forth where the ascent began.
>" *Venite, benedicti Patris mei,*"
>>Sounded within a splendour, which was there
>>Such it o'ercame me, and I could not look.

Above this last terrace stretches out the lovely Earthly Paradise, but before the poets can reach it night comes on, and Dante sleeps on the steps, guarded by Vergil and Statius, as a flock is watched over by its shepherd. The passage which describes this scene, and Dante's vision, is a beautiful one: —

>And ere in all its parts immeasurable
>>The horizon of one aspect had become,
>>And Night her boundless dispensation held,
>Each of us of a stair had made his bed;
>>Because the nature of the mount took from us
>>The power of climbing, more than the delight.
>Even as in ruminating passive grow
>>The goats, who have been swift and venturesome
>>Upon the mountain-tops ere they were fed,
>Hushed in the shadow, while the sun is hot,
>>Watched by the herdsman, who upon his staff
>>Is leaning, and in leaning tendeth them;
>And as the shepherd, lodging out of doors,
>>Passes the night beside his quiet flock,
>>Watching that no wild beast may scatter it,
>Such at that hour were we, all three of us,
>>I like the goat, and like the herdsmen they,
>>Begirt on this side and on that by rocks.

THE GREAT POETS OF ITALY

Little could there be seen of things without;
 But through that little I beheld the stars
 More luminous and larger than their wont.
Thus ruminating, and beholding these,
 Sleep seized upon me,—sleep, that oftentimes
 Before a deed is done has tidings of it.
It was the hour, I think, when from the East
 First on the mountain Citherea beamed,
 Who with the fire of love seems always burning;
Youthful and beautiful in dreams methought
 I saw a lady walking in a meadow,
 Gathering flowers; and singing she was saying:
"Know whosoever may my name demand
 That I am Leah, and go moving round
 My beauteous hands to make myself a garland.
To please me at the mirror, here I deck me,
 But never does my sister Rachel leave
 Her looking-glass and sitteth all day long.
To see her beauteous eyes as eager is she,
 As I am to adorn me with my hands;
 Her, seeing, and me, doing satisfies."
And now before the antelucan splendours
 That unto pilgrims the more grateful rise,
 As home-returning, less remote they lodge,
The darkness fled away on every side,
 And slumber with it; whereupon I rose,
 Seeing already the great Masters risen.
"That apple sweet, which through so many branches
 The care of mortals goeth in pursuit of,
 To-day shall put in peace thy hungerings."
Speaking to me, Virgilius of such words
 As these made use; and never were there guerdons
 That could in pleasantness compare with these.

THE DIVINE COMEDY

Such longing upon longing came upon me
    To be above, that at each step thereafter
    For flight I felt in me the pinions growing.
When underneath us was the stairway all
    Run o'er, and we were on the highest step,
    Virgilius fastened upon me his eyes,
And said: " The temporal fire and the eternal,
    Son, thou hast seen, and to a place art come
    Where of myself no farther I discern.
By intellect and art I here have brought thee;
    Take thine own pleasure for thy guide henceforth;
    Beyond the steep ways and the narrow art thou.
Behold the sun, that shines upon thy forehead;
    Behold the grass, the flowerets, and the shrubs
    Which of itself alone this land produces.
Until rejoicing come the beauteous eyes
    Which weeping caused me to come unto thee,
    Thou canst sit down, and thou canst walk among them.
Expect no more or word or sign from me;
    Free and upright and sound is thy free-will,
    And error were it not to do its bidding;
Thee o'er thyself I therefore crown and mitre!"

Thus Dante, having been led by reason (represented by Vergil) to purge himself of sin and vice, is now to put himself under the guidance of heavenly wisdom (represented by Beatrice), by whom he is to visit the homes of the blessed. First, however, he lingers in the Earthly Paradise which forms the summit of Purgatory, and sees strange sights before Beatrice reveals herself to him.

THE GREAT POETS OF ITALY

The descriptions of the landscape in the Earthly Paradise are of surpassing beauty, and choice of quotation is exceedingly difficult. Only a few passages can be given here: —

>Eager already to search in and round
>>The heavenly forest, dense and living-green,
>>Which tempered to the eyes the new-born day,
>Withouten more delay I left the bank,
>>Taking the level country, slowly, slowly,
>>Over the soil that everywhere breathes fragrance.
>A softly breathing air, that no mutation
>>Had in itself, upon the forehead smote me
>>No heavier blow than of a gentle wind,
>Whereat the branches, lightly tremulous,
>>Did all of them bow downward toward that side
>>Where its first shadow casts the Holy Mountain,
>Yet not from their upright direction swayed,
>>So that the little birds upon their tops
>>Should leave the practice of each art of theirs;
>But with full ravishment the hours of prime,
>>Singing, received they in the midst of leaves,
>>That ever bore a burden to their rhymes,
>Such as from branch to branch goes gathering on
>>Through the pine forest on the shore of Chiassi,[1]
>>When Eolus unlooses the Sirocco.
>Already my slow steps had carried me
>>Into the ancient wood so far, that I
>>Could not perceive where I had entered it.
>And lo! my further course a stream cut off,
>>Which tow'rd the left hand with its little waves
>>Bent down the grass that on its margin sprang.

[1] On the seashore, near Ravenna.

THE DIVINE COMEDY

All waters that on earth most limpid are
    Would seem to have within themselves some mixture
    Compared with that which nothing doth conceal,
Although it moves on with a brown, brown current
    Under the shade perpetual, that never
    Ray of the sun lets in, nor of the moon.
With feet I stayed, and with mine eyes I passed
    Beyond the rivulet, to look upon
    The great variety of the fresh May.
And there appeared to me (even as appears
    Suddenly something that doth turn aside
    Through very wonder every other thought)
A lady all alone, who went along
    Singing and culling floweret after floweret,
    With which her pathway was all painted over.
"Ah, beauteous lady, who in rays of love
    Dost warm thyself, if I may trust to looks,
    Which the heart's witnesses are wont to be,
May the desire come unto thee to draw
    Near to this river's bank," I said to her,
    "So much that I may hear what thou art singing.
Thou makest me remember where and what
    Proserpina that moment was when lost
    Her mother her, and she herself the Spring."
As turns herself, with feet together pressed
    And to the ground, a lady who is dancing,
    And hardly puts one foot before the other,
On the vermilion and the yellow flowerets
    She turned towards me, not in other wise
    Than maiden who her modest eyes casts down;
And my entreaties made to be content,
    So near approaching, that the dulcet sound
    Came unto me together with its meaning.

THE GREAT POETS OF ITALY

As soon as she was where the grasses are
    Bathed by the waters of the beauteous river,
    To lift her eyes she granted me the boon.
I do not think there shone so great a light
    Under the lids of Venus, when transfixed
    By her own son, beyond his usual custom!
Erect upon the other bank she smiled,
    Bearing full many colours in her hands,
    Which that high land produces without seed.
Apart three paces did the river make us;
    But Hellespont, where Xerxes passed across,
    (A curb still to all human arrogance,)
More hatred from Leander did not suffer
    For rolling between Sestos and Abydos,
    Than that from me, because it oped not then.
"Ye are new-comers; and because I smile,"
    Began she, "peradventure, in this place
    Elect to human nature for its nest,
Some apprehension keeps you marvelling;
    But the psalm *Delectasti* giveth light [1]
    Which has the power to uncloud your intellect."

. . . . . .

Singing like unto an enamoured lady
    She, with the ending of her words, continued:
    "*Beati quorum tecta sunt peccata.*"
And even as Nymphs, that wandered all alone
    Among the sylvan shadows, sedulous
    One to avoid and one to see the sun,
She then against the stream moved onward, going
    Along the bank, and I abreast of her,
    Her little steps with little steps attending.

---

[1] Psalm xcii. 4: "For thou, Lord, hast made me glad through thy work."

THE DIVINE COMEDY

Between her steps and mine were not a hundred,
  When equally the margins gave a turn,
  In such a way, that to the East I faced.
Nor even thus our way continued far
  Before the lady wholly turned herself
  Unto me, saying, "Brother, look and listen!"
And lo! a sudden lustre ran across
  On every side athwart the spacious forest,
  Such that it made me doubt if it were lightning.
But since the lightning ceases as it comes,
  And that continuing brightened more and more,
  Within my thought I said, "What thing is this?"
And a delicious melody there ran
  Along the luminous air, whence holy zeal
  Made me rebuke the hardihood of Eve;
For there where earth and heaven obedient were,
  The woman only, and but just created,
  Could not endure to stay 'neath any veil;
Underneath which had she devoutly stayed,
  I sooner should have tasted those delights
  Ineffable, and for a longer time.
While 'mid such manifold first-fruits I walked
  Of the eternal pleasure all enrapt,
  And still solicitous of more delights,
In front of us like an enkindled fire
  Became the air beneath the verdant boughs,
  And the sweet sound as singing now was heard.

The poet now beholds a mystical procession of strange and wonderful beasts, venerable old men, beautiful maidens dressed in red, white, green, and purple, all accompanying a chariot drawn by a grif-

THE GREAT POETS OF ITALY

fin and representing the Church of Christ. On the chariot itself stands Beatrice.

>And one of them, as if by Heaven commissioned,
>>Singing, " *Veni, sponsa, de Libano* "
>>Shouted three times, and all the others after.
>Even as the Blessed at the final summons
>>Shall rise up quickened each one from his cavern,
>>Uplifting light the reinvested flesh,
>So upon that celestial chariot
>>A hundred rose *ad vocem tanti senis*,
>>Ministers and messengers of life eternal.
>They all were saying, "*Benedictus qui venis*,"
>>And, scattering flowers above and round about,
>>"*Manibus o date lilia plenis*."
>Ere now have I beheld, as day began,
>>The eastern hemisphere all tinged with rose,
>>And the other heaven with fair serene adorned;
>And the sun's face, uprising, overshadowed
>>So that by tempering influence of vapours
>>For a long interval the eye sustained it;
>Thus in the bosom of a cloud of flowers
>>Which from those hands angelical ascended,
>>And downward fell again inside and out,
>Over her snow-white veil with olive cinct
>>Appeared a lady under a green mantle,
>>Vested in colour of the living flame.
>And my own spirit, that already now
>>So long a time had been, that in her presence
>>Trembling with awe it had not stood abashed,
>Without more knowledge having by mine eyes,
>>Through occult virtue that from her proceeded
>>Of ancient love the mighty influence felt.

THE DIVINE COMEDY

> As soon as on my vision smote the power
>   Sublime, that had already pierced me through
>   Ere from my boyhood I had yet come forth,
> To the left hand I turned with that reliance
>   With which the little child runs to his mother,
>   When he has fear, or when he is afflicted,
> To say unto Virgilius: "Not a drachm
>   Of blood remains in me, that does not tremble;
>   I know the traces of the ancient flame."

After Beatrice has rebuked Dante for his wayward conduct in life, and he has repented in bitter tears, he is led by Matilda to the streams of Lethe and Eunoë, and bathing therein, is made "pure and apt for mounting to the stars."

As we have already seen, the Paradise of Dante is composed of nine spheres enclosed by the Empyrean, which itself is boundless, and is the seat of the Godhead, surrounded by the celestial hierarchy of seraphim, cherubim, thrones, dominions, virtues, powers, principalities, archangels, and angels. The Blessed are likewise here, seated on thrones which are arranged in the form of a rose, surrounding a lake of liquid light, in which they, gazing, see all the fullness of the glory of God. These souls, however, by a mystical virtue of ubiquity, are likewise seen by Dante in the various heavens through which he, with Beatrice, passes, manifesting themselves to him in various forms of light, flames, flashes, sparkles, or shapes made of fiery particles. The souls of the Blessed which are thus distributed over the nine heavens have varying degrees of felicity. Thus, in the first heaven, — that of the moon, — Piccarda, sister of Corso Donati, appears to Dante, faint and dim in that tenuous atmosphere, as a "pearl set on a white forehead," and tells him how, having been forced by her brother to break her vows as a nun, and not having shown tenacity of purpose in opposing his tyranny, she now occupies the lowest sphere of Paradise. Yet this she does with perfect content and happiness, since such is the will of God, for, she says, to quote that one incomparable line, as Matthew Arnold calls it: —

"In la sua voluntade è nostra pace." [1]

Rising from heaven to heaven with Beatrice, Dante passes through Mercury and Venus, — in the former of which are the souls of Christians who sought with overmuch zeal for earthly glory, and in the latter those who were inclined too much to mere human love, — and finally reaches the sun, where he sees the great doctors of theology. Here St. Thomas Aquinas, a Dominican himself, tells in beautiful language the story of St. Francis of Assisi and the establishment of his order; while the Fran-

[1] In His will is our peace.

THE DIVINE COMEDY

ciscan, St. Bonaventura, with the same exquisite courtesy, tells the story of St. Dominic.

In Mars, Dante sees the souls of Christian martyrs and warriors, many of whom form themselves before the eyes of the poet into a wonderful cross of roseate light, flashing in countless splendors. Here, as we have already seen, he meets and converses with his ancestor, Cacciaguida. In Saturn the poet beholds a ladder of light, with spirits mounting and descending upon it, a ladder such as

> " Crowded with angels unnumbered
> By Jacob was seen as he slumbered
> Alone in the desert at night."

Here Peter Damian tells of the mystery of predestination, and St. Benedict describes the founding of his order at Montecassino.

In the heaven of the fixed stars Dante beholds the triumph of Christ : —

> Even as a bird, 'mid the beloved leaves,
>   Quiet upon the nest of her sweet brood
>   Throughout the night, that hideth all things from us,
> Who, that she may behold their longed-for looks
>   And find the food wherewith to nourish them,
>   In which, to her, grave labours grateful are,
> Anticipates the time on open spray
>   And with an ardent longing waits the sun,
>   Gazing intent as soon as breaks the dawn:

THE GREAT POETS OF ITALY

Even thus my Lady standing was, erect
    And vigilant, turned round towards the zone
    Underneath which the sun displays less haste;
So that beholding her distraught and wistful,
    Such I became as he is who desiring
    For something yearns, and hoping is appeased.
But brief the space from one When to the other;
    Of my awaiting, say I, and the seeing
    The welkin grow resplendent more and more.
And Beatrice exclaimed: "Behold the hosts
    Of Christ's triumphal march, and all the fruit
    Harvested by the rolling of these spheres!"
It seemed to me her face was all aflame;
    And eyes she had so full of ecstasy
    That I must needs pass on without describing.
As when in nights serene of the full moon
    Smiles Trivia [1] among the nymphs eternal
    Who paint the firmament through all its gulfs,
Saw I, above the myriads of lamps,
    A Sun [2] that one and all of them enkindled,
    E'en as our own doth the supernal sights,
And through the living light transparent shone
    The lucent substance so intensely clear
    Into my sight, that I sustained it not.

   .   .   .   .   .   .

Dazzled as he is Dante is encouraged to look again at the glorious vision,—

    and I, who to her counsels
Was wholly ready, once again betook me
Unto the battle of the feeble brows.

[1] The moon.   [2] Christ.

THE DIVINE COMEDY

As in the sunshine, that unsullied streams
    Through fractured cloud, ere now a meadow of flowers
    Mine eyes with shadow covered o'er have seen,
So troops of splendours manifold I saw
    Illumined from above with burning rays,
    Beholding not the source of the effulgence.
O power benignant that dost so imprint them![1]
    Thou didst exalt thyself to give more scope
    There to mine eyes that were not strong enough.
The name of that fair flower[2] I e'er invoke
    Morning and evening utterly enthralled
    My soul to gaze upon the greater fire.
And when in both mine eyes depicted were
    The glory and greatness of the living star
    Which there excelleth, as it here excelled,
Athwart the heavens a little torch descended[3]
    Formed in a circle like a coronal,
    And cinctured it, and whirled itself about it.
Whatever melody most sweetly soundeth
    On earth, and to itself most draws the soul,
    Would seem a cloud that, rent asunder, thunders,
Compared unto the sounding of that lyre
    Wherewith was crowned the sapphire beautiful,
    Which gives the clearest heaven its sapphire hue.
" I am Angelic Love, that circle round
    The joy sublime which breaths from out the womb
    That was the hostelry of our Desire;
And I shall circle, Lady of Heaven, while
    Thou followest thy Son, and mak'st diviner
    The sphere supreme, because thou enterest there."

[1] Christ had re-ascended.   [2] The Virgin Mary.
    [3] The Angel Gabriel.

THE GREAT POETS OF ITALY

Thus did the circulated melody
    Seal itself up ; and all the other lights
    Were making to resound the name of Mary.
The regal mantle of the volumes all [1]
    Of that world, which most fervid is and living
    With breath of God and with his works and ways,
Extended over us its inner border,
    So very distant that the semblance of it
    There where I was not yet appeared to me.
Therefore mine eyes did not possess the power
    Of following the incoronated flame,
    Which mounted upward near to its own seed.[2]
And as a little child, that towards its mother
    Stretches its arms, when it the milk has taken,
    Through impulse kindled into outward flame,
Each of those gleams of whiteness upward reached
    So with its summit, that the deep affection
    They had for Mary was revealed to me.
Thereafter they remained there in my sight,
    Regina cœli singing with such sweetness,
    That ne'er from me has the delight departed.

After the passing away of this glorious vision Dante is examined as to his faith by St. Peter, his hope by St. James, and his love by St. John; then being found worthy of being admitted into the presence of God, he rises to the Empyrean, beholds the Blessed Rose, where are seated the saints of all ages, and finally catches an instantaneous glimpse of the glory and mystery of the Trinity.

[1] The *Primum Mobile*.
[2] The Virgin Mary ascending to her Son.

THE DIVINE COMEDY

In this supreme vision his desires find full fruition, and his spirit, overcome by the overwhelming glory of the Godhead, fails him, and thus his vision comes to an end: —

> Here vigour failed the lofty fantasy:
> But now was turning my desire and will,
> Even as a wheel that equally is moved,
> The Love which moves the sun and the other stars.

Such is the "Divine Comedy" of Dante, which has won undying admiration in the realm of literature from the poet's own time down to the present. It would lead us too far to go into a detailed analysis of its greatness here, but with one consent men like Carlyle, Ruskin, Gladstone, Browning, and Tennyson in England; Tholuck, Witte, and Kraus, in Germany; Longfellow and Lowell in America, attribute the title of supreme genius to this poem.

"The Divine Comedy" is universal in its compass, containing the elements of dramatic, epic, and lyric poetry; full of sublime imaginations, touching and pathetic episodes, and not deficient even in humor, grotesque at times, but often of a strangely sweet and tender nature. The language is astonishingly simple and concise, and invariably represents the thought of the poet with absolute truth and fidelity. We find in this wonderfully condensed poem no unmeaning epithets, no mere arabesques of style such as adorn the lesser thoughts of lesser men. Each word is in its right place. The metaphors of Dante are especially famous, for the most part simple and drawn from everyday life, yet unexcelled in beauty and especially in their perfect and complete adaptation to the point they are meant to illustrate. Such are those of the old tailor threading his needle, the sheep leaving the fold in huddling groups, the fish disappearing from view in the depths of clear water, and the pearl faintly discernible on a white forehead.

Above all, the personality of the author lends a dramatic interest to the poem and exercises a fascination on the reader. As Lowell says, "The man behind the verse is far greater than the verse itself."[1] In the midst of the wonderful landscapes of his own creation, dark and terrible, soft and beautiful, he walks among the men and women of all ages; he talks to them and hears their stories of half-forgotten crimes and tragedies; he brands them with infamy or sets upon their brows the wreath of praise. It is his love for Beatrice — now become the symbol of spiritual life — which

[1] Carducci says Dante is a "most great poet because he is a great man, and a great man because he had a great conscience."

THE DIVINE COMEDY

leads him through the realms of sin over the steep rocks of Purgatory to the glory ineffable of God.

Completely a man of his age, Dante incorporates into the " Divine Comedy " all its science and learning, its theology, philosophy, astronomy, its use of classical authors, and its way of regarding the present life as insignificant in comparison with the life to come. All these things have still a distinct mediæval stamp. Yet Dante is at the same time the most original of poets. It is his mighty individuality which, rising above the conventionality of his age and country, has made him a world-poet, as true to-day as ever in his depiction of the human heart in all its sin and sorrow, virtue and vice, in its love and hate and its inextinguishable aspiration toward a better and happier existence in the world beyond the grave.[1]

---

[1] No poet in Italian literature is better adapted to special study than Dante, nor is any other so profitable. The material is abundant. The reader should provide himself with Scartazzini's *Companion to Dante*, translated by A. J. Butler, or Symonds' *Introduction to Dante*. These will furnish all necessary facts concerning the life and works of the poet. It must be remembered that the *Divine Comedy* is a difficult poem, and that it takes many readings and much study to master it. It will be best to begin by reading Maria F. Rossetti's *A Shadow of Dante*, which gives a general outline of the story with copious extracts. Then one of the numerous translations should be taken up and studied carefully,

THE GREAT POETS OF ITALY

canto by canto — Cary's, Longfellow's, and Norton's translations (the latter in prose) are the best. An edition of Cary's translation has been made by the writer of this book (published by T. Y. Crowell & Co.), with special reference to the general reader. It contains an introduction, Rossetti's translation of the *New Life*, and a revised reprint of Cary's version of the *Divine Comedy*, furnished with a popular commentary in the form of foot notes. The number of essays and critical estimates of Dante in English is legion; perhaps the three best are those by Carlyle (in *Heroes and Hero Worship*), Dean Church, and Lowell. Two excellent books recently published are *Aids to the Study of Dante*, and *The Teachings of Dante*, both by Charles A. Dinsmore, and both published by Houghton, Mifflin & Co.

IV

PETRARCH AND BOCCACCIO

It is hard for people to-day to realize the enormous difference between the mediæval and modern world. The former was full of superstition and naïve belief; authority reigned supreme; in religion no one dreamed of questioning the decrees of church and pope; in philosophy a question was settled by a quotation from Aristotle or his scholastic representative, St. Thomas Aquinas. This same blind following of authority was exemplified in art — painters imitated slavishly their predecessors, and up to the appearance of Cimabue and Giotto there was no thought of improving the stiff conventionalities of the Byzantine artists. In scholarship, criticism (*i. e.*, individual judgment) was unknown; in science, all such old-world fables as those which told of the mandragora, dragons, phenix, and unicorn were devoutly received as true zoölogy, while the Ptolemaic system of astronomy was unquestioned. The idea of progress was utterly unknown; the world had been created

THE GREAT POETS OF ITALY

exactly as it was, and would remain so till the coming of Christ, when a new heaven and a new earth would be formed. So, in the political and social world, the thought that the existing state of things could change would have seemed absurd. It needs no words of mine to demonstrate the vast difference between these conceptions and the present world, with its idea of illimitable progress, its criticism of all things high and low, its denial that authority in church and state is just, simply because it is old; its eager acceptation of innovations; its cultivation of the individual in all departments of life; to say nothing of the vast field opened up by the discoveries of positive science.

Dante stands at the end of the old order of things, rising like a mighty mountain peak over the dead plain of mediæval mediocrity. He is not an innovator; he does not inaugurate a new period of civilization. When he died he left no school of followers to carry on his work; he closed an epoch rather than opened one. It is true that for a hundred years or more men did imitate his "Divine Comedy," but only in the outward form, neglecting the poetical and æsthetical side, for which indeed Dante's contemporaries had little or no appreciation. It is only in the nineteenth

PETRARCH AND BOCCACCIO

century that Dante has become a power in Italy as voicing the universal desire for a united fatherland.

The man who begins the mighty movement of the Renaissance, from which modern civilization takes its rise, is Francesco Petrarch. It is strange to think that he, so utterly different in mental attitude from Dante, was seventeen years old when the latter died. Yet the change which he represents had been slowly prepared by his predecessors. As we have seen, the study of the Latin language and authors had never fully died out in the Middle Ages; especially in the twelfth and thirteenth centuries the classic writers, Vergil, Ovid, Statius, Livy, were read more and more, not, however, as examples of literary excellence, or as revealing the culture of antiquity, but as mines of practical wisdom, or as supplying quotations and examples for philosophical and theological discussions. The classic writers were made to fit in with mediæval ways of thinking, and thus subordinated to the then existing state of civilization. With Petrarch, however, comes a complete change in all these respects. For him the classic writers were the *ne plus ultra* of elegant form; he strove to penetrate into their spirit, to appreciate fully the peculiar excellence of each one;

THE GREAT POETS OF ITALY

and above all to clear antiquity from its barnacle-like covering of mediæval traditions and superstitions and to present Roman civilization, its learning, science, and art, as it was. To him the Middle Ages were a period of degradation, which had long hidden from view the past glories of Rome ; and he now, for the first time in history, broke away from the present and immediate past, and turned his eyes back to ancient times. In so doing he founded the Renaissance in Italy, and laid down the lines in which all subsequent students of classical antiquity were to follow. In all these respects Petrarch is justly regarded, not only as the founder of modern classical scholarship, but as the founder of modern civilization as well. He has been referred to by more than one historian as the Columbus of a new intellectual world.

The life of Petrarch is intensely interesting, and the difficulty in giving an outline of it consists not in the absence of well-ascertained facts, as in the case of Dante, but in an embarrassment of riches. For we know more of the details of Petrarch's life than we do of any other writer who lived before the Renaissance.

Francesco Petrarch was born in 1304 at Arezzo, whither his father, a prominent lawyer of Florence,

PETRARCH

PETRARCH AND BOCCACCIO

had gone on being exiled in 1302, at the same time as Dante. After moving about some time in Italy, the family finally settled at Avignon, in Southern France, then famous as the seat of the Roman papacy during the so-called Babylonian captivity. From 1315 to 1319 Francesco was sent to school at the neighboring town of Charpentras; in 1319 he went to the University of Montpellier to study law, and in 1323 went to the University of Bologna. At the university, however, he neglected law for the classic writers, and he tells us how one day his father appeared and burnt all his Latin books, with the exception of Vergil and Cicero's "Rhetoric," which by means of tears and entreaties he succeeded in saving from the flames.

After the death of his parents, in 1326, Petrarch settled down in Avignon and devoted himself to his favorite studies. As he was without means he entered the church, and henceforth was relieved of all anxiety in regard to money. From this time on his life was spent in study, in the collection of a library, in writing books, in travel, and in visits to his friends. Petrarch was very fond of traveling, and his letters abound with interesting descriptions of the places he had seen. Yet, in spite of this passion for travel, he loved also the quiet and tranquil existence of country life. Here he could indulge to his heart's content his love for nature, the beauty of which he was practically the first to describe in sympathetic language. It was to satisfy this love for nature and the "quiet life," that Petrarch bought a small property in Vaucluse, near Avignon, and here he never failed to return from time to time during all his later life, when tired of travel, weighed down by care, or depressed by the loss of friends and the "creeping steps of age."

Petrarch seems to have had a peculiar faculty for making friends; he was loved and admired by high and low. Among these numerous friends are worthy of especial mention the powerful Colonna family, father and two sons, who played so important a part in the history of Italy; King Robert of Naples; the Emperor Charles IV., who wished to have Petrarch accompany him to Germany; King John of France, who wished to retain him in Paris; Pope Urban IV., who offered him the position of papal secretary. There were scores of others of humbler rank, among them Boccaccio, his faithful admirer and life-long friend. Not only kings and princes lavished honors on Petrarch, but cities as well; Florence offered to restore his father's property and make him professor at the university if he would live there; Venice

PETRARCH AND BOCCACCIO

gave him a palace in return for his library, and in 1340 the cities of Paris and Rome, at the same time, invited him to receive the laurel crown of poet.

After due deliberation Petrarch accepted the invitation of Rome, and on Easter Sunday, 1340, in the presence of an immense company of people, he was crowned at the capitol, amid the blare of trumpets and the acclamation of the assembled multitudes. This scene may be considered as the climax of Petrarch's victorious career.

No man outwardly ever had a happier life than he. He was well-to-do; was handsome and amiable; surrounded by friends; admired and flattered by all Europe; looked on as a great poet and a prodigy of learning. Surely, if any man could be content, Petrarch was that man. And yet he was not happy. Owing to his peculiar character, his sensitiveness, his streak of melancholy, his immense vanity which could never be fully satisfied, and especially owing to the constant struggle that went on in his soul between the mediæval ascetic view of life (which he could never wholly shake off) and the more worldly modern view, which he himself inaugurated; owing to all these things, I say, there is a tinge of sadness in all his writings. Perhaps no man ever lived who

THE GREAT POETS OF ITALY

illustrated so well the well-known words of the old Latin poet : —

> E'en where the founts of pleasure flow,
> A bitter something bubbles up.

Indeed, Petrarch's character presents us with strange contrasts. He who loved travel so much is forever writing about the joys of country life; constantly seen in the gay and often licentious courts of princes, he wrote a treatise in praise of solitude; receiving his living from the church and naturally religious, many of his acts were contrary to both religion and morality.

And yet Petrarch was not a hypocrite. No one can doubt his sincerity; these things are only the outward expression of that struggle which was constantly going on in his heart. Like St. Paul, he seemed always to be crying out, "The good that I would, I do not, but the evil which I would not, that I do."

The latter part of his life was thus spent in ever-increasing sadness. In 1347 his friend, Colonna, died; in 1348, Laura; in 1347 his high hopes concerning the restoration of the ancient glory of the Roman Republic through Rienzi, the "last of the tribunes," were suddenly dashed by the fall and death of the latter. Henceforth Petrarch spent his

PETRARCH AND BOCCACCIO

life wandering from city to city, from court to court, surrounded by an aureole of glory, yet never at rest, except when he retired to the quiet seclusion of Vaucluse.

In 1370 he went to the university town of Padua, then the centre of an active intellectual life. In the spring of the same year he started for Rome, in response to an invitation of the pope, but fell so grievously ill at Ferrara that he gave up his journey and settled down at Arquà, a village not far from Padua, where he died July 18, 1374. He was found dead in his library, bending over a folio volume.

As may be supposed from Petrarch's enthusiasm for the Latin authors, most of his own works were written in that language. It is a generous trait of literary and scholarly, as well as of religious, enthusiasts that they are not content merely to receive the treasures of art and learning, but feel impelled to impart their own joys to others. Petrarch was not only an eager student, but devoted his life to making known to others the riches and glory of ancient Rome. All this he does in his numerous Latin works. These include, — in poetry, — bucolics and eclogues, imitated from Vergil; poetic epistles, imitated from Horace; and especially his "Africa," an epic poem on the life of Scipio Africanus, from which he expected immortality. Of especial importance in the development of the Renaissance and the Revival of Learning are his prose Latin works. Chief among these we may mention his history of "Illustrious Men," his moral and religious tractates, "The Remedy of Fortune," the "Solitary Life," and especially his letters, six hundred in number, written in a Latin style which infinitely surpassed anything produced till then, and which founded a branch of literature which was very popular throughout all the Renaissance.

For our purpose here, however, we can only discuss in detail Petrarch's Italian poetry — he wrote no Italian prose. It is this which gives him his place in literature as the first great lyric poet of modern times.

We have seen that Italian lyrical poetry began in Sicily, and that, carried thence to Bologna and Tuscany, it formed a new school, which found its highest expression in Dante. Petrarch once more founds a new school of lyric writers which, while still in some respects recalling the poetry of his predecessors, is yet in spirit far different from them. With him poetry is no longer a matter of chivalrous ideals, as with the troubadours, or of symbolism and philosophy, as with Guido Guinicelli and

PETRARCH AND BOCCACCIO

Dante, but the expression of his own genuine feelings. His Laura is not like the Beatrice of the "Divine Comedy," a mere abstraction, a personification of virtue and symbol of religion, but is a woman of flesh and blood, beautiful and virtuous, but not ethereal and mystical — a woman, in fact, —

> Not too bright or good
> For human nature's daily food.

In his songs, then, Petrarch describes real things — the beauty of Laura in all its details; her coldness and his suffering; and especially the conflicting feelings which tormented his soul. In his subjectivity, his psychological analysis of feelings, his use of poetry to express his own mental experiences; in his lovely descriptions of nature; and especially in his melancholy, the far-off anticipation of the "Weltschmerz," Petrarch is indeed the first modern lyrical poet.

He himself confidently expected immortality from his Latin works, which, alas for the vanity of human expectations! are now forgotten by all except special students. He apparently looked with contempt on his Italian lyrics; yet this was only affectation, for even in his later years he carefully revised them. These songs and sonnets are still unsurpassed in Italian literature. Many,

THE GREAT POETS OF ITALY

it is true, are artificial, and on account of puns, antitheses, and conceits are repugnant to modern taste; yet the large number of his best poems are exquisite pictures of womanly beauty, with a charming landscape as a background, all enveloped in an atmosphere of lovely poetry, full of tenderness, pathos, and genuine feeling. Above all, they are written in a style and with a harmony of numbers unknown till then and not surpassed since.

Petrarch's Italian poetry consists of some three hundred and seventy-five ballads, songs, and sonnets (the latter forming the vast majority), and in the twelve chapters, or books, of the so-called "Triumphs." These are, with but few exceptions, consecrated to the story of his love for a certain woman named Laura, concerning whose actual existence as much contest has been waged as over that of Beatrice. It seems now pretty definitely ascertained that Laura was no mere fancy-picture, but a real being. She was the daughter of Audibert de Noves, and the wife of Ugo de Sade, to whom she bore eleven children. She died April 6, 1348, probably of the pest, which was then raging. Petrarch saw her for the first time April 6, 1327, and for twenty-one years worshiped her from a respectful distance. There is little story or action

PETRARCH AND BOCCACCIO

in all these sonnets. Petrarch's love is not returned by Laura, he makes no progress in her affections, and his poems are devoted for the most part to descriptions of her beauty, coldness, and indifference, and his own state of wretchedness.

Among the many sonnets descriptive of Laura's beauty we may take the following, in which she is declared to be the most perfect example of Nature's handiwork: —

> The stars, the elements, and Heaven have made
> With blended powers a work beyond compare;
> All their consenting influence, all their care,
> To frame one perfect creature lent their aid.
> Whence Nature views her loveliness displayed
> With sun-like radiance sublimely fair;
> Nor mortal eye can the pure splendor bear:
> Love, sweetness, in unmeasured grace arrayed.
> The very air illumed by her sweet beams
> Breathes purest excellence; and such delight
> That all expression far beneath it gleams.
> No base desire lives in that heavenly light,
> Honor alone and virtue! — fancy's dreams
> Never saw passion rise refined by rays so bright.[1]

In another sonnet he tells how he was affected the first time he saw her: —

> Sun never rose so beautiful and bright
> When skies above most clear and cloudless showed,

[1] Capel Lofft.

THE GREAT POETS OF ITALY

Nor, after rain, the bow of heaven e'er glowed
With tints so varied, delicate, and light,
As in rare beauty flashed upon my sight,
The day I first took up this am'rous load,
That face whose fellow ne'er on earth abode —
Even my praise to paint it seems a slight!
Then saw I Love, who did her fine eyes bend
So sweetly, every other face obscure
Has from that hour till now appeared to me.
The boy-god and his bow, I saw them, friend,
From whom life since has never been secure,
Whom still I madly yearn again to see.[1]

Wherever he goes he is pursued by his love: —

Alone, and pensive, near some desert shore,
Far from the haunts of men I love to stray,
And, cautiously, my distant path explore
Where never human footsteps marked the way.
Thus from the public gaze I strive to fly,
And to the winds alone my griefs impart;
While in my hollow cheek and haggard eye
Appears the fire that burns my inmost heart.
But ah, in vain to distant scenes I go;
No solitude my troubled thoughts allays.
Methinks e'en things inanimate must know
The flame that on my soul in secret preys;
Whilst Love, unconquered, with resistless sway
Still hovers round my path, still meets me on my way.[2]

Yet Laura is not only beautiful, but good; a virtuous heart, a lofty mind, a happy spirit, all these are united in her with natural grace and beauty.

[1] Macgregor.   [2] J. B. Taylor.

PETRARCH AND BOCCACCIO

> High birth in humble life, reserved yet kind,
> On youth's gay flower ripe fruits of age and rare,
> A virtuous heart, therewith a lofty mind,
> A happy spirit in a pensive air;
> Her planet, nay, heaven's king, has fitly shrined
> All gifts and graces in this lady fair,
> True honor, purest praises, worth refined,
> Above what rapt dreams of best poets are.
> Virtue and Love so rich in her unite,
> With natural beauty dignified address,
> Gestures that still a silent grace express,
> And in her eyes I know not what strange light,
> That makes the noonday dark, the dusk night clear,
> Bitter the sweet, and e'en sad absence dear.[1]

Petrarch not only gives general descriptions of the beauty of his lady and their effect as his predecessors had done, but he gives over and over again details thereof, especially her eyes and hair: —

> Say, from what vein did Love procure the gold
> To make those sunny tresses? From what thorn
> Stole he the rose, and whence the dew of morn,
> Bidding them breathe and live in Beauty's mould?
> What depth of ocean gave the pearls that told
> Those gentle accents sweet, though rarely born?
> Whence came so many graces to adorn
> That brow more fair than summer skies unfold?
> Oh! say what angels lead, what spheres control
> The song divine which wastes my life away?
> (Who can with trifles now my senses move?)
> What sun gave birth unto the lofty soul

[1] Macgregor.

THE GREAT POETS OF ITALY

> Of those enchanting eyes, whose glances stray
> To burn and freeze my heart — the sport of Love?[1]

He is especially fond of describing the scenes where she is, thus combining with her own charms those of lovely nature. Thus he sees her on the banks of clear streams, sitting on the green grass, with blossoms falling upon her from the trees in springtime, as in the following lines from one of his most beautiful songs: —

> Clear, fresh, and dulcet streams,
> Which the fair shape who seems
> To me, sole woman, haunted at noontide;
> Fair bough, so gently fit,
> (I sigh to think of it),
> Which lent a pillar to her lovely side;
> And turf, and flowers bright-eyed,
> O'er which her folded gown
> Flowed like an angel's down;
> And you, O holy air and hushed,
> Where first my heart at her sweet glances gushed;
> Give ear, give ear, with one consenting,
> To my last words, my last and my lamenting.
>
> . . . .
>
> How well I call to mind,
> When from those boughs the wind
> Shook down upon her bosom flower on flower;
> And there she sat meek-eyed,
> In midst of all that pride,
> Sprinkled and blushing through an amorous shower.
> Some to her hair paid dower,

[1] Wrottesley.

PETRARCH AND BOCCACCIO

And seemed to dress the curls,
Queenlike, with gold and pearls;
Some, snowing, on her drapery stopped,
Some on the earth, some on the water dropped;
While others, fluttering from above,
Seemed wheeling round in pomp, and saying, "Here reigns Love."
How often then I said,
Inward, and filled with dread,
"Doubtless this creature came from Paradise!"
For at her look the while,
Her voice, and her sweet smile,
And heavenly air, truth parted from mine eyes;
So that, with long-drawn sighs,
I said, as far from men,
"How came I here, and when?"
I had forgotten; and alas!
Fancied myself in heaven, not where I was;
And from that time till this, I bear
Such love for the green bower, I cannot rest elsewhere.[1]

Yet, in spite of all her beauty, he is not happy; the thought of her never leaves him. When absent from her he is most miserable: —

Never was bird, spoiled of its young, more sad,
Or wild beast in his lair, more lone than me,
Now that no more that lovely face I see,
The only sun my fond eyes ever had.
In ceaseless sorrow is my chief delight;
My food to poison turns, to grief my joy;
The night is torture, dark the clearest sky,
And my lone pillow a hard field of fight.

[1] Leigh Hunt.

THE GREAT POETS OF ITALY

> Sleep is indeed, as has been well expressed,
> Akin to death, for it the heart removes
> From the dear thought in which alone I live.
> Land above all with plenty, beauty blessed!
> Ye flowery plains, green banks, and shady groves!
> Ye hold the treasure for whose loss I grieve![1]

Night, which brings rest and peace to others, brings it not to him:—

> O'er earth and sky her lone watch silence keeps,
> And bird and beast in stirless slumber lie,
> Her starry chariot Night conducts on high,
> And in its bed the waveless ocean sleeps.
> I wake, muse, burn, and weep; of all my pain
> The one sweet cause appears before me still;
> War is my lot, which grief and anger fill,
> And thinking but of her some rest I gain.
> Thus from one bright and living fountain flows
> The bitter and the sweet on which I feed;
> One hand alone can harm me or can heal;
> And thus my martyrdom no limit knows,
> A thousand deaths and lives each day I feel,
> So distant are the paths to peace which lead.[1]

Above all, his torment is increased by the contest between his religious feelings and his love, which, earthly as it was, seemed to be inconsistent with his duty as a Christian. Yet he cannot tear his heart away from the object of his affection. Hence arises a constant warring of the flesh against the

[1] Macgregor.

PETRARCH AND BOCCACCIO

spirit, and a vacillation which finds expression in sentiments diametrically opposite. Thus at times he declares that his love for Laura is a blessing to him, leading him to a virtuous and religious life: —

> Lady, in your bright eyes
> Soft glancing round, I mark a holy light,
> Pointing the arduous way that heavenward lies;
> And to my practised sight,
> From thence, where Love enthroned, asserts his might,
> Visibly, palpably, the soul beams forth.
> This is the beacon guides to deeds of worth,
> And urges me to seek the glorious goal;
> This bids me leave behind the vulgar throng,
> Nor can the human tongue
> Tell how those orbs divine o'er all my soul
> Exert their sweet control,
> Both when hoar winter's frosts around are flung,
> And when the year puts on his youth again,
> Jocund, as when this bosom first knew pain.[1]

And again: —

> Throned on her angel brow, when love displays
> His radiant form among all other fair,
> Far as eclipsed their choicest charms appear,
> I feel beyond its wont my passion blaze.
> And still I bless the day, the hour, the place,
> When first so high mine eyes I dared to rear;
> And say, "Fond heart, thy gratitude declare,
> That then thou hadst the privilege to gaze.

[1] Dacre.

THE GREAT POETS OF ITALY

'T was she inspired the tender thought of love,
Which points to heaven, and teaches to despise
The earthly vanities that others prize:
She gave the soul's light grace, which to the skies
Bids thee straight onward in the right path move;
Whence buoyed by hope e'en now I soar to worlds above."[1]

Then comes another mood, in which his love seems sinful and he prays God to lead him to a better life: —

Father of heaven! after the days misspent,
After the nights of wild tumultuous thought,
In that fierce passion's strong entanglement,
One, for my peace too lovely fair, had wrought;
Vouchsafe that, by thy grace, my spirit bent
On nobler aims, to holier ways be brought;
That so my foe, spreading with dark intent
His mortal snares, be foiled, and held at nought.
E'en now th' eleventh year its course fulfils,
That I have bowed me to the tyranny
Relentless most to fealty most tried.
Have mercy, Lord! on my unworthy ills;
Fix all my thoughts in contemplation high;
How on the cross this day a Saviour died.[2]

Once he made a pilgrimage to Rome, and the sight of the holy city increases the conviction he has that he ought to tear himself from Laura: —

The solemn aspect of this sacred shore
Wakes for the misspent past my bitter sighs;

[1] Wrangham.   [2] Dacre.

PETRARCH AND BOCCACCIO

"Pause, wretched man! and turn," as conscience cries,
  Pointing the heavenward way where I should soar.
  But soon another thought gets mastery o'er
The first, that so to palter were unwise;
E'en now the time, if memory err not, flies,
  When we should wait our lady-love before.
  I, for his aim then well I apprehend,
Within me freeze, as one who sudden hears
News unexpected, which his soul offend.
Returns my first thought then, that disappears;
  Nor know I which shall conquer, but till now
Within me they contend, nor hope of rest allow! [1]

This state of his mind, divided against itself, finds its best expression in the song, which is regarded as one of the most beautiful of his poems. In the various strophes conflicting sentiments arise, develop, and reach a climax, only to be overthrown by a sudden revulsion of feeling; fame, happiness, the sweetness of love beckon the poet on; then comes the chilling thought of death to show that all things earthly are nothing but vanity. Unfortunately this song is too long to be quoted here entire. We give the first strophe and the refrain: —

    Ceaseless I think, and in each wasting thought
    So strong a pity for myself appears,
    That often it has brought
    My harassed heart to new yet natural tears;

[1] Macgregor.

THE GREAT POETS OF ITALY

Seeing each day my end of life draw nigh,
Instant in prayer, I ask of God the wings
With which the spirit springs,
Freed from its mortal coil, to bliss on high;
But nothing to this hour, prayer, tear, or sigh,
Whatever man could do, my hopes sustain;
And so indeed in justice should it be;
Able to stay, who went and fell, that he
Should prostrate, in his own despite, remain.
But, lo! the tender arms
In which I trust are open to me still,
Though fears my bosom fill
Of other's fate, and my own heart alarms,
Which worldly feelings spur, haply to utmost ill.

. . . .

Song! I am here, my heart the while more cold
With fear than frozen snow,
Feels in its certain core death's coming blow;
For thus, in weak self-communing has rolled
Of my vain life the better portion by:
Worse burden surely ne'er
Tried mortal man than that which now I bear;
Though death be seated nigh,
For future life still seeking councils new,
I know and love the good, yet, ah! the worse pursue.[1]

The finest of Petrarch's sonnets are those written after the death of Laura. With this dread event he loses all joy in life; the thought of her beauty returns softened by memory and the lapse of time:—

[1] Macgregor.

PETRARCH AND BOCCACCIO

Where is the brow whose gentlest beckonings led
My raptured heart at will, now here, now there?
Where the twin stars, lights of this lower sphere,
Which o'er my darkling path their radiance shed?
Where is true worth, and wit, and wisdom fled?
The courteous phrase, the melting accent, where?
Where, grouped in one rich form, the beauties rare,
Which long their magic influence o'er me shed?
Where is the shade, within whose sweet recess
My wearied spirit still forgot its sighs,
And all my thoughts their constant record found?
Where, where is she, my life's sole arbitress?
Ah, wretched world! and wretched ye, mine eyes
(Of her pure light bereft) which aye with tears are drowned.[1]

Yet, in his affliction there is a certain comfort, for now that she is dead she seems no longer cold to him, and he often sees and converses with her in heaven: —

Fond fancy raised me to the spot where strays
She whom I seek but find on earth no more;
There, fairer still and humbler than before,
I saw her, in the third heaven's blessèd maze.
She took me by the hand, and "Thou shalt trace,
If hope not errs," she said, "this happy shore;
I, I am she, thy breast with slights who tore,
And ere its evening closed my day's brief space.
What human heart conceives my joys exceed;
Thee only I expect, and (what remain
Below) the charms, once objects of thy love."
Why ceased she? Ah! my captive hand why freed?

[1] Wrangham.

THE GREAT POETS OF ITALY

    Such of her soft and hallowed tones the chain,
    From that delightful heaven my soul could scarcely move.[1]

She treats him kindly, bending over him from her heavenly seat, as a mother over her child: —

    Ne'er did fond mother to her darling son,
    Or zealous spouse to her belovèd mate,
    Sage counsel give, in perilous estate,
    With such kind caution, in such tender tone,
    As gives that fair one, who, oft looking down
    On my hard exile from her heavenly seat,
    With wonted kindness bends upon my fate
    Her brow, as friend or parent would have done :
    Now chaste affection prompts her speech, now fear,
    Instructive speech, that points what several ways
    To seek or shun, while journeying here below;
    Then all the ills of life she counts, and prays
    My soul ere long may quit this terrene sphere;
    And by her words alone I'm soothed and freed from woe.[2]

When spring returns, it brings a renewal of his grief : —

    The spring returns, with all her smiling train:
    The wanton Zephyrs breathe along the bowers,
    The glistening dewdrops hang on bending flowers,
    And tender green light-shadows o'er the plain;
    And thou, sweet Philomel, renew'st thy strain,
    Breathing thy wild notes to the midnight grove;
    All nature feels the kindling fire of love,
    The vital force of spring's returning reign.
    But not to me returns the cheerful spring!
    O heart! that know'st no period to thy grief,

[1] Wrangham.   [2] Nott.

PETRARCH AND BOCCACCIO

> Nor nature's smiles to thee impart relief,
> Nor change of mind the varying seasons bring:
> She, she is gone! All that e'er pleased before,
> Adieu! ye birds, ye flowers, ye fields, that charm no more! [1]

The charms of Vaucluse only embitter his sense of loss: —

> Once more, ye balmy gales, I feel you blow;
> Again, sweet hills, I mark the morning beams
> Gild your green summits: while your silver streams
> Through vales of fragrance undulating flow.
> But you, ye dreams of bliss, no longer here
> Give life and beauty to the glowing scene;
> For stern remembrance stands where you have been,
> And blasts the verdure of the blooming year.
> O Laura! Laura! in the dust with thee,
> Would I could find a refuge from despair!
> Is this thy boasted triumph, Love, to tear
> A heart thy coward malice dares not free;
> And bid it live, while every hope is fled,
> To weep, among the ashes of the dead? [2]

His only comfort now is in thinking that he, too, must soon die: —

> Oh! swifter than the hart my life hath fled,
> A shadowed dream; one wingèd glance hath seen
> Its only good; its hours (how few serene!)
> The sweet and bitter tide of thought have fed:
> Ephemeral world! in pride and sorrow bred,
> Who hope in thee, are blind as I have been;
> I hoped in thee, and thus my heart's loved queen
> Hath borne it mid her nerveless, kindred dead.

[1] Woodhouselee.   [2] Anne Bannerman.

THE GREAT POETS OF ITALY

<blockquote>
Her form decayed — its beauty still survives;
For in high heaven that soul will ever bloom,
With which each day I more enamoured grow:
Thus though my locks are blanched, my hope revives
In thinking on her home — her soul's high doom:
Alas! how changed the shrine she left below! [1]
</blockquote>

Weary of life, now that he is left alone, he devotes himself to God; he directs all his thought to heaven, where Laura awaits and beckons him: —

<blockquote>
The chosen angels, and spirits blest,
Celestial tenants, on that glorious day
My lady joined them, thronged in bright array
Around her, with amaze and awe imprest.
"What splendour, what new beauty stands confest
Unto our sight?" — among themselves they say;
"No soul, in this vile age, from sinful clay
To our high realms has risen so fair a guest."
Delighted to have changed her mortal state,
She ranks amid the purest of her kind;
And ever and anon she looks behind,
To mark my progress and my coming wait;
Now my whole thought, my wish to heaven I cast;
'T is Laura's voice I hear, and hence she bids me haste. [2]
</blockquote>

His love thus purified and his thoughts now turned to God alone, the poet awaits in resignation the coming of the inevitable hour of death. The "Book of Songs and Sonnets," as his Italian poetry may be called, ends in a beautiful hymn to

[1] Wollaston. [2] Nott.

PETRARCH AND BOCCACCIO

the Virgin Mary, in which the poet breathes forth his chastened sorrow and his hopes.

>   Beautiful Virgin! clothed with the sun,
>   Crowned with the stars, who so the Eternal Sun
>   Well pleasedst that in thine his light he hid;
>   Love pricks me on to utter speech of thee,
>   And — feeble to commence without thy aid —
>   Of Him who on thy bosom rests in love.
>   Her I invoke who gracious still replies
>   To all who ask in faith,
>   Virgin! if ever yet
>   The misery of man and mortal things
>   To mercy moved thee, to my prayer incline;
>   Help me in this my strife,
>   Though I am but of dust, and thou heaven's radiant Queen!
>   . . . .
>
>   Bright Virgin! and immutable as bright,
>   O'er life's tempestuous ocean the sure star
>   Each trusting mariner that truly guides,
>   Look down, and see amid this dreadful storm
>   How I am tost at random and alone,
>   And how already my last shriek is near,
>   Yet still in thee, sinful although and vile,
>   My soul keeps all her trust;
>   Virgin! I thee implore
>   Let not thy foe have triumph in my fall;
>   Remember that our sin made God himself,
>   To free us from its chain,
>   Within thy virgin womb our image on Him take!
>
>   Virgin! what tears already have I shed,
>   Cherished what dreams and breathed what prayers in vain,

THE GREAT POETS OF ITALY

But for my own worse penance and sure loss;
Since first on Arno's shore I saw the light
Till now, whate'er I sought, wherever turned,
My life has passed in torment and in tears;
For mortal loveliness in air, act, speech,
Has seized and soiled my soul:
O Virgin! pure and good,
Delay not till I reach my life's last year;
Swifter than shaft and shuttle are, my days
'Mid misery and sin
Have vanished all, and now Death only is behind!

Virgin! She now is dust, who, living, held
My heart in grief, and plunged it since in gloom;
She knew not of my many ills this one,
And had she known, what since befell me still
Had been the same, for every other wish
Was death to me and ill renown for her;
But, Queen of heaven, our Goddess — if to thee
Such homage be not sin —
Virgin! of matchless mind,
Thou knowest now the whole; and that, which else
No other can, is nought to thy great power:
Deign then my grief to end,
Thus honor shall be thine, and safe my peace at last!

. . . .

Virgin! benevolent, and foe of pride,
Ah! let the love of our one Author win,
Some mercy for a contrite humble heart:
For, if her poor frail mortal dust I loved
With loyalty so wonderful and long,
Much more my faith and gratitude for thee.
From this my present sad and sunken state
If by thy help I rise,

PETRARCH AND BOCCACCIO

Virgin! to thy dear name
I consecrate and cleanse my thoughts, speech, pen,
My mind, and heart with all its tears and sighs;
Point then that better path,
And with complacence view my changed desires at last.

The day must come, nor distant far its date,
Time flies so swift and sure,
O peerless and alone!
When death my heart, now conscience struck, shall seize;
Commend me, Virgin! then to thy dear Son,
True God and Very Man,
That my last sigh in peace may, in his arms, be breathed! [1]

We have hitherto discussed the development of poetry almost exclusively; and this is justifiable, for in Italy, as in all other countries, the development of prose as a form of literature comes after that of poetry. Petrarch wrote no prose in Italian; and although Dante wrote his "Banquet" and, in part, his "New Life" in prose, yet the former is couched in scholastic phraseology and the prose portion of the latter is of small compass. Giovanni Boccaccio, although not so great a poet as Dante, or so great a scholar and master of form as Petrarch, is yet of high importance in the history of

[1] Macgregor. A collection of translations of Petrarch's Italian poems, together with an extended life of the poet, is published in the Bohn Library. Very important are the Latin letters of Petrarch, an English translation of a number of which was published a short time ago by Putnam & Co., of New York.

THE GREAT POETS OF ITALY

Italian literature from a double point of view, as the first great writer of prose and the founder of the modern novel.

We can only give here a brief outline of his life and character, before passing on to his works. He was born in Paris in 1313, the son of a Florentine merchant and a young French gentlewoman. Returning to Florence with his father, he was sent to school and is said to have written verses before the age of seven. His father, a merchant himself, wished his son to follow the same career, and at the age of fourteen the boy was taken to Naples with this purpose in view. In this " great, sinful city " Boccaccio passed his youth, at first in business, then in the study of law, both of which, however, he heartily disliked. Making the acquaintance of some well-known scholars, he was inducted into a love for study, and resolved to devote himself to a literary career.

About 1340 he left Naples and returned to Florence, which henceforth became his residence, although he was frequently absent from it on matters of business and pleasure. For he soon became known as a scholar and poet, and, in accordance with the customs of the times, he was honored by his city by being sent on frequent embassies. In

BOCCACCIO

PETRARCH AND BOCCACCIO

this capacity he went, in 1350, to Ravenna, to the daughter of Dante; in 1354, to Pope Innocent VI., at Avignon; and in 1351, to Petrarch at Padua, in order to induce the great poet and scholar to reside in Florence. This meeting with the great apostle of the New Learning was an important event in Boccaccio's life, who from henceforth became one of his most enthusiastic admirers.

He plunged still more eagerly into the study of classic antiquity; and although, as we have said, not so great a scholar as Petrarch, he accomplished some things which the latter had not been able to do. Thus he learned Greek, imperfectly, however, and introduced to the Western world a knowledge of that language (unknown to the Middle Ages) by bringing Leontius Pilatus to Florence as a professor in the university. It was at the dictation of the latter that Boccaccio wrote down his Latin translation of the Homeric poems, which, worthless as it now seems, then excited widespread admiration.

Boccaccio differed from Petrarch in being an ardent admirer and indefatigable student of Dante. Petrarch had once declared that he had never read the "Divine Comedy," and he scarcely ever mentions the name of his mighty predecessor. This was

THE GREAT POETS OF ITALY

undoubtedly due to a sort of jealousy, for Petrarch in his inordinate pride and vanity could not endure the thought of a rival, even among the dead. Boccaccio generously tried to reconcile these two great poets, the one dead, the other still living, and in 1359 he sent to Petrarch a copy of the "Divine Comedy," written with his own hand. He only succeeded, however, in calling forth a cold letter, in which Petrarch defended himself against the accusation of jealousy, and accorded to Dante a small measure of perfunctory praise.

The influence of Dante on Boccaccio himself is seen on almost every page of his poetry, and it was in reward of his services in promoting the study of the former's works that in 1373 he was invited by Florence to lecture on the "Divine Comedy" in the Church of Santo Stefano. The results of this professorship, which Boccaccio only held for a short time, are recorded in his life of Dante and the commentaries on part of the "Inferno."

Boccaccio's character was in many respects an attractive one; he was honest, sincere, and modest; a faithful friend, a lover of true literature; and, above all, of a lovable and gentle disposition; *Giovanni della Tranquillità*, his friends called him — "John of the quiet mind," as we may translate it.

PETRARCH AND BOCCACCIO

The gravest accusation made against him, and one, alas! only too well founded, is his immorality. In his early years, and even later in life, his manners were light, and the effects thereof are too often reflected in his books. Before condemning him too harshly, however, we must bear in mind the low state of morals that marked all society at that time. Toward the end of his life Boccaccio became converted by a strange event. It seems that a certain Carthusian monk, Pietro de' Petroni, who, by the austerity of his life and his religious exaltation, had won a reputation for holiness, died at Siena, May 29, 1361. Fourteen days before his death he entered into a trance, in which he had a vision of the saints in heaven and the damned in hell. When he awoke he declared that he had been commanded by Christ to warn a number of distinguished men of the error of their ways. Among these was Boccaccio. Being too ill to go himself, Petroni sent his disciple Gioachino Ciani to fulfill his commission. The latter came to Florence, told Boccaccio of his master's vision, and then, in fiery language, urged him to see to the salvation of his soul, and to repudiate his immoral writings, else he would soon die and his soul be lost forever. Boccaccio was deeply affected by this strange embassy. In the

THE GREAT POETS OF ITALY

first moments of depression he resolved to give up all study, burn his books, write no more, and spend the rest of his life in religious exercises. From this violent action, however, he was saved by a sensible letter from Petrarch. Yet the effect did not pass away. Ever after this he was more serious and thought more of religious matters. He lost his former zest in life; his gayety and serenity of temper became clouded. After a youth of enjoyment the evening of life came on gray and cold.

He died December 21, 1375, in Certaldo, not far from Florence.

Boccaccio, like Petrarch, wrote much in Latin, chief among such writings being the historical or biographical compilations on "Illustrious Women" and the "Vicissitudes of Great Men," and especially his "Genealogy of the Gods," which for one hundred years and more became the standard handbook of mythology. His work in Italian is extensive, both in prose and poetry. The one book, however, by which he is known to-day, not only in Italy, but the world over, is his "Decameron," a collection of short stories in prose. In this book he becomes epoch-making in a double sense, for it begins both Italian prose and the modern novel. The name of the book is composed of two Greek words, meaning "ten days," and is explained by the fact that there are one hundred stories in all, told ten at a time, on ten successive days.

Neither the various stories themselves nor the idea of uniting them in a framework is original with Boccaccio. The latter device was especially popular in the Orient, and is illustrated in the "Seven Wise Men," so vastly popular in the Middle Ages. The sources of the stories in the "Decameron" are various. Such tales were among the most popular kinds of literature of the times, as may be seen in the *Fabliaux* in France and the well-known collection, known as the *Novellino*, in Italy. Boccaccio gathers them from all sides, and adds many he had heard told orally, especially anecdotes of his contemporaries. All these are changed, however, by the alchemy of his own genius, and become original in style, in delineation of character, and in local color.

The framework of the "Decameron" is as follows: During the terrible pestilence which raged in Europe in 1348, a famous description of which is given in the opening chapter of the book, seven young ladies and three young men meet in one of the churches at Florence, agree to forsake the plague-stricken city, and retire to their villas in the country to forget in pleasant converse the terrors that surround them. The plan is carried out. Each day a leader is chosen, whom all must obey. After breakfast they betake themselves to the garden, and here on green lawns covered with flowers, beneath shady trees and beside clear-running streams, they dance, play, and sing; and then, comfortably seated on the soft grass, they pass the hours away in cheerful conversation and story-telling.

Each one of these one hundred stories has an individual character of its own. While reading them we see passing in picturesque procession before our eyes the whole of Italian society of the times, kings and princes, knights and peasants, merchant, artist, mechanic, priest, and monk. There are not wanting earnest and serious stories, but the comic and satirical element prevails; especially are the vices of the clergy scourged, that fruitful source of all mediæval European literature. The avaricious and licentious priests and monks are everywhere held up to the scornful laughter of his readers.

All this is expressed in an admirable prose style, with perfect adaptation of local color, with excellent delineation of character and insight into human nature, and with the inimitable skill in narration of the born story-teller.

PETRARCH AND BOCCACCIO

The popularity of Boccaccio was, and is still, enormous, in spite of the immorality of certain of his stories. He is read to-day in elementary schools (in emendated editions) and his influence on modern literature is incalculable. In English literature alone most of the great writers have found subjects for poems, stories, and dramas in the "Decameron," among them Chaucer, Dryden, Shakespeare, Keats, Tennyson, and Longfellow.[1]

In Italian poetry he was far more voluminous than Petrarch. Among the best known of his poems are the "Vision of Love;" "Filostrato," which tells the story of Troilus and Cressida, afterwards imitated by Chaucer and Shakespeare; and the "Theseid," imitated by Chaucer in his "Knight's Tales." His "Ninfale Fiesolana" describes the beautiful suburbs of Florence, while his pastoral poem, "Ameto," is the first example of that popular branch of poetry, which found its highest development in Sannazaro's "Arcadia," Tasso's "Aminta," and Guarini's "Pastor Fido."

None of the above poems are easily accessible in English, but fortunately we have several of Boc-

[1] A selection of stories from the *Decameron* fit for the general public has been made by Joseph Jacobs and published by the Macmillan Co.

caccio's sonnets translated by Rossetti so beautifully that his versions almost surpass the originals. Two of these sonnets are devoted to the object of his early love, to whom he gives the name of Fiammetta. He first records his feelings on hearing her sing : —

> Love steered my course, while yet the sun rode high,
>   On Scylla's waters to a myrtle-grove :
>   The heaven was still and the sea did not move ;
> Yet now and then a little breeze went by
> Stirring the tops of trees against the sky :
>   And then I heard a song as glad as love,
>   So sweet that never yet the like thereof
>   Was heard in any mortal company.
> "A nymph, a goddess, or an angel sings
>   Unto herself, within this chosen place,
>   Of ancient loves ; " so said I at that sound.
>   And there my lady, 'mid the shadowings
>   Of myrtle-trees, 'mid flowers and grassy space,
>   Singing I saw, with others who sat round.

The second sonnet is on his last sight of Fiammetta : —

> Round her red garland and her golden hair
>   I saw a fire about Fiammetta's head ;
>   Thence to a little cloud I watched it fade,
> Than silver or than gold more brightly fair ;
> And like a pearl that a gold ring doth bear,
>   Even so an angel sat therein, who sped
>   Alone and glorious throughout heaven arrayed
> In sapphires and in gold that lit the air.

PETRARCH AND BOCCACCIO

> Then I rejoiced as hoping happy things,
>   Who rather should have then discerned how God
>   Had haste to make my lady all His own,
> Even as it came to pass. And with these stings
>   Of sorrow, and with life's most weary load
>   I dwell, who fain would be where she is gone.

Boccaccio's love and admiration for Dante is well shown in the sonnet written as an inscription for a portrait of the great Florentine: —

> Dante Alighieri, a dark oracle
>   Of wisdom and of art, I am; whose mind
>   Has to my country such great gifts assigned
> That men account my powers a miracle.
> My lofty fancy passed as low as Hell,
>   As high as Heaven, secure and unconfined;
>   And in my noble book doth every kind
> Of earthly lore and heavenly doctrine dwell.
> Renownèd Florence was my mother, — nay,
>   Stepmother unto me her piteous son,
>   Through sin of cursèd slander's tongue and tooth.
> Ravenna sheltered me so cast away;
>   My body is with her, — my soul with One
>   For whom no envy can make dim the truth.

These two affections which made so large a part of Boccaccio's life, — love for his master in the art of song, and love for Fiammetta, — are joined together in the following beautiful sonnet: —

> Dante, if thou within the sphere of Love,
>   As I believe, remain'st contemplating
>   Beautiful Beatrice, whom thou didst sing
> Erewhile, and so wast drawn to her above;

THE GREAT POETS OF ITALY

Unless from false life true life thee remove
  So far that Love's forgotten, let me bring
  One prayer before thee : for an easy thing
This were, to thee whom I do ask it of.
I know that where all joy doth most abound
  In the Third heaven,[1] my own Fiammetta sees
    The grief which I have borne since she is dead.
O pray her (if mine image be not drowned
  In Lethe) that her prayers may never cease
    Until I reach her and am comforted.

[1] Heaven of Venus.

V

THE RENAISSANCE

WE have seen in a preceding chapter how Petrarch may be considered as the founder of the Renaissance in Italy. He died in 1374, and it took a century and more to complete the work he inaugurated. The whole of this period, while of immense importance for the history of modern civilization in general, is chiefly important in the history of Italian literature, not so much for what it produced itself, as for the fact that it prepared the way for the so-called "Golden Age" of the sixteenth century.

It may be well here to distinguish, as far as possible, between the terms Renaissance, Revival of Learning, and Humanism, — terms which are often used vaguely, and at times synonymously. According to the consensus of recent opinion, however, Renaissance is much the broadest term, and is applied to the whole process of transition from the mediæval to the modern world. It thus includes not merely the intellectual re-birth due to the new study of the ancient classics, but those other equally mighty forces which arose at the same time, such as the decay of the Holy Roman Empire, the loss of prestige on the part of the Papacy, the disappearance of the feudal system and the rise of free cities, the great upheaval of the Reformation, the discovery of the New World, and the invention of printing. The Revival of Learning is more strictly applied to the intellectual, philosophical and literary movement incident upon and caused by the re-discovery of Greek and Roman literature and antiquities. Humanism is a much narrower term than either of the above, and is used to indicate that period in the Revival of Learning, when the leadership of the process above mentioned fell into the hands of a narrow class of technical scholars who devoted themselves exclusively to the study and the teaching of the classic authors, and whose chief efforts were directed to the restoration of the noble monuments of antiquity, whether of literature, architecture or sculpture.

This whole movement was a slow process of development, — the material (manuscripts, statuary, inscriptions, coins, vases) was first collected, then carefully studied, and finally the principles of modern art and scholarship were laid down, based on

THE RENAISSANCE

the newly discovered treasures of the ancient world. When the process was completed, the Humanists as a class lost prestige and disappeared, while another class arose, that of the poets, painters, and sculptors, who, entering into the glorious heritage left by their predecessors, produced those masterpieces of art and literature which are the glory of the sixteenth century in Italy, and among the priceless treasures of the world.

It is hard for us to-day to get an idea of the eager enthusiasm and intense delight in study of these men of the Renaissance; they must have felt as Wordsworth did when he cried out: —

> Bliss was it in these days to be alive,
> But to be young was very heaven.

The scholars of the time enjoyed an immense popularity. A new caste of society arose, not dependent on birth or wealth, but on learning and intelligence. Princes and cities sought for their services, for which they paid large sums. Everywhere they were received as equal to the noblest in the land. At the feudal court of Ferrara, in the republic of Florence, under the Papacy at Rome, and in the monarchy of Naples, the Humanists occupied first rank. They became secretaries to the pope, ambassadors of kings and princes, and chancellors of the

THE GREAT POETS OF ITALY

republics. The cities of their birth were proud to claim them, and the honors formerly bestowed upon saints now fell to their lot.

At first these Humanists were wandering teachers, moving about from city to city, preaching the faith that was in them after the manner and often with the enthusiasm of the early Methodist circuit riders. Afterward, however, they settled down in some intellectual centre, where they lectured in the university or held some public office. The moral and religious character of these men was not in general very high. Although their writings abound in lofty sentiments, their private life was irregular, if not immoral. They were for the most part vain to excess, insincere, given to flattery, and many of them openly acknowledged their illegitimate children. Such books as the "Hermaphroditus" of Panormita and the "Facetiae" of Poggio were read and praised by all.

Humanism is in a certain sense a revolt not only against the scholastic philosophy of the Middle Ages, but against the authority of Christianity itself. The philosophers of antiquity were sceptics, and the natural effect of their writings on the Humanists was to cultivate within them a spirit of scepticism. Thus the scholars of the Renaissance for the

THE RENAISSANCE

most part scorned the traditions and the superstitions of the church, hated the monks, and either disbelieved in, or " slept out the thought " of the life to come. For them the joy of this life was enough, for in nothing does the contrast between the Middle Ages and the Renaissance show itself so much as in the different ways of looking at life. War, famine, pestilence, oppression, had made life to the men of the Middle Ages a long pilgrimage over a dreary desert. They turned their eyes to the world to come, seeking there a reward and comfort for their present sorrows. St. Bernard expressed the feeling of all his contemporaries in the well-known hymn : —

>Brief life is here our portion,
>   Brief sorrow, short-lived care ;
>The life that knows no ending,
>   The tearless life is there.
>O happy retribution!
>   Short toil, eternal rest;
>For mortals and for sinners,
>   A mansion with the blest.

Now, however, a new spirit arose, the world was re-discovered, the joy in life so characteristic of the ancients once more was cultivated. Hence came a revival of luxury which manifested itself in festivities of all sorts, in gorgeous garments, costly jewels, and stately palaces, adorned with almost barbaric splendor. No wonder that with all these things to dazzle the senses, the necessity of a future life was not keenly felt. Earthly fame now took the place of a desire for the glory of heaven. Dante had himself been touched with that "last infirmity of noble minds," but yet he says: —

> Non é il mondan remore altro che un fiato
> Di vento, ch'or vien quinci'ed or vien quindi,
> E muta nome, perche muta lato.[1]

Now the Humanists made fame the chief object of their lives, — nay, they sought it not only for themselves, but they claimed to possess the ability to bestow it on others, a claim which for many of them became the chief instrument in the acquisition of wealth and power.

Yet, if the Humanists were irreligious, they did not dare openly to revolt against the church. They had no desire to become martyrs. They simply were indifferent. Besides, the whole life of the times was inextricably mixed up with the outward observances of the church. Many of the

---

[1] Naught is this mundane rumor but a breath
Of wind, that comes now this way and now that,
And changes name, because it changes side.

THE RENAISSANCE

Humanists themselves belonged to the clergy, and still more had relatives there. Hence it came to pass that the spasmodic revolt of Savonarola found no abiding place in the hearts of the Italians.

The Humanistic movement began at Florence, which indeed remained its chief centre during the whole period. Later, however, it spread through nearly all the chief cities of Italy, with the exception of Genoa and Venice, although the latter became the great centre for printing. In Ferrara the movement was not so learned, and as we shall see later, was more closely connected with literature in the vernacular. After Florence, the two most important centres of the Renaissance were Rome and Naples. In the former, such Popes as Nicholas V., Julius II., and Leo X., entered into the movement with enthusiasm; Nicholas V. sought to add to the glory of the Roman Church the glory of classical antiquity, hoping thus to strengthen the tottering foundations of the ecclesiastical authority. His chief motive was a personal one. Not merely was he inspired by a desire for the glory of God, but he desired to be great and famous himself as a patron of art and learning. The chief results of Humanism in Rome were the translation of a large number of Greek authors into Latin, the founding

THE GREAT POETS OF ITALY

of great libraries and museums, and the building of magnificent churches. The movement reached its climax under Leo X., a Medici and son of Lorenzo the Magnificent.

In Naples the movement came latest of all. Here it was largely a matter of imitation. Yet through men like Lorenzo Valla, Panormita and Pontano were laid the foundations of scientific grammar and of literary criticism.

Two of the earliest followers of Petrarch, belonging, indeed, to the same generation, were the Florentines, Luigi Marsigli and Coluccio Salutato. The former was an Augustinian friar, who combined a love for theology with a love for the new learning, then fast absorbing the attention of all men. In the cloister of San Spirito, which contained the library of Boccaccio, he gathered about him a group of Florentines, young and old, who were themselves to be later the torch-bearers of classical learning. Still more important was Salutato, who, having been appointed chancellor of the Signoria of Florence, began the long line of learned men who for an hundred years were at the head of state affairs in Florence, and who brought the doctrines of the new learning to bear upon the transaction of public business. Salutato was kind toward all young

THE RENAISSANCE

students, whom he helped in many ways, gaining thus the title of "father of scholars."

Among the disciples of Marsigli and Salutato may be mentioned Leonard Bruni (1369-1444), called Aretino from his birth-place Arezzo, who after having been secretary of the pope at Rome, succeeded Salutato as chancellor in Florence. His chief literary work was the translation of Greek authors into Latin. Niccolo Niccoli is an excellent example of the enthusiastic scholar of the Renaissance. The son of a Florentine merchant, he spent all his patrimony in the acquisition and copying of new manuscripts, and had to receive pecuniary aid from Cosimo de' Medici. Like Chaucer's Clerk, he had —

> but litel gold in cofre;
> But all that he mighte of his freendes hente,
> On bokes and on lerninge he it spente.

Not a writer himself, Niccoli's influence was purely personal. His books, after serving his friends, were purchased at his death by Cosimo de' Medici, and formed the nucleus of the famous Laurentian library in Florence.

One of the most distinguished of the earlier Humanists was Poggio Bracciolini (1380-1459) who was the true disciple of Petrarch in his eager and successful search after new manuscripts. The record of his achievements in this respect is of great interest. He himself traveled abroad even as far as England. Everywhere he went he inquired after manuscripts. As secretary of the pope he resided in Rome many years and devoted himself eagerly to the discovery and investigation of the antiquities of the world-city. His book, "Urbis Romae Descriptio," is the first work on the subject. In a similar way the "Roma Instaurata" of Flavio Biondo (1388–1468), founded the subject of Roman topography.

The most typical example of the Humanists, however, was the learned, but not very amiable Francesco Filelfo (1398–1481), who was equally famous as a Greek and a Latin scholar. Having gone to Constantinople on business he learned Greek there, married the daughter of Johannes Chrysoloras, and, returning to Italy, began his wandering life as a professor of Greek and Latin. At Florence he was hailed as the greatest living Greek scholar and the most distinguished of modern Latin poets. His lectures were attended by crowds who came hither from all parts of Italy and even from foreign lands. Among his students were Popes Nicholas V. and Pius II. From Florence he went to Milan, where he

THE RENAISSANCE

received a large salary from the Duke, in return for which he wrote the most extravagant eulogies of his princely patron. Later, when he visited Naples and Rome, he was received with unbounded enthusiasm, his progress resembling a triumphal procession. Filelfo, while one of the greatest scholars of the Renaissance, was one of the most contemptible of men. He was fickle, mercenary, and of incredible vanity, while his quarrelsome disposition constantly involved him in unseemly broils.

Of far nobler character was Marsiglio Ficino (1433–1499), son of the physician of Cosimo de' Medici, who had the young man educated with the intention of placing him at the head of the Platonic Academy which he had founded.

A peculiar charm attaches to another member of this Academy, the young, beautiful, nobly-born and marvellously learned Pico della Mirandola (1464–1494), the intellectual ideal of whose short life is summed up in his often quoted phrase: "Philosophia veritatem quaerit, scientia invenit, religio possidet."[1]

The greatest of all Humanists, however, was Angelo Ambrogini (1454–1494), called Politian,

[1] Philosophy seeks truth, knowledge finds it, and religion possesses it.

from his native town of Montepulciano. His lectures on subjects of classical criticism were not only enormously popular in his own day, but are still of the greatest value, many of his annotations and emendations remaining the standard down to the present time.

Glancing over the fifteenth century as a whole, we see that a vast advance has been made over Petrarch and Boccaccio. The whole distance between antiquity and the Middle Ages has been bridged; not only classical scholarship, but archæology, topography and literary criticism have been founded and brought to perfection. In short, ancient civilization has once more been brought to life, and, uniting with the elements of Romanticism introduced by Christianity, has produced the modern spirit. It is worthy of note that all this was accomplished by Italy, alone and without aid. While the brilliant movement was going on there, the rest of Europe was still sitting in darkness, and only when the Renaissance was about to end in Italy did it begin in Germany, England, and France.

During the greater part of the fifteenth century, whatever literature there was in prose and poetry was in Latin, which was looked upon by the

THE RENAISSANCE

Humanists as their true mother-tongue, of which Italian was only a corruption, fit for the uses of everyday life, but not fit to be the medium of literature. At the beginning of the century, some even went so far as to despise the Italian works of Petrarch and Boccaccio, and even the "Divine Comedy" of Dante. Such a feeling, however, never became general in Florence, where, indeed, the chair on Dante begun by Boccaccio in 1373 lasted till 1472.

And yet, while Latin was the language chiefly cultivated in the fifteenth century, it had a mighty influence on Italian literature of the following century. The careful study of the great Latin writers, especially of Cicero, the critical and grammatical labors of such men as Valla and Politian, affecting first the Latin style of these and other writers, by a natural process was transferred to Italian style, as soon as that language became the chief medium of the literature.

A literature in the vernacular came more and more to the front as the fifteenth century wore away. Great credit for the rehabilitation of Italian as a literary language is due to Leon Battista Alberti (1404–1472), that shining example of the type *uomo universo* so characteristic of the Renaissance.

THE GREAT POETS OF ITALY

He not only wrote most of his works in Italian, but on all occasions boldly defended the rights of the Tuscan tongue to be regarded as the natural medium of literary art; and it was largely due to his initiative that the poetical tournament took place in the Cathedral of Florence, October 22, 1401, in which the poems submitted were to be composed in the Italian tongue.

The impulse given by Alberti was carried to a successful conclusion by Politian and Lorenzo de' Medici, who not only advocated the use of Italian, but produced genuine literature of a high quality, and thus opened the way for the great writers of the following century.

During the whole of the fifteenth century, side by side with the learned movement, there existed a humble form of literature among the people. This *Volkspoesie* was of two sorts, one profane, the other religious. The former consisted largely of songs, often humorous, often coarse, but at times full of naïve freshness and grace, as in the following lines translated by Symonds: —

> O, swallow, swallow, flying through the air,
> Turn, turn, I prithee, from thy flight above.
> Give me one feather from thy wing so fair,
> For I will write a letter to my love.

THE RENAISSANCE

When I have written it and made it clear,
I'll give thee back thy feather, swallow dear;
When I have written it on paper white,
I'll make, I swear, thy missing feather right;
When once 't is written on fair leaves of gold,
I'll give thee back thy wings and flight so bold.

Such songs were lifted from the lower ranks of society and given a permanent place in literature, by Lionardo Giustiniani (1388-1446), many of whose lyrics are popular, even to-day. Giustiniani likewise cultivated the branch of popular poetry, known as *Laudi* and Sacred Representations, which, as we have already seen, were a prominent feature of literature in the thirteenth and fourteenth centuries. These religious songs were enormously popular in the fifteenth century, for, notwithstanding the pagan ideas of the Humanists, and the pomp and luxury of life among the rich and noble, religion still held sway over the hearts of the people. In the beginning of the century a movement of repentance, similar to those of the thirteenth and fourteenth centuries, already described, swept over Italy. The *Laudi* were the literary representatives of this movement, and often showed real lyric beauty, especially those written by Giustiniani, Lorenzo, Politian, Belcari, and Benivieni. As an example of this interesting kind of litera-

THE GREAT POETS OF ITALY

ture, we give here a *Lauda* by Girolamo Benivieni (1453–1542), translated by Symonds:—

> Jesus, whoso with Thee
> Hangs not in pain and loss,
> Pierced on the cruel cross,
> At peace shall never be.
>
> Lord, unto me be kind;
> Give me that peace of mind,
> Which in this world so blind
> And false, dwells but with Thee.
>
> Give me that strife and pain,
> Apart from which 't were vain
> Thy love on earth to gain
> Or seek a share in Thee.
>
> If, Lord, with Thee alone
> Heart's peace and love be known,
> My heart shall be Thine own,
> Ever to rest with Thee.
>
> Here in my heart be lit
> Thy fire, to feed on it,
> Till burning bit by bit
> It dies to live with Thee.
>
> Jesus, whoso with Thee
> Hangs not in pain or loss,
> Pierced on the cruel cross,
> At peace shall never be.

It was the combination of this popular poetry with the results of the classical revival and the

THE RENAISSANCE

influence of Petrarch and Dante, which produced the efflorescence of Italian poetry in the sixteenth century.

The first important writer to combine these elements was Angelo Politian, already mentioned as the greatest of the Humanists and one of the most graceful poets in Italian literature. He was born in Montepulciano in 1454. He studied in Florence under Marsiglio Ficino, and the Greek Argyropoulos, being the companion in study of Lorenzo de' Medici, who afterwards became his friend and protector. The friendship thus begun between the humble scholar and the wealthy citizen-prince was genuine on both sides, and lasted till the death of Lorenzo in 1492. Politian soon became known as the foremost scholar of his time, and was looked upon as a prodigy of learning. For the skill with which he translated a part of the "Iliad" into Latin, his master, Ficino, called him the "Homeric Youth." His Italian poetry is marked by a perfection of style hitherto unknown in Italian. He had no originality, no creative power — everything he wrote was imitation, yet so completely fused together was what he borrowed that it seemed to be the creation of his own mind. He used his knowledge of Greek and Latin as well as of early Italian poetry with consummate skill. A good example of Politian's style is seen in the following Dance-Song: —

> I went a-roaming, maidens, one bright day,
> In a green garden in mid-month of May.
>
> Violets and lilies grew on every side
> Mid the green grass, and young flowers wonderful,
> Golden and white and red and azure-eyed;
> Toward which I stretched my hands, eager to pull
> Plenty to make my fair curls beautiful,
> To crown my rippling curls with garlands gay.
>
> I went a-roaming, maidens, one bright day,
> In a green garden in mid-month of May.
>
> But when my lap was full of flowers, I spied
> Roses at last, roses of every hue;
> Therefore I ran to pluck their ruddy pride,
> Because their perfume was so sweet and true
> That all my soul went forth with pleasure new,
> With yearning and desire too soft to say.
>
> I went a-roaming, maidens, one bright day,
> In a green garden in mid-month of May.
>
> I gazed and gazed. Hard task it were to tell
> How lovely were the roses in that hour;
> One was but peeping from her verdant shell,
> And some were faded, some were scarce in flower.
> Then Love said: Go, pluck from the blooming bower
> Those that thou seest ripe upon the spray.
> I went a-roaming, maidens, one bright day,
> In a green garden in mid-month of May.

POLITIAN

THE RENAISSANCE

For when the full rose quits her tender sheath,
When she is sweetest and most fair to see,
Then is the time to place her in thy wreath,
Before her beauty and her freshness flee.
Gather thee, therefore, roses with great glee,
Sweet girls, or ere their perfume pass away.

I went a-roaming, maidens, one bright day,
In a green garden in mid-month of May.[1]

His two best poems, however, are the "Orfeo," and the "Stanzas" on the tournament held in 1475 by Giuliano de' Medici, in honor of his lady Simonetta. The "Orfeo," recited in 1471 at a festival held to welcome Galeazzo Sforza to Mantua, relates the well-known story of how Eurydice died and descended into Hades, how her husband Orpheus followed her thither, obtained her release on condition of not looking upon her until she is among the living, and how, having broken this condition, Eurydice was lost to him forever, and he himself torn to pieces by the Bacchantes, enraged at his vow never to love woman again.

Equally famous are the "Stanzas" above alluded to, in which a description of the tournament held by Giuliano de' Medici in 1475 was to be given. Part only, however, of the poem was finished, but

[1] Symonds.

THE GREAT POETS OF ITALY

this part, containing masterpieces of description of the beauty of Nature and of woman, full of exquisite music and written in an elegant and refined style, is justly esteemed as the very flower of poetic art of the Renaissance. The following stanzas of this poem describe the island of Cyprus, the home of Venus: —

> Now, in his proud revenge exulting high,
> Through fields of air, Love speeds his rapid flight,
> And in his mother's realms, the treacherous boy
> Rejoins his kindred band of flutterers light;
> That realm, of each bewitching grace the joy,
> Where Beauty wreaths with sweets her tresses bright,
> Where Zephyr importunes, on wanton wing,
> Flora's coy charms, and aids her flowers to spring.
>
> Thine, Erato! to Love's a kindred name!
> Of Love's domain instruct the bard to tell;
> To thee, chaste Muse! alone 't is given to claim
> Free ingress there, secure from every spell;
> Thou rul'st of soft amours the vocal frame,
> And Cupid, oft, as childish thoughts impel
> To thrill with wanton touch its golden strings,
> Behind his winged back his quiver flings.
>
> A mount o'erlooks the charming Cyprian Isle,
> Whence, toward the morn's first blush, the eye sublime
> Might reach the sevenfold course of mighty Nile;
> But ne'er may mortal foot that prospect climb;
> A verdant hill o'erhangs its highest pile,
> Whose base, a plain, that laughs in vernal prime;

THE RENAISSANCE

Where gentlest airs, midst flowers and herbage gay,
Urge o'er the quivering blade their wanton way.

A wall of gold secures the utmost bound,
And, dark with viewless shade, a woody vale;
There, on each branch, with youthful foliage crown'd,
Some feathered songster chants his amorous tale;
And joined in murmurs soft, with grateful sound,
Two rivulets glide pellucid, through the dale;
Beside whose streams, this sweet, that bitter found,
His shafts of gold Love tempers for the wound.

No flow'rets here decline their withered heads,
Blanched with cold snows, or fringed with hoar-frost sere;
No Winter, wide, his icy mantle spreads;
No tender scion rends the tempest drear.
Here Spring eternal smiles; nor varying leads
His change quadruple, the revolving year:
Spring with a thousand blooms her brows entwined,
Her auburn locks light fluttering in the wind.

The inferior band of Loves, a childish throng,
Tyrants of none, save hearts of vulgar kind,
Each other gibing with loquacious tongue,
On stridulous stones their barbed arrows grind;
Whilst Pranks and Wiles, the rivulet's marge along,
Ply at the whirling wheel their task assigned;
And on the sparkling stone, in copious dews,
Vain Hopes and vain Desires the lymph effuse.

There pleasing Pain and fluttering fond Delight,
Sweet broils, caresses sweet, together go;
Sorrows that hang their heads in doleful plight,
And swell with tears the bitter streamlet's flow;

THE GREAT POETS OF ITALY

Paleness all wan, and dreaming still of slight,
Affection fond, with Leanness, Fear and Woe;
Suspicion, casting round his peering eye
And o'er the midway dancing wanton Joy.

Pleasure with Beauty gambols: light in air
Bliss soars inconstant; Anguish sullen sits;
Blind Error flutters bat-like, here and there,
And Frenzy raves, and strikes his thigh by fits;
Repentance, of past folly late aware,
Her fruitless penance there ne'er intermits;
Her hand with gore fell Cruelty distains,
And seeks Despair in death to end his pains.

Gestures and nods, that inmost thoughts impart,
Illusions silent, smiles that guile intend,
The glance, the look, that speak th' impassioned heart,
Mid flowery haunts, for youth their toils suspend:
And never from his griefs Complaint apart,
Prone on his palm his face is seen to bend;
Now hence — now thence — in unrestrained guise,
Licentiousness on wing capricious flies.

Such ministers thy progeny attend,
Venus! fair mother of each fluttering power:
A thousand odors from those fields ascend,
While Zephyr brings in dews the pearly shower,
Fanned by his flight, what time their incense blend
The lily, violet, rose, or other flower;
And views, with conscious pride, the exulting scene,
Its mingled azure, vermeil, pale and green.

The trembling pansy virgin fears alarm;
Downward, her modest eye she blushing bends;

THE RENAISSANCE

> The laughing rose, more specious, bold and warm,
> Her ardent bosom ne'er from Sol defends;
> Here from the capsule bursts each opening charm,
> Full-blown, th' invited hand she here attends;
> Here she, who late with fires delightful glowed,
> Droops languid, with her hues the mead bestrewed.
>
> In showers descending, courts th' enamoured air
> The violet's yellow, purple, snowy hues;
> Hyacinth! thy woes thy bosom's marks declare;
> His form Narcissus in the stream yet views;
> In snowy vest, but fringed with purple glare,
> Pale Clytia still the parting sun pursues;
> Fresh o'er Adonis, Venus pours her woes;
> Acanthus smiles; her lovers Crocus shows.[1]

Closely connected with Politian, not only by ties of intimate friendship, but as a poet, is Lorenzo de' Medici (1448–1492), called the Magnificent, son of Piero and grandson of Cosimo. He is one of the most interesting characters of this wonderful age. He was a consummate statesman, who managed to keep the balance of power in Italy during the last years of his life, and thus gave to Florence that peace and prosperity so necessary to the development of culture and literature. And yet while he was a man of affairs, he was endowed with a love for all forms of art, especially of literature. He gathered

[1] From Roscoe's translation of Sismondi's *Literature of the South of Europe*.

about him either at his palace in the city, or in his villas near Florence, the most distinguished men of the day. His chief importance for us, however, is as a poet. While not so polished as Politian, he was more original, and stood closer to the spirit of the people. He was an ardent admirer of the early Italian poets, not only of Dante and Petrarch, but of the humbler writers of popular songs. His own poetry is of two kinds, — profane and religious. The influence of Petrarch is seen in the following sonnet on the violet : —

> Thy beauty, gentle violet, was born
>   Where for the look of Love I first was fain,
>   And my bright stream of bitter tears was rain
> That beauty to accomplish and adorn.
> And such desire was from compassion born,
>   That from the happy nook where thou wert lain
>   The fair hand gathered thee, and not in vain,
> For by my own it willed thee to be borne.
> And as to me appears, thou would'st return
>   Once more to that fair hand, whence thee upon
>   My naked breast I have securely set :
> The naked breast that doth desire and burn,
>   And holds thee in her heart's place, that hath gone
>   To dwell where thou wert late, my Violet.[1]

The longest and most important of Lorenzo's love-

---

[1] Garnett, in his *History of Italian Literature*, published by Appleton & Co.

THE RENAISSANCE

songs are contained in the sequence of stanzas known as *Selve*,[1] from which we quote the following description of his first meeting with his lady Lucrezia.

> What time the chain was forced which then I bore,
> Air, earth, and heavens were linked in one delight;
> The air was never so serene before,
> The sun ne'er shed such pure and tranquil light;
> Young leaves and flowers upon the grassy floor
> Gladdened the earth where ran a streamlet bright,
> Where Venus in her father's bosom lay
> And smiled from heaven upon the spot that day.
>
> She from her brows divine and amorous breast
> Took with both hands roses of many a hue,
> And showered them through the heavens that slept in rest,
> Covering my lady with their gracious dew;
> Jove, full of gladness, on that day released
> The ears of men that they might hear the true
> Echoes of melody and dance divine,
> Which fell from heaven in songs and sounds benign.
>
> Fair women to that music moved their feet,
> Inflamed with gentle fire by Love's breath fanned:
> Behold yon lover with his lady sweet —
> Her hand long yearned for clasped in his loved hand;
> Their sighs, their looks, which pangs of longing cheat;
> Brief words that none but they can understand;
> The flowers that she lets fall, resumed and pressed,
> With kisses covered, to his head or breast.

[1] From *selva*, a forest; so called because the mind of the poet is allowed to wander at will, as one wanders through a forest.

THE GREAT POETS OF ITALY

Amid so many pleasant things and fair,
My loveliest lady with surpassing grace
Eclipsed and crowned all beauties that were there;
Her robe was white and delicate as lace;
And still her eyes, with silent speech and rare,
Talked to the heart, leaving the lips at peace:
Come to me, come, dear heart of mine, she said:
Here shall thy long desires at rest be laid.[1]

The literature of the Italian Renaissance, which was inaugurated by Petrarch and Boccaccio, reached its highest point with Ariosto. Tasso, equally great with Ariosto, lived at the beginning of a long period of decline, the "Jerusalem Delivered" projecting the last rays of the glories of the Renaissance into this new period. The sixteenth century, or rather the first half of it, is the golden age of Italian literature, comparable to that of Augustus in Rome, of Louis XIV. in France, and of Queen Elizabeth in England. In the narrow confines of this sketch we shall only be able to treat in some detail the great writers thereof, Boiardo, Ariosto, and Tasso. Yet the number of men of genius and talent is legion — giants indeed lived in those days — not only in the field of art and scholarship but in literature. In the pastoral poem, besides Tasso, there were Sannazaro and Guarini, the former (whose "Arcadia"

[1] Symonds.

THE RENAISSANCE

was imitated in England by Sidney and Spenser) on the border-line between the fifteenth and sixteenth century, the latter on that between the sixteenth and seventeenth. In comic poetry there was Francesco Berni, who also worked over Boiardo's "Orlando Innamorato," which has since then been read almost wholly in his version. In prose was developed an especially rich literature, among the great masters of which we may mention in history, Guicciardini, Varchi, Nardi and Nicholas Machiavelli, who, in his "Prince," introduced a new philosophy of politics; in the history of art, Vasari; in novels and stories, Luigi da Porto, who first told the story of Romeo and Juliet, Giraldo Cinzio, and Matteo Bandello, who continued the work of Boccaccio and Sacchetti.[1] Forming a special group are Benvenuto Cellini, whose autobiography has made him famous; Firenzuola, who wrote on the beauty of woman; Baldasarre Castiglione, the Lord Chesterfield of his day, who in his book on the Courtier depicted the character of the perfect gentleman according to the ideals of the times.

The two chief forms of the literature of this period, however, were the epic and the lyric. We

[1] Franco Sacchetti (1335–1400), lyrical poet and writer of stories (*Novelle*).

THE GREAT POETS OF ITALY

shall discuss the former in the next two chapters. Here we shall briefly mention some of the best known lyric poets.

The most celebrated literary man of the day was Pietro Bembo (1470–1547), who exerted a vast influence in making Italian once more the vehicle for the highest kind of literature. An accomplished Latin scholar himself, he urged by doctrine and example the necessity of having a national literature expressed in the national tongue. His dialogues on this subject, as well as those on the subject of love, both in Italian, influenced prose, while his lyrical poetry placed him at the head of the followers of Petrarch. Owing to the fact that he sought his highest honor in imitating Petrarch as closely as possible, his poetry seems monotonous to modern taste, exhibiting as it does the weakness of Petrarchism in exaggerated form.

Among the followers of Bembo in his exaggerated Petrarchism are the female poets Gaspara Stampa (1523–1554), Veronica Gambara (1485–1550), and Vittoria Colonna (1490–1547), famous as the friend of Michael Angelo, who addressed to her some of his best sonnets.

All these writers, however, were utterly without originality, and the slavish imitators of Petrarch.

THE RENAISSANCE

Michael Angelo (1475-1564), on the other hand, who might perhaps have been as great in poetry as he was in sculpture, painting, and architecture, if he had devoted his life to it, also wrote a number of sonnets, which by their native strength and originality separate him from the common crowd of songsters about him. In these sonnets we no longer find mere conventional themes, treated in pretty language and conceits, but deep, sincere and original thoughts. If we are to seek for any predecessor it must be Dante, his intense admiration for whom is expressed in the following sonnet: —

> What should be said of him cannot be said;
> By too great splendor is his name attended;
> To blame is easier those who him offended,
> Than reach the faintest glory round him shed.
> This man descended to the doomed and dead
> For our instruction; then to God ascended;
> Heaven opened wide to him its portals splendid,
> Who from his country's, closed against him, fled,
> Ungrateful land! To its own prejudice
> Nurse of his fortunes; and this showeth well
> That the most perfect most of grief shall see.
> Among a thousand proofs let one suffice,
> That as his exile hath no parallel,
> Ne'er walked the earth a greater man than he.[1]

His love for Vittoria Colonna finds expression in the following two sonnets, — the first of which

[1] Longfellow.

THE GREAT POETS OF ITALY

both in thought and expression might have been written by Dante, — while the second, on the death of his lady, reminds us of Petrarch's expression of grief for the loss of Laura : —

> The might of one fair face sublimes my love,
>   For it hath weaned my heart from low desires;
>   Nor death I need, nor purgatorial fires.
> Thy beauty, antepast of joys above,
> Instructs me in the bliss that saints approve;
>   For oh! how good, how beautiful, must be
>   The God that made so good a thing as thee,
> So fair an image of the heavenly Dove.
> Forgive me if I cannot turn away
>   From those sweet eyes that are my earthly heaven,
>   For they are guiding steps, benignly given
> To tempt my footsteps to the upward way;
>   And if I dwell too fondly in thy sight,
>   I live and love in God's peculiar light.[1]

> When the prime mover of my many sighs
>   Heaven took through death from out her earthly place,
>   Nature, that never made so fair a face,
> Remained ashamed, and tears were in all eyes.
> O fate, unheeding my impassioned cries!
>   O hopes fallacious! O thou spirit of grace,
>   Where art thou now? Earth holds in its embrace
> Thy lovely limbs, thy holy thoughts the skies.
> Vainly did cruel death attempt to stay
>   The rumor of thy virtuous renown,
>   That Lethe's waters could not wash away!

[1] J. E. Taylor.

MICHELANGELO

THE RENAISSANCE

> A thousand leaves since he hath stricken thee down,
>   Speak of thee, nor to thee could Heaven convey,
>   Except through death, a refuge and a crown.[1]

Very beautiful are the lines in which the aged poet and artist looks back over the past, and realizing with the Preacher of old, that all life is vanity, turns his eyes forward to the life beyond the grave, of which the crucifixion and the resurrection of the Saviour are the pledge.

> The course of my long life hath reached at last,
>   In fragile bark o'er a tempestuous sea,
>   The common harbor where must rendered be
> Account of all the actions of the past.
> The impassioned phantasy, that, vague and vast,
>   Made art an idol and a king to me,
>   Was an illusion, and but vanity
> Were the desires that lured me and harassed.
> The dreams of love, that were so sweet of yore,
>   What are they now, when two deaths may be mine,
>   One sure, and one forecasting its alarms?
> Painting and sculpture satisfy no more
>   The soul now turning to the Love Divine,
>   That oped, to embrace us, on the cross its arms.[1]

[1] Longfellow. The best books in English on the Renaissance are those written by John Addington Symonds.

VI

ARIOSTO

IN the preceding chapter we have seen how the Renaissance after an hundred years and more of slow development reached its climax, and produced that wonderful efflorescence of art and intellectual activity which marks the first half of the sixteenth century. Among the supreme representatives in art of this brilliant period may be mentioned Raphael in painting, Michael Angelo in sculpture and architecture, and Ariosto in poetry.

In discussing the romantic poetry of Ariosto, we must go back a number of years in order to get the proper perspective. Among the brilliant men of letters of the court of the Medici in Florence was a certain Luigi Pulci, of a poor but noble family. It was he who was the first to introduce into elegant literature the old romances of the Carlovingian cycle, which for centuries had been sung and recited by rude, wandering minstrels in the public streets of Italy.

ARIOSTO

ARIOSTO

We have seen in Chapter I. how in the thirteenth century the old French *chansons de geste* had been introduced into North Italy and had there become popular. These had been rewritten and worked over in rude forms for the amusement of the common folk, but up to the time of Pulci they had found no place in literature proper. Now it is the glory of Pulci to have brought this popular material into the realm of artistic poetry. This he is said to have done at the request of Lorenzo's mother, the result being the poem known as "Morgante." In this poem Pulci introduces as the chief character Orlando,[1] the nephew of Charlemagne, and the hero of Roncesvalles, who plays so large a rôle in the French romances. The title of the poem is derived from the name of a giant whose life has been saved by Orlando, whom he, full of gratitude, follows as a faithful servant; he drops out of the story in the twentieth canto.

Pulci, in his "Morgante," follows closely the popular poetry of his predecessors, but differs from them in language, style, and especially in the comic treatment of his theme; in all these respects he is the forerunner of Boiardo and Ariosto. As we have seen, he was a native of Florence, which, up to the

[1] The Italian form of Roland.

THE GREAT POETS OF ITALY

end of the fifteenth century, had been the chief centre of the literary glory of Italy. The scene now changes to Ferrara, where the house of Este had for generations held a brilliant court. It was here that the three great poets Boiardo, Ariosto, and Tasso lived and produced their works.

The fame of Boiardo has been so eclipsed by that of Ariosto that he is not known as well as he ought to be, considering his services to Italian literature. To him belongs the credit of having invented the romantic epic, and Ariosto, who followed in the same lines, added but little to the general groundwork of his predecessor.

Matteo Maria Boiardo was born of a noble family at Reggio in 1434, and having early gone to Ferrara, remained there till his death in 1494. A scholar, poet, administrator, and courtier, his position at the court of the Duke of Este reminds us involuntarily of that of Goethe, three hundred years later, at Weimar. His first essays in literature were in Latin, but when he was about forty years old he began his poem of " Orlando Innamorato " (Roland in Love). He was led naturally thereto. Ferrara had early favored chivalrous poetry, and the library of the Duke contained a large number of romances, belonging especially to the Arthurian cycle, which

ARIOSTO

pleased the elegant society of the court more than the Carlovingian stories so popular with the common people. These romances of King Arthur and the Round Table, however, were in French.

Boiardo's great merit consists in the fact that he united in one the various characteristics of both the Carlovingian and the Arthurian romances, and thus combined the popular and the courtly element. He chose the characters of his poem from the former, but changed them to true knights of chivalry, and added all the paraphernalia of the Arthurian tales. Of especial importance was the introduction of romantic love as the motive of all action.

The general theme of "Orlando Innamorato" is the war between Charlemagne and the Saracens, yet there is no one definite action as in the case of the regular epic. Rather, the poem consists of a series of independent, or at least very loosely connected episodes, in which the adventures of the various knights-errant are recounted with great skill and interest. Chief among these episodes is that of Orlando and his love for Angelica, the daughter of the king of Cathay, who comes to the court of Charlemagne in Paris, and by means of her beauty and coquetry succeeds in drawing away a number of the best Christian warriors. Other important characters are Astolfo, Rodomonte, Rinaldo, and the latter's sister, Bradamante, who falls in love with the pagan Roger, who, according to Boiardo, was the founder of the house of Este. Vast as the poem is in its present state, Boiardo left it only half finished when he died, in 1494.

At the time of Boiardo's death Ludovico Ariosto was a youth of twenty. Born in Reggio, in 1474, of a family that had long been in the service of the Este family, he, too, after an irregular and tardy education came to Ferrara and entered the service of the Cardinal Este. At the death of his father, in 1500, Ariosto found himself at the head of a family of ten, and nobly performed his duty by caring and providing for all his brothers and sisters. His position in the household of the cardinal was not at all to his liking; he was often sent on embassies and business trips, a function which, to a man who loved quiet and leisure as much as Ariosto did, was utterly distasteful. In 1517 he refused to accompany the cardinal to Hungary, on the ground of ill-health, and was thereupon summarily dismissed. He found soon, however, more congenial employment in the household of Duke Alfonso. His life now was more quiet and afforded him more

ARIOSTO

opportunity for study and writing. Yet even here he was not content. His inclinations were all against court life, and he only retained his position on account of his poverty. His character, as depicted in his satires, was very different from that of Petrarch, who was a successful courtier. Ariosto could not bow and smile and make himself agreeable. He was sincere and independent by nature, modest in his desires, kindly and amiable, loved nature, quiet study, and rural occupations. In 1527 he succeeded in saving enough to buy a small house at Ferrara, with a garden attached. Over the door he placed the inscription which has become famous: "Small, but suited to me; harmful to no one; bought with my own money."[1] Here he spent the remainder of his days, happy and contented, amusing himself with almost childish joy in the cultivation of his garden. He died June 6, 1533.

Ariosto's literary work consists of comedies, which are among the first of modern literature, satires, and the "Orlando Furioso" (Mad Roland). The satires rank next in literary value to his masterpiece, and are charming examples of the poetic epistle rather than of biting satire. They contain

[1] Parva sed apta mihi : sed nulli obnoxia, sed non sordida, parta meo sed tamen aere domus.

many details of the society of the day, and are our best source for a knowledge of the life and character of their author. They are all inspired by kindly humor and full of worldly wisdom and common sense. No one can read these satires without feeling a respect and affection for the poet who wrote them.

Ariosto's most famous work, however, is the "Orlando Furioso." When he came to Ferrara everybody was talking about the "Orlando Innamorato" of Boiardo. Ariosto himself admired it immensely, for it harmonized perfectly with his own genius and literary tastes. Hence when there came to him that mysterious command, " Write," which all men of poetical genius hear some day or other, it was only natural that he should turn to the unfinished poem of his predecessor, with the thought of completing it.

Yet it would be a mistake to think Ariosto was a mere plagiarist or that he lacked originality. No writer ever lived who has so impressed his own individuality on his works as he. He took the data furnished by his predecessors and joined to them all the culture of his time, its ideas, aspirations, and conception of life; these he fused into one vast work which reflects the age of the Renaissance as

ARIOSTO

completely as the "Divine Comedy" reflects the closing period of the Middle Ages.

It is practically impossible to give a clear yet brief outline of "Orlando Furioso." It does not, like the "Iliad," "Æneid," "Paradise Lost," and "Jerusalem Delivered," contain one central action, with which all parts are logically connected, but is rather a vast arena on which take place many different and independent actions at the same time. The wars between Charlemagne and the Saracens, which had been begun in Boiardo's poem, are here continued and brought to an end. In similar manner Ariosto takes up the history of the various knights-errant introduced by his predecessor, and either continues their adventures or introduces new ones himself. In the first canto the poet shows us the army of Agramante before the walls of Paris, in which Charlemagne and his army are shut up, and in the course of the poem he shows us the city freed, the enemy defeated, and Christianity saved from the dominion of the Saracen. Yet this is not the real centre of action; often it is entirely lost sight of in the confusing crowd of individual adventures. It only serves as a factitious means of joining from time to time the scattered threads of the various episodes. When the poet does not know what to do with any particular character, he dispatches him forthwith to Paris, there to await the final dénouement.

The individual heroes are free, not bound by any ties of discipline to Charlemagne; they leave at any moment, in obedience to individual caprice, and wander forth in search of love and honor. It is in these various episodes or adventures that the true interest of the poem resides. At first sight there seems to be an inextricable confusion in the way they are told; but after careful study we find that the poet always controls them with a firm hand. A constant change goes on before our eyes. When one story has been told for a time, the poet, apparently fearing lest he weary the reader, breaks it off, always at an interesting point, to begin another, which, in its turn, yields to another, and this to still another; from time to time these stories are taken up again, continued, and finished. All these transitions are marvels of skill and ingenuity.

Among the crowd of minor episodes three stand out with especial distinctness, the story of Cloridan and Medoro, Angelica's love for the latter and the consequent madness of Orlando, and the death of Zerbino.

Cloridan and Medoro are two brave young pagans,

ARIOSTO

whose lord and master, Dardinello, has been slain in battle with Charlemagne's army outside the walls of Paris. The two youths, as they stand on guard at night, lament that their master's body lies unburied and dishonored on the field of battle, and resolve to go and find it and, if possible, to bring it back to camp.[1]

> Two Moors amid the paynim army were,
>   From stock obscure in Ptolomita grown;
>   Of whom the story, an example rare
>   Of constant love, is worthy to be known;
>   Medoro and Cloridan were named the pair;
>   Who, whether Fortune pleased to smile or frown,
>   Served Dardinello with fidelity,
>   And late with him to France had crossed the sea.
>
> These two were posted on a rampart's height,
>   With more to guard the encampment from surprise,
>   When 'mid the equal intervals, at night,
>   Medoro gazed on heaven with sleepy eyes.
>   In all his talk, the stripling, woful wight,
>   Here cannot choose, but of his lord devise,
>   The royal Dardinel; and evermore
>   Him, left unhonoured on the field, deplore.
>
> Then, turning to his mate, cries: "Cloridane,
>   I cannot tell thee what a cause of woe
>   It is to me, my lord upon the plain
>   Should lie, unworthy food for wolf or crow!

[1] Rose's translation has been used in the following quotations.

Thinking how still to me he was humane,
Meseems, if in his honour I forego
This life of mine, for favours so immense
I shall but make a feeble recompense.

"That he may lack not sepulture, will I
   Go forth, and seek him out among the slain;
   And haply God may will that none shall spy
   Where Charles's camp lies hushed. Do thou remain;
   That, if my death be written in the sky,
   Thou may'st the deed be able to explain,
   So that if Fortune foil so fair a feat,
   The world, through Fame, my loving heart may weet."

Amazed was Cloridan a child should show
   Such heart, such love, and such fair loyalty;
   And fain would make the youth his thought forego,
   Whom he held passing dear; but fruitlessly
   Would move his steadfast purpose; for such woe
   Will neither comforted nor altered be.
   Medoro is disposed to meet his doom,
   Or to enclose his master in the tomb.

Seeing that nought would bend him, nought would move,
   "I too will go," was Cloridan's reply,
   "In such a glorious act myself will prove;
   As well such famous death I covet, I:
   What other thing is left me, here above,
   Deprived of thee, Medoro mine? To die
   With thee in arms is better, on the plain,
   Than afterwards of grief, should'st thou be slain."

So they go forth on their generous enterprise, and after slaying many distinguished warriors among

ARIOSTO

the sleeping Christians, they approach the tent of Charlemagne, near which they find the body of their master : —

> Rearing the insidious blade, the pair are near
>   The place, where round King Charles's pavilion
>   Are tented warlike paladin and peer,
>   Guarding the side that each is camped upon.
>   When in good time the paynims backward steer,
>   And sheathe their swords, the impious slaughter done;
>   Deeming impossible, in such a number,
>   But they must light on one who does not slumber.
>
> And though they might escape well charged with prey,
>   To save themselves they think sufficient gain.
>   Thither by what he deems the safest way
>   (Medoro following him) went Cloridane,
>   Where, in the field, mid bow and faulchion, lay,
>   And shield and spear, in pool of purple stain,
>   Wealthy and poor, the king and vassal's corse,
>   And overthrown the rider and his horse.
>
> The horrid mixture of the bodies there
>   Which heaped the plain where roved these comrades sworn,
>   Might well have rendered vain their faithful care
>   Amid the mighty piles, till break of morn,
>   Had not the moon, at young Medoro's prayer,
>   Out of a gloomy cloud put forth her horn.
>   Medoro to the heavens upturns his eyes
>   Towards the moon, and thus devoutly cries:
>
> " O holy goddess! whom our fathers well
>   Have styled as of a triple form, and who

THE GREAT POETS OF ITALY

    Thy sovereign beauty dost in heaven, and hell,
    And earth, in many forms reveal; and through
    The greenwood holt, of beast and monster fell,
    — A huntress bold — the flying steps pursue,
    Show where my king, amid so many, lies,
    Who did, alive, thy holy studies prize."

At the youth's prayer from parted cloud outshone
    (Were it the work of faith or accident)
The moon, as fair, as when Endymion
    She circled in her naked arms: with tent,
Christian or Saracen, was Paris-town
    Seen in that gleam, and hill and plain's extent
With these Mount Martyr and Mount Lery's height,
This on the left and that upon the right.

The silvery splendour glistened yet more clear,
    There where renowned Almontes' son lay dead.
Faithful Medoro mourned his master dear,
    Who well agnized [1] the quartering white and red,
With visage bathed in many a bitter tear,
    (For he a rill from either eyelid shed),
And piteous act and moan, that might have whist [2]
The winds, his melancholy plaint to list.

Hurrying their steps, they hastened, as they might,
    Under the cherished burden they conveyed;
And now approaching was the lord of light,
    To sweep from heaven the stars, from earth the shade,
When good Zerbino, he whose valiant sprite
    Was ne'er in time of need by sleep down-weighed,
From chasing Moors all night, his homeward way
Was taking to the camp at dawn of day.

[1] Recognized.   [2] Hushed or silenced.

ARIOSTO

He has with him some horsemen in his train,
   That from afar the two companions spy;
   Expecting thus some spoil or prize to gain,
   They, every one, towards that quarter hie.
   " Brother, behoves us, " cries young Cloridane,
   " To cast away the load we bear, and fly:
   For 'twere a foolish thought (might well be said)
   To lose *two* living men, to save *one* dead."

And dropped the burden, weening his Medore
   Had done the same by it, upon his side:
   But that poor boy, who loved his master more,
   His shoulders to the weight, alone, applied;
   Cloridan hurrying with all haste before,
   Deeming him close behind him or beside;
   Who, did he know his danger, him to save
   A thousand deaths, instead of one, would brave.

So far was Cloridan advanced before,
   He heard the boy no longer in the wind;
   But when he marked the absence of Medore,
   It seemed as if his heart was left behind.
   " Ah! how was I so negligent (the Moor
   Exclaimed), so far beside myself, and blind,
   That I, Medoro, should without thee fare,
   Nor know when I deserted thee or where ? "

So saying, in the wood he disappears,
   Plunging into the maze with hurried pace;
   And thither, whence he lately issued, steers,
   And, desperate, of death returns in trace;
   Cries and the tread of steeds this while he hears,
   And word and threat of foemen, as in chase;
   Lastly Medoro by his voice is known,
   Disarmed, on foot, 'mid many horse, alone.

A hundred horsemen who the youth surround,
　Zerbino leads, and bids his followers seize
　The stripling; like a top, the boy turns round
　And keeps him as he can: among the trees,
　Behind oak, elm, beech, ash, he takes his ground,
　Nor from the cherished load his shoulders frees.
　Wearied, at length, the burden he bestowed
　Upon the grass, and stalked about his load.

Cloridan, who to aid him knows not how,
　And with Medoro willingly would die,
　But who would not for death this being forego,
　Until more foes than one should lifeless lie,
　Ambushed, his sharpest arrow to his bow
　Fits, and directs it with so true an eye,
　The feathered weapon bores a Scotchman's brain,
　And lays the warrior dead upon the plain.

Enraged at this, Zerbino leaps forward to wreak vengeance on Medoro, but he, begging to be allowed to bury his master, so touches Zerbino with his youthful beauty that he is inclined to spare him; but one of his own followers smiting Medoro, who stands in suppliant attitude, Zerbino, in a rage, pursues him, and followed by his companions disappears, leaving Cloridan dead and Medoro gravely wounded.

In the mean time —

　By chance arrived a damsel at the place,
　　Who was (though mean and rustic was her wear)

ARIOSTO

> Of royal presence and of beauteous face,
> And lofty manners, sagely debonair;
> Her have I left unsung so long a space,
> That you will hardly recognize the fair
> Angelica, in her (if known not) scan,
> The lofty daughter of Cathay's great khan.

This is Angelica, who having despised the love of Orlando and abandoned her former lover Rinaldo, now finally meets her fate in the person of Medoro; she —

> . . . above every other deed repented,
> That good Rinaldo she had loved of yore;
> And that to look so low she had consented,
> (As by such choice dishonoured) grieved her sore.
> Love, hearing this, such arrogance resented,
> And would the damsel's pride endure no more
> Where young Medoro lay he took his stand,
> And waited her, with bow and shaft in hand.

> ·When fair Angelica the stripling spies,
> Nigh hurt to death in that disastrous fray,
> Who for his king, that there unsheltered lies,
> More sad than for his own misfortune lay,
> She feels new pity in her bosom rise,
> Which makes its entry in unwonted way.
> Touched was her haughty heart, once hard and cursed,
> And more when he his piteous tale rehearsed.

> And calling back to memory her art,
> For she in Ind had learned chirurgery,

THE GREAT POETS OF ITALY

(Since it appears such studies in that part
Worthy of praise and fame are held to be,
And, as an heirloom, sires to sons impart,
With little aid of books, the mystery)
Disposed herself to work with simples' juice,
Till she in him should healthier life produce.

She succeeds in curing him, and falling desperately in love, marries him and departs for Cathay, of which she now designs to make her husband king.

After some time Orlando comes that way and finds engraved on trees in love-knots and intertwined names, the evidence of the love of Angelica and Medoro: —

Turning him round, he there, on many a tree,
Beheld engraved, upon the woody shore,
What as the writing of his deity
He knew, as soon as he had marked the lore.
This was a place of those described by me,
Whither ofttimes, attended by Medore,
From the near shepherd's cot had wont to stray
The beauteous lady, sovereign of Cathay.

In a hundred knots, amid those green abodes,
In a hundred parts, their cyphered names are dight;
Whose many letters are so many goads,
Which Love has in his bleeding heart-core pight.[1]
He would discredit in a thousand modes,
That which he credits in his own despite;
And would parforce persuade himself, *that* rhind [2]
Other Angelica than his had signed.

[1] Fixed. [2] Rhyme.

ARIOSTO

He thus tries to convince himself that his suspicions are unfounded; but in vain, for, meeting the shepherd to whose house Angelica had brought Medoro, he learns in detail the whole story : —

> Little availed the count his self-deceit;
> For there was one who spake of it unsought;
> The shepherd-swain, who to allay the heat,
> With which he saw his guest so troubled, thought:
> The tale which he was wonted to repeat
> — Of the two lovers — to each listener taught,
> A history which many loved to hear,
> He now, without reserve, 'gan tell the peer.
>
> "How at Angelica's persuasive prayer,
> He to his farm had carried young Medore,
> Grievously wounded with an arrow; where,
> In little space she healed the angry sore.
> But while she exercised this pious care,
> Love in her heart the lady wounded more,
> And kindled from small spark so fierce a fire,
> She burnt all over, restless with desire:
>
> "Nor thinking she of mightiest king was born,
> Who ruled in the East, nor of her heritage,
> Forced by too puissant love, had thought no scorn
> To be the consort of a poor foot-page."
> — His story done, to them in proof was borne
> The gem, which, in reward for harbourage,
> To her extended in that kind abode,
> Angelica, at parting, had bestowed.

THE GREAT POETS OF ITALY

A deadly axe was this unhappy close,
  Which, at a single stroke, lopped off the head;
  When, satiate with innumerable blows,
  That cruel hangman Love his hate had fed.
  Orlando studied to conceal his woes;
  And yet the mischief gathered force and spread,
  And would break out parforce in tears and sighs,
  Would he, or would he not, from mouth and eyes.

He rushes forth from the cottage and hastens to the forest, where he can give full vent to the sorrow that fills his heart, and where he gradually loses all control of himself, finally becoming raging mad : —

  All night about the forest roved the count,
    And, at the break of daily light, was brought
    By his unhappy fortune to the fount,
    Where his inscription young Medoro wrought.
    To see his wrongs inscribed upon that mount,
    Inflamed his fury so, in him was nought
    But turned to hatred, frenzy, rage, and spite;
    Nor paused he more, but bared his faulchion bright,

  Cleft through the writing; and the solid block,
    Into the sky, in tiny fragments sped.
    Wo worth each sapling and that caverned rock,
    Where Medore and Angelica were read!
    So scathed, that they to shepherd or to flock
    Thenceforth shall never furnish shade or bed;
    And that sweet fountain, late so clear and pure,
    From such tempestuous wrath was ill secure.

ARIOSTO

For he turf, stone, and trunk, and shoot, and lop
    Cast without cease into the beauteous source;
    Till, turbid from the bottom to the top,
    Never again was clear the troubled course.
    At length, for lack of breath, compelled to stop,
    (When he is bathed in sweat, and wasted force,
    Serves not his fury more) he falls, and lies
    Upon the mead, and, gazing upward, sighs.

Wearied and woe-begone, he fell to ground,
    And turned his eyes toward heaven; nor spake he aught,
    Nor ate, nor slept, till in his daily round
    The golden sun had broken thrice, and sought
    His rest anew; nor ever ceased his wound
    To rankle, till it marred his sober thought.
    At length, impelled by frenzy, the fourth day,
    He from his limbs tore plate and mail away.

Here was his helmet, there his shield bestowed;
    His arms far off, and, farther than the rest,
    His cuirass; through the greenwood wide was strowed
    All his good gear, in fine; and next his vest
    He rent; and, in his fury, naked showed
    His shaggy paunch, and all his back and breast.
    And 'gan that frenzy act, so passing dread,
    Of stranger folly never shall be said.

Thus begins the madness of Orlando, who, after performing prodigious deeds of strength on men, cattle, and trees, is seized with restlessness, and wanders far and wide: —

THE GREAT POETS OF ITALY

> Now right, now left, he wandered far and wide,
>   Throughout all France, and reached a bridge one day;
>   Beneath which ran an ample water's tide,
>   Of steep and broken banks; a turret gray
>   Was builded by the spacious river's side,
>   Discerned, from far and near, and every way.
>   What here he did I shall relate elsewhere,
>   Who first must make the Scottish prince my care.

The Scottish prince, to whom the poet refers in these last lines, is the same Zerbino whom we have left pursuing the wretch who wounded the young Medoro. Zerbino is young, handsome, and brave, and has married Isabella, daughter of the king of Gallicia, whom he loves and by whom he is loved with tender conjugal affection. Now his time has come to die. He, with Isabella, arrives on the scene of Orlando's madness, and finding the scattered arms of the unfortunate knight, he gathers them together and hangs them on a tree, with an inscription telling whose they are, and forbidding all to touch them. Just then up comes Mandricardo, emperor of Tartary, accompanied by Doralice, his lady-love, and attempts to take possession of Orlando's sword Durindane. The two warriors fight, and Zerbino being fatally wounded, Doralice, at the prayer of Isabella, prevails on Mandricardo to end the battle. Yet it is too late to save the life of Zerbino : —

ARIOSTO

Now, when his anger and his heat secede,
    After short interval, his anguish grows;
    His anguish grows, with such impetuous pains,
    He feels that life is ebbing from his veins.

For weakness can the prince no further hie,
    And so beside a fount is forced to stay;
    Him to assist the pitying maid would try,
    But knows not what to do, nor what to say.
    For lack of comfort she beholds him die;
    Since every city is too far away,
    Where in this need she could resort to leech,
    Whose succour she might purchase or beseech.

She, blaming Fortune, and the cruel sky,
    Can only utter fond complaints and vain.
    "Why sank I not in ocean (was her cry),
    When first I reared my sail upon the main?"
    Zerbino, who on her his languid eye
    Had fixed, as she bemoaned her, felt more pain
    Than that enduring and strong anguish bred,
    Through which the suffering youth was well-nigh dead.

"So be thou pleased, my heart (Zerbino cried),
    To love me yet, when I am dead and gone,
    As to abandon thee without a guide,
    And not to die, distresses me alone.
    For did it me in place secure betide
    To end my days, this earthly journey done,
    I cheerful, and content, and fully blest
    Would die, since I should die upon thy breast.

"But since to abandon thee, to whom a prize
    I know not, my sad fate compels, I swear,

THE GREAT POETS OF ITALY

My Isabella, by that mouth, those eyes,
By what enchained me first, that lovely hair;
My spirit, troubled and despairing, hies
Into hell's deep and gloomy bottom; where
To think, thou wert abandoned so by me,
Of all its woes the heaviest pain will be."

At this the sorrowing Isabel, declining
Her mournful face, which with her tears o'erflows,
Towards the sufferer, and her mouth conjoining
To her Zerbino's, languid as a rose:
Rose gathered out of season, and which, pining,
Fades where it on the shadowy hedgerow grows,
Exclaims, " Without me think not so, my heart,
On this your last, long journey to depart.

" Of this, my heart, conceive not any fear,
For I will follow thee to heaven or hell;
It fits our souls together quit this sphere,
Together go; for aye together dwell.
No sooner closed thine eyelids shall appear,
Than either me internal grief will quell,
Or has it not such power, I here protest,
I with this sword to-day will pierce my breast.

" I of our bodies cherish hope not light,
That they shall have a happier fate when dead;
Together to entomb them, may some wight,
Haply by pity moved, be hither led."
She the poor remnants of his vital sprite
Went on collecting, as these words she said:
And while yet aught remains, with mournful lips,
The last faint breath of life devoutly sips.

ARIOSTO

'T was here his feeble voice Zerbino manned,
    Crying, "My deity, I beg and pray,
    By that love witnessed, when thy father's land
    Thou quittedst for my sake; and, if I may
    In any thing command thee, I command,
    That, with God's pleasure, thou live out thy day;
    Nor ever banish from thy memory,
    That, well as man can love, have I loved thee.

"God haply will provide thee with good aid,
    To free thee from each churlish deed I fear;
    As when in the dark cavern thou wast stayed,
    He sent, to rescue thee, Anglante's peer;
    So he (grammercy!) succoured thee dismayed
    At sea, and from the wicked Biscayneer.
    And if thou must choose death, in place of worse,
    Then only choose it as a lesser curse."

I think not these last words of Scotland's knight
    Were so expressed, that he was understood;
    With these, he finished, like a feeble light,
    Which needs supply of wax, or other food.
    — Who is there, that has power to tell aright
    The gentle Isabella's doleful mood?
    When stiff, her loved Zerbino, with pale face,
    And cold as ice, remained in her embrace.

On the ensanguined corse, in sorrow drowned,
    The damsel throws herself, in her despair,
    And shrieks so loud that wood and plain resound
    For many miles about; nor does she spare
    Bosom or cheek; but still, with cruel wound,
    One and the other smites the afflicted fair;
    And wrongs her curling locks of golden grain,
    Aye calling on the well-loved youth in vain.

THE GREAT POETS OF ITALY

Neither the wars of Charlemagne nor the madness of Orlando gives a real unity to the poem; the nearest thing to such a unity is to be found in the story of Roger and Bradamante, the former a pagan, the latter a Christian, daughter of Aymon and sister of Rinaldo. They love each other, seek each other, and after countless adventures by land and sea, are united in marriage, thus founding the House of Este. It is with Roger's conversion to Christianity and his marriage that the poem ends. All the different heroes are gathered together before the walls of Paris; Orlando's madness has been cured by Astolfo, who has made his famous visit to the moon, where, in the Paradise of Fools, he recovers the lost brains of his friend; Roger on his wedding day slays Rodomonte, the truculent and hitherto unconquerable enemy of the Christians, and with his fall the war and the poem are ended.

Hard as it is to give a clear conception of the complicated adventures, told in the "Orlando Furioso," it is perhaps still harder to give an idea of its charm to those who have not read it. We are introduced at once into a world of fancy, a sort of fairy-book for grown-up people. The poem is not

ARIOSTO

deeply impressive like the "Divine Comedy;" it has no elements of tragedy. Ariosto did not aim at moral effect, but merely sought to amuse his readers. Dante represents the deep, mystical religious feeling of his times; Ariosto represents the worldliness of the neo-paganism of the Renaissance. The asceticism of the Middle Ages now gives way to intense delight in the life that now is. The artist and poet sought to represent the pomp and circumstance of life, man in his physical and intellectual power, woman in her beauty, nature in all its picturesque variety, art in its magnificence. This was the ideal of the Italian Renaissance; this was the ideal followed by Ariosto.

The great charm of Ariosto is his style. Here form reaches its highest expression. He worked over and polished his verses unceasingly, yet so natural are they that they seem to have been written spontaneously. The "Orlando" is full of beautiful descriptions, of pathetic scenes, alternating skillfully with humorous ones. Ariosto's humor, however, is not coarse or grotesque, but refined and elegant. He does not caricature the stories of chivalry, as Cervantes does in "Don Quixote;" but living in a sceptical age he cannot take seriously the creatures of his own fancy, and accompanies the prodigious deeds of his heroes with a smile of good-natured irony.

We have already said that Ariosto was a man of good sense. From the quiet of his own home he looked out upon the ruffled sea of life and mused on what he saw. His reflections are chiefly contained in his satires; but they likewise add a peculiar and original charm to the "Orlando Furioso." Among the parts most popular with the serious reader are the short introductions to the various cantos, each containing some wise reflection, some rule of life, or some kindly satire; this charm is well known to the lover of Thackeray.[1]

---

[1] For the romantic poets, Leigh Hunt's book, *Stories from the Italian Poets*, may be read. The first canto of Pulci's *Morgante Maggiore* was translated by Byron and may be found in his works. A complete translation of *Orlando Furioso*, translated by Rose, is published in the Bohn Library.

VII

TASSO

From the beginning of Italian literature to the death of Ariosto nearly three hundred years had elapsed. In that period four of its greatest writers had appeared. Yet no literature can attain the highest rank in which the drama and epic are not represented. Italy hitherto lacked these two important branches. The "Divine Comedy" of Dante is, strictly speaking, not an epic, but forms a class by itself, being an imaginative journey to the supernatural world, with a record of things seen and heard therein; Ariosto's "Orlando Furioso" was a revival of the old chivalrous romances in a new and elegant form, adapted to the conditions and taste of his times; a huge fresco, rather than an epic. As we shall see in the next chapter, comedy and tragedy had to wait nearly two hundred years after the death of Ariosto before finding worthy representatives in Alfieri and Goldoni. The regular epic, however, was given to Italy by Tasso toward the end of the sixteenth century.

THE GREAT POETS OF ITALY

The story of Tasso's life is of great though painful interest. It is a tragedy of suffering like that of Dante; yet how vast the difference between the two! Dante bore his sufferings with unparalleled nobility of character, exciting our admiration. Tasso, weak and vacillating by nature, lives wretched and miserable, not from the decrees of fortune, but owing to his unfitness to bear the trials of ordinary life.

He was born March 11, 1544, at Sorrento, near Naples, the son of Bernardo Tasso, a man of affairs, a courtier and a poet, who, although of noble family, was forced by straitened circumstances to pass his life in the service of others. Tasso's education was varied enough; he spent a few years at a Jesuit school in Naples, an experience which left a lasting impression on his sensitive and melancholy temperament; then after studying under private teachers at Rome, he devoted himself for several years to the study of law at the universities of Padua and Bologna. He was compelled to leave the latter as a result of certain satires against the university authorities, which he was accused of having written.

The important period of his life begins in 1565, when he went to Ferrara, then, as in the days of

TASSO

TASSO

Boiardo and Ariosto, the centre of a rich and brilliant court. His life here for the next seven or eight years was a prosperous one. Fortune seemed to have showered her fairest gifts on this young, handsome, and gentle-mannered poet. He was treated on terms of intimacy by the Duke and his sisters, Lucretia and Leonora. He was accustomed to take his meals with the two ladies, and to them he read the poetry which he wrote from time to time. It was undoubtedly due to their influence that he composed his famous pastoral poem, "Aminta" (1572–73), full of exquisite pictures of rural life, and bathed in an atmosphere of tender and refined love. This poem had an unprecedented success, and made its author famous throughout all Europe.

Not long after this, however, the first germs of the terrible mental disease which wrecked his life began to show themselves. For many years after his death Tasso was made the hero of a romance, in which he was depicted as a martyr to social caste; the victim of his own love for a woman beyond his sphere. According to this romance, Tasso fell in love with the sister of the Duke of Ferrara, and for this crime was shut up in prison and falsely treated as insane. The results of modern scholarship, however, have dissipated the sentimental halo from the brow of the unfortunate poet, and reduced his case to one of pathological diagnosis. Leonora was some ten years older than Tasso, and the affection which at first undoubtedly existed between them was that of an elder sister and a younger brother. The Duke was not cruel to Tasso, but on the contrary treated him at first kindly, and only when his patience was at last worn out by the vagaries of the poet, did he decide to drop him and to bother himself no more about him.

The secret of Tasso's sufferings and vicissitudes of fortune lay in himself; he was, during the later part of his life, simply insane. All his actions during this period illustrate perfectly the various phases of the persecution mania, which in his case was aggravated by religious hallucination. To this terrible mental disease he was predisposed from early life; his Jesuit education, the mysterious death of his mother (suspected of having been poisoned), overwork and worriment, and especially his morbidly sensitive and melancholy temperament, all helped to prepare the way for the catastrophe that was to darken his life.

The first open manifestations of insanity occurred in 1577 (probably as the result of a fever), about

TASSO

the time he had finished the first draft of the
" Jerusalem Delivered." Very foolishly for a man
as sensitive as he was, he turned over the manuscript of his poem to a number of friends for sug-
gestions. The heartless criticisms he received from
them filled him with bitterness and fostered the
rising irritability of his nascent disease. He was
especially hurt by the brutal and stupid criticism
of the Inquisitor Antoniano, who advised him to cut
out all the romantic episodes, which form the real
beauty of the poem. This put into his mind the
thought that the Inquisition might refuse him per-
mission to print his poem, and made him fear that
he might be a heretic. The lessons of his early
teachers, the Jesuits, now began to bear fruit. In
1577, tormented by religious doubts, he went to
the Inquisitor of Bologna and laid his case before
him. Although the latter absolved him from his
self-charge of heresy, Tasso was not satisfied.
Henceforth religious fear was added to the fear of
assassination — a double torment to his soul.

Under these circumstances he became more and
more moody and irritable; he was suspicious of all
about him and subject to frequent outbursts of
violence. On the evening of June 17, 1577, he
was discoursing of his troubles to the Princess

Lucretia, when he suspected a passing servant of spying him, and flung a knife at him. In order to prevent further acts of violence he was shut up, at first in his own room, and later in the monastery of St. Francis, under the care of a physician. On July 27 he broke the door and escaped. Horsemen were sent after him, but being disguised as a peasant, he escaped, and after many adventures, often begging his way as a common beggar, he reached Sorrento, where, in the quiet seclusion of his sister's house, surrounded by all the tokens of her love and sympathy, he enjoyed a short period of rest and peace.

He soon became restless, however, and yearned for the brilliant life of the court, which presented itself to his fancy, enhanced by the charms of distance and of those things which were once possessed and have been lost. He was like a butterfly, always attracted toward the light that was to destroy him. He returned to Ferrara, but again ran away, wandering from city to city, yet finding nowhere a warm welcome. "The world's rejected guest," Shelley called him, who knew himself only too well the meaning of these words.

In February, 1579, Tasso once more returned to Ferrara, this time without previous warning, and asked to be received by the Duke. It was a singu-

TASSO

larly unpropitious moment; the Duke was then in the midst of preparations for his marriage with Margaret Gonzaga, his third wife, and naturally enough, the obscure, half-insane poet was neglected. This neglect completely turned Tasso's mind, and losing all self-control, he broke out into violent invectives in the presence of the court. He was immediately taken out, shut up in the insane asylum of St. Anna, and, in accordance with the barbarous customs of the age in the treatment of the insane, was put in chains. Here he remained in utter misery, a prey to the double nightmare of his sick brain, — fear of death by the assassin's knife, and of everlasting damnation as a heretic. The letters which he wrote by scores during this period are of heartbreaking pathos.

He remained in St. Anna nearly eight years, being released in 1586 at the solicitation of Prince Vincenzo Gonzaga, brother-in-law of the Duke of Ferrara. From now on to the end, the story of Tasso's life becomes a mere repetition of melancholy incidents. Once more he went from city to city, visiting in turn Milan, Florence, Naples, and Rome, and moving restlessly hither and thither —

> Like spirits of the wandering wind,
> Who seek for rest, yet rest can never find.

THE GREAT POETS OF ITALY

Finally, fortune seemed about to smile upon him; a faint ray of sunshine broke through the thick clouds that for so long had hung over his life. In November, 1594, he was invited to Rome, there to be crowned poet, as Petrarch had been. The Pope assigned him a pension, and it seemed as if at last some measure of happiness might again be his. It was only a brief gleam of sunshine, however; the clouds soon closed again, and the sun of Tasso's life hastened to its setting shrouded in gloom. The coronation was put off on account of the ill health of Cardinal Cinzio and the inclemency of the season. In March, 1595, Tasso himself fell sick, and in April was taken to the monastery of St. Onofrio on the Janiculum hill. To the monks who came to meet him he uttered the pathetic words: "My fathers, I have come to die among you." The Pope sent his own physician to attend him, but in vain. The world-weary poet passed away April 25, 1595. His body lies buried in the adjacent church. The visitor to-day can still see his room, furnished as in his lifetime, and on the wall of which is hanging a framed copy of his last letter, in which he foretells his speedy death.

Tasso's works are comparatively voluminous, and consist of lyrical poems, a pastoral drama

TASSO

("Aminta"), a tragedy ("Torrismondo"), dialogues, letters, and the "Jerusalem Delivered." In this brief sketch we can only discuss the latter, by which alone he is known the world over.

Already when only sixteen years old, he had felt the ambition to write a poem which should combine the merits of the regular epic (such as the "Iliad" and "Æneid"), and the romantic interest of the poems of Boiardo and Ariosto. His "Rinaldo," written when he was only nineteen years old, was remarkable both on account of the youth of its author and as a promise of what was to follow. For a number of years after this, however, he devoted himself almost exclusively to the task of preparing himself, by reading, study, and thought, to write the great poem which he had in mind.

His choice of a subject was a happy one. The fear of the Turk at that time was widespread; the wars between Christian and Saracen, which filled the old romances, were now occurring again on the eastern borders of Europe. The Turks had conquered Hungary, and their piratic ships had ravaged the coast of Italy, often destroying entire populations; a short time before, Sorrento, Tasso's birthplace, had been attacked, and his sister escaped only by a miracle. Tasso himself must have heard

THE GREAT POETS OF ITALY

many a story of the crusades when a child at Sorrento, where Pope Urban, who had published the first crusade, was buried. His choice of the deliverance of Jerusalem from the unbeliever then was a natural one.

The story of " Jerusalem Delivered," unlike that of the " Orlando Furioso," is a simple one. Yet the main plot, *i. e.*, the military operations of Godfrey, the various battles, and the final capture of Jerusalem, are not so effective or interesting as the various romantic episodes introduced from time to time; the reader to-day is disposed to hurry over the early cantos and to linger over the beautiful pages which tell the loves of Tancred and Clorinda, Olinda and Sofronia, Rinaldo, Armida, and Erminia.

The poem begins with the usual invocation : [1] —

> I sing the pious arms and Chief, who freed
> The Sepulchre of Christ from thrall profane:
> Much did he toil in thought, and much in deed;
> Much in the glorious enterprise sustain
> And hell in vain opposed him; and in vain
> Afric and Asia to the rescue poured
> Their mingled tribes ; — Heaven recompensed his pain,
> And from all fruitless sallies of the sword,
> True to the Red-Cross flag his wandering friends restored.
>
> O, thou, the Muse, that not with fading palms
> Circlest thy brows on Pindus, but among

[1] Wiffen's translation is used in the following quotations.

TASSO

> The Angels warbling their celestial psalms,
> Hast for thy coronal a golden throng
> Of everlasting stars! make thou my song
> Lucid and pure; breathe thou the flame divine
> Into my bosom; and forgive the wrong,
> If with grave truth light fiction I combine,
> And sometimes grace my page with other flowers than thine.

The poet then plunges into the midst of the action. We learn how the Christian army has been in Holy Land for six years, and how it has made many conquests: —

> Six summers now were past, since in the East
> Their high Crusade the Christians had begun;
> And Nice by storm, and Antioch had they seized
> By secret guile, and gallantly when won,
> Held in defiance of the myriads dun,
> Pressed to its conquest by the Persian king;
> Tortosa sacked, when now the sullen sun
> Entered Aquarius, to breme [1] winter's wing
> The quartered hosts give place, and wait the coming spring.

In the spring of the seventh year the archangel Gabriel appears to Godfrey of Bouillon and orders him to assemble the chiefs of the army and prepare for a new and vigorous prosecution of the war. Godfrey obeys and is himself elected commander-in-chief. Then, after a review of the troops, which furnishes the poet an opportunity of giving a cata-

[1] Fierce.

logue of the various Christian forces (after the manner of Homer), the whole army starts for Jerusalem.

The scene then changes to the Holy City itself, where King Aladine and his followers are seized with consternation at the news of the advance of the Christians. We now see the first of the famous episodes of the "Jerusalem Delivered." The magician Ismeno urges the king to seize a certain image of the Virgin Mary and shut it up in the royal mosque (thus converting it into a palladium for Jerusalem). The king does so; but immediately the image disappears from the mosque. Aladine is wild with rage, and being unable to discover the perpetrator of the outrage, resolves to destroy all the Christians in the city. Now there was in the city a beautiful Christian girl.

> Of generous thoughts and principles sublime,
> Amongst them in the city lived a maid,
> The flower of virgins, in her ripest prime,
> Supremely beautiful! but that she made
> Never her care, or beauty only weighed
> In worth with virtue; and her worth acquired
> A deeper charm from blooming in the shade;
> Lovers she shunned, nor loved to be admired,
> But from their praises turned, and lived a life retired.

Although she was unconscious of love herself,

TASSO

there was a noble Christian youth who had long loved her in secret: —

> Sophronia hers, Olindo was his name;
> Born in one town, by one pure faith illumed;
> Modest — as she was beautiful, his flame
> Feared much, hoped little, and in nought presumed;
> He could not, or he durst not speak, but doomed
> To voiceless thought his passion; him she slighted,
> Saw not, or would not see; thus he consumed
> Beneath the vivid fire her beauty lighted;
> Either not seen, ill known, or, known, but ill requited.

Sophronia resolves to save her people: —

> And thus it was, when like an omen drear
> That summoned all her kindred to the grave,
> The cruel mandate reached Sophronia's ear,
> Who, brave as bashful, yet discreet as brave,
> Mused how her people she from death might save;
> Courage inspired, but virginal alarm
> Repressed the thought, till maiden shyness gave
> Place to resolve, or joined to share the harm;
> Boldness awoke her shame, shame made her boldness charm.

She makes her way to the king's palace, and declares that she alone is guilty of having stolen the sacred image from the mosque.

> Thus she prepares a public death to meet,
> A people's ransom at a tyrant's shrine:
> Oh glorious falsehood! beautiful deceit!
> Can Truth's own light thy loveliness outshine?

THE GREAT POETS OF ITALY

To her bold speech misdoubting Aladine
With unaccustomed temper calm replied:
"If so it were, who planned the rash design,
Advised thee to it, or became thy guide?
Say, with thyself who else his ill-timed zeal allied?"

"Of this my glory not the slightest part
Would I," said she, "with one confederate share;
I needed no adviser; my full heart
Alone sufficed to counsel, guide, and dare."
"If so," he cried, "then none but thou must bear
The weight of my resentment, and atone
For the misdeed." "Since it has been my care,"
She said, "the glory to enjoy alone,
'T is just none share the pain; it should be all mine own."

To this the tyrant, now incensed, returned,
"Where rests the Image?" and his face became
Dark with resentment; she replied, "I burned
The holy image in the holy flame,
And deemed it glory; thus at least no shame
Can e'er again profane it — it is free
From farther violation; dost thou claim
The spoil or spoiler? this behold in me;
But that, whilst time rolls round, thou never more shalt see.

"Albeit no spoiler I; it was no wrong
To repossess what was by force obtained."
At this the tyrant loosed his threatening tongue,
Long-stifled passion raging unrestrained:
No longer hope that pardon may be gained,
Beautiful face, high spirit, bashful heart!
Vainly would Love, since mercy is disdained,
And Anger flings his most envenomed dart,
In aid of you his else protecting shield impart!

TASSO

    Doomed in tormenting fire to die, they lay
    Hands on the maid; her arms with rough cords twining,
    Rudely her mantle chaste they tear away,
    And the white veil that o'er her drooped declining:
    This she endured in silence unrepining,
    Yet her firm breast some virgin tremors shook;
    And her warm cheek, Aurora's late outshining,
    Waned into whiteness, and a colour took,
Like that of the pale rose, or lily of the brook.

    The crowd collect; the sentence is divulged;
    With them Olindo comes, by pity swayed;
    It might be that the youth the thought indulged,
    What if his own Sophronia were the maid!
    There stand the busy officers arrayed
    For the last act, here swift the flames arise;
    But when the pinioned beauty stands displayed
    To the full gaze of his inquiring eyes,—
'T is she! he bursts through all, the crowd before him flies.

    Aloud he cries: "To her, oh not to her
    The crime belongs, though frenzy may misplead!
    She planned not, dared not, could not, king, incur
    Sole and unskilled the guilt of such a deed!
    How lull the guards, or by what process speed
    The sacred Image from its vaulted cell?
    The theft was mine! and 't is my right to bleed!"
    Alas for him! how wildly and how well
He loved the unloving maid, let this avowal tell.

    "I marked where your high Mosque receives the air
    And light of heaven; I climbed the dizzy steep,
    I reached a narrow opening; entered there,
    And stole the Saint, whilst all were hushed in sleep:

THE GREAT POETS OF ITALY

Mine was the crime, and shall another reap
The pain and glory? grant not her desire!
The chains are mine; for me the guards may heap
Around the ready stake the penal fire;
For me the flames ascend; 't is mine, that funeral pyre!"

Sophronia raised to him her face, — her eye
Was filled with pity and a starting tear;
She spoke — the soul of sad humanity
Was in her voice, "What frenzy brings thee here,
Unhappy innocent! is death so dear,
Or am I so ill able to sustain
A mortal's wrath, that thou must needs appear?
I have a heart, too, that can death disdain,
Nor ask for life's last hour companionship in pain."

Thus she appeals to him; but scorning life,
His settled soul refuses to retreat:
Oh glorious scene, where in sublimest strife
High-minded Virtue and Affection meet!
Where death 's the prize of conquest, and defeat
Seals its own safety, yet remains unblest!
But indignation at their fond deceit,
And rage, the more inflames the tyrant's breast,
The more this constant pair the palm of guilt contest.

He deems his power despised, and that in scorn
Of him they spurn the punishment assigned:
"Let," he exclaimed, "the fitting palm adorn
The brows of both! both pleas acceptance find!"
Beckoning he bids the prompt tormentors bind
Their galling chains around the youth — 't is done;
Both to one stake are, back to back, consigned,
Like sunflowers twisted from their worshiped sun,
Compelled the last fond looks of sympathy to shun.

TASSO

Thus both are about to die, when a knight appears: —

> In midst of their distress, a knight behold,
> (So would it seem) of princely port! whose vest,
> And arms of curious fashion, grained with gold,
> Bespeak some foreign and distinguished guest;
> The silver tigress on the helm impressed,
> Which for a badge is borne, attracts all eyes, —
> A noted cognizance, the accustomed crest
> Used by Clorinda, whence conjectures rise,
> Herself the stranger is — nor false is their surmise.
>
> All feminine attractions, aims, and parts,
> She from her childhood cared not to assume;
> Her haughty hand disdained all servile arts,
> The needle, distaff, and Arachne's loom;
> Yet, though she left the gay and gilded room
> For the free camp, kept spotless as the light
> Her virgin fame, and proud of glory's plume,
> With pride her aspect armed; she took delight
> Stern to appear, and stern, she charmed the gazer's sight.

This is the first appearance of Clorinda, who is destined to play so large a part in the poem, and who shows the nobility of her character by interceding for the lovers with the king: —

> The throng falls back, and she awhile remains,
> The fettered pair more closely to survey;
> One she sees silent, one, she sees, complains,
> The stronger spirit nerves the weaker prey:

She sees him mourn like one whom the sad sway
Of powerful pity doth to tears chastise,
Not grief, or grief not for himself; but aye
Mute kneels the maid, her blue beseeching eyes
So fixed on heaven, she seems in heaven ere yet she dies.

Clorinda melts, and with them both condoles;
Some tears she sheds, but greater tenderness
Feels for her grief who most her grief controls, —
The silence moves her much, the weeping less;
No longer now does she delay to press
For information; turning towards one
Of reverend years, she said with eagerness,
"Who are they? speak! and oh, what crime has won
This death? in Mercy's name, declare the deed they 've done!"

Thus she entreats; a brief reply he gives,
But such as well explains the whole event:
Amazed she heard it, and as soon conceives
That they are both sincerely innocent;
Her heart is for them, she is wholly bent
To avert their fate, if either arms can aid,
Or earnest prayers secure the king's consent;
The fire she nears, commands it to be stayed,
Which now approached them fast, and to the attendants said:

" Let none of you presume to prosecute
Your barbarous office, till the king I see;
My word I pledge that at Clorinda's suit,
Your fault he will forgive, if fault it be."
Moved by her speech and queenlike dignity
The guards obey, and she departs in quest
Of the stern monarch, urgent of her plea;
Midway they met; the monarch she addressed;
And in this skilful mode her generous purpose pressed.

TASSO

The king, delighted at having so powerful an auxiliary in his hour of danger and need, willingly grants Clorinda's request, and the lovers are saved.

In the mean time the Christian army approach Jerusalem, which they reach at early dawn, and which they greet with deep emotion: —

  The odorous air, morn's messenger, now spread
  Its wings to herald, in serenest skies,
  Aurora issuing forth, her radiant head
  Adorned with roses plucked in Paradise;
  When in full panoply the hosts arise,
  And loud and spreading murmurs upward fly,
  Ere yet the trumpet sings; its melodies
  They miss not long, the trumpet's tuneful cry
Gives the command to march, shrill sounding to the sky.

  The skilful Captain with a gentle rein
  Guides their desires and animates their force;
  And though 't would seem more easy to restrain
  Charybdis in its mad volubile course,
  Or bridle Boreas in, when gruffly hoarse
  He tempests Apenninus and the grey
  Ship-shaking Ocean to its deepest source, —
  He ranks them, urges, rules them on the way;
Swiftly they march, yet still with swiftness under sway.

  Winged is each heart, and wingèd every heel;
  They fly, yet notice not how fast they fly;
  But by the time the dewless meads reveal
  The fervent sun's ascension in the sky,

THE GREAT POETS OF ITALY

  Lo, towered Jerusalem salutes the eye!
  A thousand pointing fingers tell the tale!
  " Jerusalem! " a thousand voices cry,
   " All hail, Jerusalem ! " hill, down, and dale
Catch the glad sounds, and shout, " Jerusalem, all hail ! "

  Thus, when a crew of fearless voyagers,
  Seeking new lands, spread their audacious sails
  In the hoar Arctic, under unknown stars,
  Sport of the faithless waves and treacherous gales;
  If, as their little bark the billow scales,
  One views the long-wished headland from the mast,
  With merry shouts the far-off coast he hails,
  Each points it out to each, until at last
  They lose in present joy the troubles of the past.

Erminia, daughter of the deceased king of Antioch, points out to King Aladine from a high tower the famous warriors among the Christians, and especially praises Tancred, who had conquered her father, made a prisoner of herself, and by his courtesy and gentle treatment won her love. A sortie is made from the city, and Tancred, finding himself engaged in battle with Clorinda, whom he esteems a man, breaks her helmet, and discovering her to be the maiden whom he loves, refuses to fight further with her.

   Meanwhile Clorinda rushes to assail
   The Prince, and level lays her spear renowned;

TASSO

Both lances strike, and on the barred ventayle
In shivers fly, and she remains discrowned;
For, burst its silver rivets, to the ground
Her helmet leaped (incomparable blow!)
And by the rudeness of the shock unbound,
Her sex to all the field emblazoning so,
Loose to the charmèd winds her golden tresses flow.

Then blazed her eyes, then flashed her angry glance,
Sweet e'en in wrath; in laughter then what grace
Would not be theirs! — but why that thoughtful trance?
And, Tancred, why that scrutinizing gaze?
Know'st not thine idol? lo, the same dear face,
Whence sprang the flame that on thy heart has preyed!
The sculptured image in its shrine retrace,
And in thy foe behold the noble maid,
Who to the sylvan spring for cool refreshment strayed.

He who her painted shield and silver crest
Marked not at first, stood spell-bound at the sight;
She, guarding as she could her head, still pressed
Th' assault, and struck, but he forbore the fight,
And to the rest transferring his despite,
Plied fast his whirling sword; yet not the less
Ceased she to follow and upbraid his flight,
With taunt and menace heightening his distress;
And, "Turn, false knight!" she cried, loud shouting through the press.

Thus begins the most famous episode of the "Jerusalem Delivered." For the next half of the poem Tancred and Clorinda are the real hero and heroine.

THE GREAT POETS OF ITALY

In the mean time Satan has called together his followers for consultation. Among the many plans for holding the Christian army in check is the sending of the beautiful enchantress Armida to the camp of Godfrey, where she succeeds by her wiles in drawing away from the army a number of the bravest warriors. The king of Egypt, with an immense army, announces his intention to help Jerusalem, and from this time on this menace hovers like a black cloud over the horizon of the poem, ever approaching nearer and nearer, till in the last canto the storm is averted by the bravery of the Christian warriors and the aid of heaven.

Argantes, one of the pagan warriors of Jerusalem, sends a herald to Godfrey's camp, challenging any of his warriors to single combat. Tancred is appointed by Godfrey to accept the challenge, and the two doughty champions fight all day long with no result. When night comes on both retire, bearing away serious wounds. Erminia, who has been in a terrible state of anxiety during the combat, cannot rest content when night comes on, without learning the condition of Tancred's wounds. She puts on Clorinda's suit of armor, leaves the city, and makes her way to the Christian camp, first sending a messenger to Tancred, announcing

TASSO

that a lady desires to see him. The scene which follows is very picturesque, describing as it does the silence of the night and the distant view of the tents : —

> But she meanwhile impatient, in whose eyes
> Each moment seemed an age, to care a prey,
> Counts to herself each separate step, and cries,
> "Now he arrives, now speaks, now hastes away;"
> Next she upbraids his indolent delay;
> Chides his unusual want of diligence;
> And, weary grown of his eternal stay,
> Spurs till she gains the nearest eminence,
> Whence her dilating eye discerns the distant tents.
>
> On high were the clear stars; the gentle Hours
> Walked cloudless through the galaxy of space,
> And the calm moon rose, lighting up the flowers
> With frost of living pearl: like her in grace,
> Th' enamoured maid from her illumined face
> Reflected light where'er she chanced to rove;
> And made the silent Spirit of the place,
> The hills, the melancholy moon above,
> And the dumb valleys round, familiars of her love.
>
> Seeing the Camp, she whispered, " O ye fair
> Italian tents! how amiable ye show!
> The breathing winds that such refreshment bear,
> Ravish my soul, for 't is from you they blow!
> So may relenting Heaven on me bestow, —
> On me, by froward Fate so long distressed,
> A chaste repose from weariness and woe,
> As in your compass only lies my quest;
> As 't is your arms alone can give my spirit rest.

THE GREAT POETS OF ITALY

> "Receive me then, and in you let me find
> Love's gentle voice, which spoke of pity, true;
> And that delightful music of the mind,
> Which in my blest captivity I drew
> From my lord's mercy; patronized by you,
> I have no wish to re-obtain and wear
> My regal crown, — adieu, vain pomps, adieu!
> Enough for me if Tancred grants my prayer;
> More blest in you to serve, than reign a queen elsewhere."
>
> Ah, little does she think, while thus she dreams,
> What is prepared for her by Fortune's spite!
> She is so placed, that the moon's placid beams
> In line direct upon her armour light;
> So far remote into the shades of night
> The silver splendour is conveyed, and she
> Surrounded is with brilliancy so bright,
> That whosoe'er might chance her crest to see,
> Would of a truth conclude it must Clorinda be.

Two sentinels see her, and believing her to be Clorinda, pursue her. She flies, and is carried by her horse many miles away, finally reaching a shepherd's cottage on the banks of the Jordan, where for some time she takes up her abode far from war's alarms and the "pangs of despised love." The description of Erminia's life here is much admired for its delineations of the charm of rural life : —

> She slept, till in her dreaming ear the bowers
> Whispered, the gay birds warbled of the dawn;

TASSO

  The river roared; the winds to the young flowers
  Made love; the blithe bee wound its dulcet horn;
  Roused by the mirth and melodies of morn,
  Her languid eyes she opens, and perceives
  The huts of shepherds on the lonely lawn;
  Whilst seeming voices, twixt the waves and leaves
Call back her scattered thoughts, — again she sighs and grieves.

  Her plaints were silenced by soft music, sent
  As from a rural pipe, such sounds as cheer
  The Syrian shepherd in his summer tent,
  And mixed with pastoral accents, rude but clear.
  She rose and gently, guided by her ear,
  Came where an old man on a rising ground
  In the fresh shade, his white flocks feeding near,
  Twig-baskets wove, and listened to the sound
Trilled by three blooming boys, who sate disporting round.

The shepherd, pitying Erminia's distress, takes her to his wife, and she thus becomes a member of the humble but happy household.

  And straight, with all a father's love and zeal,
  He took her to his heart, soothed her distress,
  And to his wife, whose heart alike could feel
  For others' sorrows, led the fair Princess.
  Her arms she changes for a pastoral dress,
  And with rude ribbon binds her dainty hair;
  Yet still, her graceful manner of address,
  Movement of eyes and steps the truth declare, —
Was never woodland girl so delicately fair!

  Those rustic weeds hid not the princely fire
  And grandeur so instinctively her own;

THE GREAT POETS OF ITALY

In every action through her quaint attire,
The latent spirit of the Lady shone;
Whether she drove her flocks to range alone
The thymy down, or penned them in the fold;
Or to wild ditties sung in mournful tone,
The dulcet cream in churns revolving rolled,
Till firm the fluid fixed, and took the tinge of gold.

Oft when her flocks, from summer's noontide rays,
Lay in cool shades o'erarched by gadding vines,
She carved on beeches and immortal bays
Her Tancred's name, and left the mossy pines
With sad inscriptions flourished, silent signs
Of the unhappy flame her fancy fed;
And when again she saw her own fond lines,
As she the melancholy fragments read,
Fresh tears of grief, unchecked, her lovely eyes would shed.

And weeping she would say: " For ever be,
O ye dear trees, historians of my woe!
That when two faithful lovers rest, like me,
In the cool shade your verdant boughs bestow,
Their hearts with generous sympathy may glow;
And, as this volume of my griefs they view,
Say to themselves, ' Ah, never may we know
Her pangs, poor maid! 't is hard a love so true
Should be so ill repaid by Love and Fortune, too!'"

In the mean time many events are taking place between the Christians and pagans, sorties, single combats, and attacks on the walls of the city. Godfrey has caused powerful engines of war to be built, especially a mighty movable tower, so high that it

TASSO

overtops the walls of the city. Clorinda, eager for glory, undertakes one night to destroy the tower, in spite of the warning of her old servant Arsetes, who tells her the story of her birth, and reveals the fact that she is of Christian parentage. She issues forth, succeeds in setting fire to the tower, but not being able to reënter the city, flies, followed by Tancred, who not recognizing her, fights with her and, to his own eternal sorrow, slays her. This passage is regarded as the most beautiful of the whole poem:

> Faint on their swords, with like exhausted frame,
> Alike they rest, and echo gaze for gaze:
> Fades the last star; Aurora robed in flame,
> Unbars Elysium, and the morning plays;
> Tancred perceives, beneath its grateful rays,
> From her the trickling blood profusely rain,
> And glories in the languor she displays:
> Oh man, vain man! poor fool of pride and pain!
> Puffed up with every breath from Fortune's wavering vane!
>
> Why that proud smile? sad, oh how sad, shall be
> Thy acted triumphs when the illusion clears!
> Thine eyes shall weep, if still the light they see,
> For every drop of blood a sea of tears;
> Thus resting, gazing, full of hopes and fears,
> The bleeding warriors, silent as the dead,
> Stood for a space; at length some feelings fierce
> Tancred deposed, — kind thoughts rose in their stead,
> He wished her name to know, and, breaking silence, said:

THE GREAT POETS OF ITALY

"Hard is our chance, our prowess thus to spend
On deeds which silence and these shades conceal;
To which thwart Fortune yields no praise, no friend
On our viewed acts to set his speaking seal!
Yet, if amid the sullen shock of steel
Prayers may have access, courtesies find place,
Thy name, thy country, and thy rank reveal;
That I, whatever issue crown the case,
May know at least who gives my death or victory grace."

Sternly she said: "Thy prayer no access wins;
Custom forbids; but, whatsoe'er my name,
Thou seest before thee one of those brave twins,
Who gave your towering structure to the flame."
Fired at her answer, Tancred made exclaim:
"In evil hour hast thou thy guilt avowed;
Thy speech and silence are to me the same,
Discourteous wretch, contemptible as proud!
Both chide my sloth, and both for vengeance plead aloud."

Rage to their hearts returns, and spurs them on,
Though weak, to war; dire war! from which the sleights
Of art are banished, whence all strength is gone.
And in the room of both, brute fury fights;
Oh, sharp his falchion, sharp her sabre smites!
What bloody gaps they make through plate and chain,
In their soft flesh! revenge, revenge requites;
If life parts not, 't is only that disdain
Knits it in pure despite to the rebellious brain.

As the deep Euxine, though the wind no more
Blows, that late tossed its billows to the stars,
Stills not at once its rolling and its roar,
But with its coasts long time conflicting jars;

TASSO

Thus, though their quickly-ebbing blood debars
Force from their blades as vigour from their arms,
Still lasts the frenzy of the flame which Mars
Blew in their breasts; sustained by whose strong charms,
Yet heap they strokes on strokes, yet harms inflict on harms.

But now, alas! the fatal hour arrives
That must shut up Clorinda's life in shade:
In her fair bosom deep his sword he drives;
'T is done — life's purple fountain bathes the blade!
The golden flowered cymar of light brocade,
That swathed so tenderly her breasts of snow,
Is steeped in the warm stream: the hapless maid
Feels her end nigh; her knees their strength forego;
And her enfeebled frame droops languishing and low.

He, following up the thrust with taunting cries,
Lays the pierced Virgin at his careless feet;
She as she falls, in mournful tones outsighs,
Her last faint words, pathetically sweet;
Which a new spirit prompts, a spirit replete
With charity, and faith, and hope serene,
Sent dove-like down from God's pure mercy-seat;
Who, though through life his rebel she had been,
Would have her die a fond, repentant Magdalene.

"Friend, thou hast won; I pardon thee, and oh
Forgive thou me! I fear not for this clay,
But my dark soul — pray for it, and bestow
The sacred rite that laves all stains away:"
Like dying hymns heard far at close of day,
Sounding I know not what in the soothed ear
Of sweetest sadness, the faint words make way
To his fierce heart, and touched with grief sincere,
Streams from his pitying eye the involuntary tear.

THE GREAT POETS OF ITALY

    Not distant, gushing from the rocks, a rill
    Clashed on his ear; to this with eager pace
    He speeds — his hollow casque the waters fill —
    And back he hurries to the deed of grace;
    His hands as aspens tremble, whilst they raise
    The locked aventayle of the unknown knight; —
    God, for thy mercy! 't is her angel face!
    Aghast and thunderstruck, he loathes the light;
Ah, knowledge best unknown! ah, too distracting sight!

    Yet still he lived; and mustering all his powers
    To the sad task, restrained each wild lament,
    Fain to redeem by those baptismal showers
    The life his sword bereft: whilst thus intent
    The hallowing words he spoke, with ravishment
    Her face transfigured shone, and half apart
    Her bland lips shed a lively smile that sent
    This silent speech in sunshine to his heart:
"Heaven gleams; in blissful peace behold thy friend depart!"

    A paleness beauteous as the lily's mixed
    With the sweet violet's, like a gust of wind
    Flits o'er her face; her eyes on Heaven are fixed,
    And heaven on her returns its looks as kind:
    Speak she can not; but her cold hand, declined,
    In pledge of peace on Tancred she bestows;
    And to her fate thus tenderly resigned,
    In her meek beauty she expires, and shows
But as a smiling saint indulging soft repose.

    But when he saw her starlike spirit set,
    The self-possession which had manned his soul,
    Bent to the storm of anguishing regret
    That o'er his bosom burst beyond control:

TASSO

Pangs of despair convulsed his heart; life stole
As to its last recess; death's icy dew
Bathed his pale brow, his blood forebore to roll;
Till like the breathless dead the living grew,
In chillness, silence, air, and attitude, and hue.

And sure his life, impatient of the light,
Struggling had burst in its rebellious scorn
From its weak chain, and followed in its flight
The beauteous spirit, that, but just re-born,
Had spread its wings in sunshine of the morn, —
Had not a party of the Franks, dispread
In search of water o'er the gleaming lawn,
By providential guidance thither led,
Seen where he lay supine, the dying by the dead.

Their Chief, though distant, by his armour knew
The Latin Prince, and hastened to the place;
The lifeless beauty he remembered too
For Tancred's love, and mourned her fatal case;
He would not leave a form so full of grace,
Albeit a Pagan, as he deemed, a prey
To wolves, but lifting, in a little space,
To others' arms both bodies whence they lay,
Took straight to Tancred's tent his melancholy way.

Not yet the knight, so equally and slow
They marched, from his dark trance awakened was;
But feeble groans at intervals might show
Some sands still glided in his vital glass;
The Lady lay a mute and stirless mass,
Nor breath, nor pulse gave hope that life was there
Incorporate with its beauty: thus they pass;
Thus, side by side, the two, lamenting bear;
And in adjoining rooms dispose with silent care.

THE GREAT POETS OF ITALY

Clorinda being dead, Tancred has little desire to live, but is comforted by a vision of her in heaven: —

>On her at smile of morn, for her at frown
>Of eve he calls, he murmurs, and complains;
>Like a lorn nightingale when some rude clown
>Has stolen her plumeless brood; in piercing strains
>She fills the dying winds, and woods, and plains
>With her sweet quarrel; all night long she weeps,
>And to the listening stars repeats her pains,
>Till morn with rosy tears the forest steeps; —
>Then on his streaming eyes awhile calm slumber creeps.

>And, clad in starry robes, the maid for whom
>He mourned, appears amid his mourning dreams;
>Fairer than erst, but by the deathless bloom
>And heavenly radiance that around her beams,
>Graced, not disguised; in sweetest act she seems
>To stoop, and wipe away the tears that flow
>From his dim eyes: "Behold what glory streams
>Round me," she cries; "how beauteous now I show,
>And for my sake, dear friend, this waste of grief forego.

>"Thee for my bliss I thank; Earth's sordid clod
>Thou by a happy error forced to quit,
>And for the glorious Paradise of God
>By sacred baptism mad'st my spirit fit:
>There now midst angels and blest saints I sit
>In rapturous love and fellowship divine;
>There may our souls together yet be knit,
>And there in fields where suns eternal shine,
>Shalt thou at once enjoy their loveliness and mine;

TASSO

> " If by thy passions unseduced, if thou
> Grudge not thyself the bliss; live then, Sir Knight,
> Know that I love thee, far as Love can bow
> For aught of earthly mould a Child of Light ! "
> As thus she spoke, her glowing eyes shone bright
> With an immortal's fervour; rosy red
> She in the mild irradiance shut from sight
> Her face, like a sweet flower, her fans outspread,
> And in his drooping soul celestial comfort shed.

Up to this time the most prominent characters in the poem have been Tancred and Clorinda. This state of things now changes and the real hero, Rinaldo, who like Achilles has long been absent from the field of action, reappears and brings matters to a climax.

We have already seen how Armida has come to camp and carried off a number of the Christian warriors. At the same time Rinaldo, in a contest over the question as to who should succeed Dudo (killed in the first skirmish between the crusaders and the pagans), had slain Gernando in the presence of the whole army, and was forced to fly the wrath of Godfrey. He, after having freed the fifty knights from the power of Armida, is himself caught by her wiles, and carried off by her to a gorgeous palace situated in the midst of a beautiful garden, on a high mountain in the island of

THE GREAT POETS OF ITALY

Teneriffe. Here, lost in luxury and idleness, he sleeps out the thought of his duty as a Christian warrior.

In the mean time Godfrey, by various supernatural tokens, learns that Rinaldo alone can bring about the final success of the Christian arms. He is thus induced to pardon his crime, which indeed had in a certain sense been justified, and sends two messengers to bring him back. These embark on a magic vessel, traverse the Mediterranean, pass the strait of Gibraltar, enter the Atlantic, and reach the island of Teneriffe. The descriptions of this voyage and the allusion to Columbus are famous and well deserve to be quoted, if we had the space. It is especially interesting to compare this fictitious voyage into the Atlantic Ocean with that of Ulysses in Dante's "Inferno," written before — as the "Jerusalem Delivered" was written shortly after — the discovery of America.

The ambassadors arrive at the island, climb the mountain, overcome all obstacles, enter the enchanted garden, and discover Rinaldo, surrounded by all the beauty of nature and the magnificence of art.

> This is the haven of the world ; here Rest
> Dwells with Composure, and that perfect bliss,

TASSO

    Which in the Golden Age fond men possessed,
    In liberty and love, unknown to this;
    You now may lay aside th' incumbrances
    Of arms, and safely hang them on the trees,
    Sacred to Peace; all else but folly is;
    Seek then soft quiet, seek indulgent ease,
Love's the sole captain here, young Love's the lord to please.
  .   .   .   .

    Midst the same leaves and on the self-same twig
    The rosy apple with th' unripe is seen;
    Hung on one bough the old and youthful fig,
    The golden orange glows beside the green;
    And aye, where sunniest stations intervene,
    Creeps the curled vine luxuriant high o'erhead;
    Here the sour grape just springs the flowers between,
    Here yellowing, purpling, blushing ruby red,
Here black, the clusters burst, and heavenly nectar shed.

    The joyful birds sing sweet in the green bowers;
    Murmur the winds; and, in their fall and rise,
    Strike from the fruits, leaves, fountains, brooks, and flowers
    A thousand strange celestial harmonies;
    When cease the birds, the zephyr loud replies;
    When sing the birds, it faints amidst the trees
    To whispers soft as lovers' farewell sighs;
    Thus, whether loud or low, the bird the breeze,
The breeze obeys the bird, and each with each agrees.

    One bird there flew, renowned above the rest,
    With party-coloured plumes and purple bill,
    That in a language like our own expressed
    Her joys, but with such sweetness, sense, and skill,
    As did the hearer with amazement fill;
    So far her fellows she outsang, that they
    Worshipped the wonder; every one grew still

THE GREAT POETS OF ITALY

At her rich voice, and listened to the lay :
Dumb were the woods — the winds and whispers died away.

The messengers succeed in arousing the dormant nobility of Rinaldo; he tears himself away, follows them to the camp of Godfrey, is pardoned by the latter, succeeds in breaking the spell of the enchanted forest, and thus prepares the way for the building of new war-machines. The city then is assaulted and taken, and finally the Egyptian army, which now appears on the scene, is defeated, and the poem ends.[1]

[1] A complete translation of the *Jerusalem Delivered* by Wiffen is published in the Bohn Library. An older translation by Fairfax was published in 1600, and has frequently been reprinted since. Longfellow calls Fairfax's translation " a grand book " (*Life*, vol. i. p. 315).

VIII

THE PERIOD OF DECADENCE AND THE REVIVAL

In the history of Italian literature, Dante, to expand a figure already used, stands at the end of the Middle Ages like a lofty, solitary mountain peak; behind him the scene fades away into darkness; before him the landscape, shone upon by the first rays of a new epoch, slopes gradually upward until with Petrarch, Boccaccio, and the great writers of the Renaissance, we have a lofty and widely extended plateau. After Tasso there is a sudden descent to a low, level, uniform plain, in which Italian literature drags itself along until the middle of the eighteenth century, when again an upward slope is noticed, which for the next hundred years becomes more and more accentuated.

Hardly had the Renaissance reached its height in the early decades of the sixteenth century when a reaction set in. The whole movement had been intellectual rather than moral; it had been marked by "light rather than by warmth," by "ideas rather than by conscience." To the brilliant side of life so characteristic of the sixteenth century corresponded a darker side. Unbelief in religious matters was general. Morals were at a low ebb, even among the clergy, the Pope himself not excepted. The record of crimes, murder, gambling, unnatural vice, given in the histories of the times, is appalling. At the very time when the beneficent results of the Renaissance were spreading abroad (producing in Germany the Reformation), Italy was already beginning to slide down that steep incline which finally landed her in a state of degradation as low as her previous glory had been high.

When Lorenzo de' Medici died in 1492, the political equilibrium which that wise statesman had maintained in Italy was broken. In the bitter strife between the ruler of Milan, Ludovico il Moro, and the court of Naples, the former invited Charles VIII to invade Italy and to make good his rights as a descendant of Charles of Anjou to the former kingdom of Sicily. Charles accepted the invitation, and from that time on until 1748 devoted Italy became the battle-ground first of the rival powers of Spain and France, and later of the houses of Bourbon and Hapsburg.

THE DECADENCE AND REVIVAL

In the first of these long-drawn-out wars Spain was victorious, and from 1559 to 1648 its influence was predominant. This period is one of the saddest in the history of Italy. The great provinces of Milan, Naples, Sicily, and Sardinia were ruled by tyrannical Spanish viceroys, while the rest of the country was subject to Spanish influence. No government ever had less care for a subject land than did that of Spain. Justice was corrupt, the system of finance was one of extortion and oppression, taxes were enormous. The Spanish viceroys and their ignoble imitators, the Italian nobles, lived a life of luxury and vice, surrounded by bandits and brigands, and by paralyzing all commerce and industry brought on famine and pestilence.

The religious condition was no better. The Catholic reaction, or Counter Reformation, which culminated in the Council of Trent, fastened still more firmly the chains of mediæval superstition and dogmatism on the mass of the Italian people. The absolute power of the Pope was reaffirmed; two mighty instruments were forged to crush out heresy and opposition, — the Inquisition, which effectually choked free thought, and the Jesuits, who found their way stealthily into all ranks and classes of society. Such was the condition of Italy at this time, " a prolonged, a solemn, an inexpressibly heartrending tragedy." The effect on the social life of Italy was almost fatal. Everywhere, to use the almost exaggerated language of Symonds, were to be seen idleness, disease, brigandage, destitution, ignorance, superstition, hypocrisy, vice, ruin, pestilence, " while over the Dead Sea of social putrefaction floated the sickening oil of Jesuit hypocrisy."

From 1648 to 1748, the state of affairs was not much better, the only difference being that it was now the House of Hapsburg that held the balance of power in Northern and Central Italy, while the French and Spanish finally founded the Bourbon dynasty in Naples which lasted till 1860, when it was destroyed by the famous expedition of the Thousand under Garibaldi.

The literature of Italy during all this long period was in harmony with its political and moral condition. It sank to its lowest ebb. Already in the sixteenth century an impulse to a literature corrupt in style and subject had been given. Sannazaro, whose influence had been so great, was full of puerile conceits, far-fetched figures, and all the exaggerations of the school of Petrarch. This same tendency was carried to still greater excess by Cariteo and

THE DECADENCE AND REVIVAL

Tebaldeo.[1] These, not Dante or Petrarch, were the masters of the poets of the early seventeenth century, — at the head of whom was Giovanni Battista Marini (1569–1625), the author of the famous "Adone." Marini, although born in Italy, spent a number of years in Paris, where he was looked upon as a great poet, and where he wrote his version of the love of Venus for Adonis, — a subject that had already occupied the pen of Shakespere a few years before. This vast poem of some 45,000 lines contains little or no action. All is description of artificial nature and of female beauty expressed in a kind of voluptuous music of verse, in which the entire repertory

---

[1] The following is a good example of the extent to which these conceits were carried. The Lady of Tebaldeo, while dancing at a ball, begins to bleed from the nose; it is Love who has struck her. But Love, being blind, makes a mistake and instead of striking her heart, as he intended, struck her nose. His Lady is one day walking in a snowstorm; everybody is amazed to see snow falling and the sun shining. Serafino, a pupil of Tebaldeo, is still more puerile. The precious stone which his Lady wears on her finger is a flower petrified by a glance of her eyes. A missing tooth is a corridor opened by Love, who, lodged in his Lady's mouth, has torn out the tooth in order to watch the enemy. Serafino is so inflamed with love that his sighs roast the birds of the air; he flings himself into the sea, but the sea is set on fire and burns even the rocks on the shore. He swallows snow, but this is itself changed to fire in his stomach. Cf. Monnier, *Le Quattrocento*, vol. ii. pp. 403, 404.

THE GREAT POETS OF ITALY

of Preciosity runs riot. This book was enormously popular, not only in Italy but in France. It introduced, or at least exerted a mighty influence on, that peculiar phenomenon of literature known as Marinism in Italy, Preciosity in France, Gongorism in Spain, and Euphuism in England. The following extracts, in which is described the death of Adonis, will give some idea of this extravagant style, and may stand as a type of Italian poetry during the whole of the seventeenth century. Adonis attempts to slay a wild boar, but is unable to pierce the tough hide of his adversary.

> That soft white hand now hurls the threatening spear,
> Straining each nerve, against the monster's side,
> But, ah! in vain, to check his fierce career;
> Harmless it flew, nor drew the crimson tide;
> And stouter heart and stouter arm might fear
> To urge the quivering point, he vainly tried,
> Through that dark bristling shield; like some firm wall,
> Or anvil fixed it stood; no red drops fall.
>
> Adonis saw; his purple cheeks grew pale;
> The startled blood flew to his throbbing breast;
> Late he repents, late sees his bold hopes fail,
> And doubts, and turns to fly, while onward prest
> The terrors of his foe, that ever quail
> Young hunters' hearts; sharp growl, erected crest,
> And rapid pace, with eyes more fearful bright
> Than meteors seen 'mid darkest clouds of night.

THE DECADENCE AND REVIVAL

He is pursued by the monster, wounded again and again by the sharp tusks, and dies lamented by Venus and all nature.

> Soft breathing sighs, sweet languor, sweetest hue
> Of pallid flowers, Death's ensigns beautiful,
> With Love's triumphant smiles, no terrors threw
> O'er his bright face and form, and eyes late full
> Of amorous fires. Though quenched those orbs of blue,
> Their beauty doth not yet look cold or dull:
> Shining, as Love and Death, young brothers were,
> And sported midst those graces, cold as fair.
>
> Cool fountains shed their urns, warm-gushing tears,
> Proud oaks and pines low bend their mournful heads,
> And Alpine height, and forest murmuring hears,
> And pours a flood of sorrow o'er the meads.
> Now weep the Nymphs, and Dryads weep with fears
> For Venus now; her lost Adonis bleeds;
> While spring and mountain-hunting Nymphs lament;
> Through springs and mountains is a sighing sent.[1]

There is no dearth of poets in these two hundred years of decadence, but scarcely one rises above mediocrity, and however famous in their own day, they are now forgotten. Among the more prominent names, after Marini, we may mention that of Gabriello Chiabrera (1559–1637), who deserves some praise in that he opposed the extravagances of

---

[1] From Sismondi's *Literature of the South of Europe*, translated by Thomas Roscoe.

THE GREAT POETS OF ITALY

the school of Marini, and improved Italian poetry by means of Greek and Latin models. Henceforth a new style of lyric poetry ruled in Italy, — the academic or classic. Fulvio Testi (1593–1646), born in Ferrara, passed his short life in the service of the House of Este, and, being accused of secret correspondence with the French, was arrested and cast into prison, where he died in 1646. His best-known poem is the "Lament of Italy," in which he bewails the wretched state of his native land. Another well-known name is that of Vincenzo Filicaja (1642–1707), whom Macaulay considered the greatest lyrical poet of his age. His sonnet on the slavish condition of Italy as paraphrased by Byron in "Childe Harold" has become widely known to English readers.

> Italia! oh Italia! thou who hast
> The fatal gift of beauty, which became
> A funeral dower of present woes and past,
> On thy sweet brow is sorrow plough'd by shame,
> And annals graved in characters of flame.
> Oh, God! that thou wert in thy nakedness
> Less lovely or more powerful, and couldst claim
> Thy right, and awe the robbers back, who press
> To shed thy blood, and drink the tears of thy distress;
>
> Then might'st thou more appal, or less desired,
> Be homely and be peaceful, undeplored

THE DECADENCE AND REVIVAL

> For thy destructive charms; then, still untired,
> Would not be seen the armed torrents pour'd
> Down the steep Alps; nor would the hostile horde
> Of many-nation'd spoilers from the Po
> Quaff blood and water; nor the stranger's sword
> Be thy sad weapon of defence, and so
> Victor or vanquished, thou the slave of friend or foe.

In 1748, the Treaty of Aix-la-Chapelle ended Spanish rule in Italy, and the breath of free thought from England sweeping across the plains of France entered Italy and gradually weakened the power of the Jesuits, dissipated to a certain extent superstition and ignorance, and aroused the country to a sense of its degradation. By bringing Italy into connection with other nations, and with newer ideals, it planted the germs of a new intellectual life. The influence of France, England, and Germany began to make itself felt. Corneille, Racine, and Voltaire influenced Italian tragedy, while Molière, who himself had borrowed largely from the early Italian comedies, now returned the favor by becoming the master of Goldoni. English influence came later, first Addison, Pope, and Milton, then toward the end of the eighteenth century, Young, Gray, Shakespere, and Ossian. Last of all came the German influence, especially that of Klopstock and Goethe.

THE GREAT POETS OF ITALY

One of the first and greatest of the poets to show the new spirit of independence that breathed over all Europe at this time both in the world of politics and of literature was Giuseppe Parini (1729–1799), who, while an original thinker and poet, yet shows plainly the influence of the English writers of the period. He was a man of admirable character, gentle in disposition, quiet and dignified in manners, and full of sorrow at the wretched state of his beloved country. He received a good education, and having passed a number of years as tutor in the house of several members of the upper nobility, he used his opportunities there to observe carefully the corrupt and effeminate customs of the aristocratic youth of the day, and published his observations in the form of a satire, entitled " Il Giorno " (The Day), a poem which at once became famous. In this poem, which belongs to the same general class as the " Lutrin " of Boileau and the " Rape of the Lock" of Pope, the poet pretends to be the preceptor of a young man in all matters pertaining to elegant society, and undertakes to teach him the customs and duties necessary to one who wishes to obtain the name of perfect " cavalier." With happy satire he held up to ridicule the conduct, manners, and conversation of the noble classes, and rebuked their

THE DECADENCE AND REVIVAL

idleness, pride, extravagance, and vice, thus laying the foundations of that branch of patriotic literature which sought to prepare the Italian people for the task of unifying the fatherland by the cultivation of character.

In this period of awakening, however, the chief gain was in the field of the drama. Up to the middle of the eighteenth century, Italy, in this branch of literature, could not even remotely be compared with France, Spain, or England. In the sixteenth century comedies had not been wanting, and beside the purely Italian creation of improvised farce (now represented in Punch and Judy shows, pantomimes, and harlequinades), Ariosto had written literary comedies in close imitation of Plautus and Terence. Yet from Ariosto to Goldoni we find practically but one genuine writer of comedy. This, singularly enough, was Machiavelli, whose "Mandragora" enjoyed immense popularity, and was declared by Voltaire to be better than the comedies of Aristophanes and but little inferior to those of Molière. It was left for Carlo Goldoni (1707–1793), then, to give his country a number of comedies worthy of being compared with those of Molière.

Goldoni was a kindly, amiable man of the world as well as of letters, bright and witty but withal somewhat superficial. Although a keen observer of the outer form of society and of human nature, he lacked the depth and insight, and especially the subtle pathos of Molière. He was greatly influenced by the latter, whom he looked upon as his master. Like him he began with light comedy, farcical in nature, and gradually produced more and more comedies of manner and of character. Yet he is not a slavish imitator of the great Frenchman, to whom, while inferior in earnestness and knowledge of the human heart, he was equal in dialogue, in development of plot, and in comic talent. Goldoni composed rapidly (once he wrote sixteen comedies in a year), and has left behind him one hundred and sixty plays and eighty musical dramas and opera texts.

The musical drama is a peculiarly Italian invention, and almost immediately reached perfection in Pietro Metastasio (1698–1782), after whom it began rapidly to decline. Metastasio was universally admired, and was, before Goldoni and Alfieri, the only Italian who had a European reputation, and who thus won some measure of glory for his country in her period of deepest degradation. His plays, meant to be set to music (the modern opera text is a debased form of this), were superficial, had no real delineation of character, yet

THE DECADENCE AND REVIVAL

were written in verses which flowed softly along like a clear stream through flowery meads. Light, artificial in sentiment, often lax in morals, yet expressing the courtly conventionalities of the times, Metastasio's poetry enjoyed vast popularity, while he himself became the favorite of the aristocratic society of Vienna (where he lived for fifty years), and the pride and glory of Italy. After him music became the all-important element in this peculiar form of drama, which thus developed into the modern opera.

More famous, perhaps, than either of the above was Alfieri, the founder of modern Italian tragedy. In the intellectual movement of the sixteenth century, tragedy, like comedy, had not been neglected, and many translations and imitations had been made from the Greek and Latin dramatists. The first regular tragedy, not only of Italian but of modern European literature, was the "Sofonisba" of Trissino, which became the model of all succeeding writers. Published first in 1524, it was soon translated into all European languages and imitated, among many others, by Corneille and Voltaire in France, Alfieri in Italy, and Geibel in Germany. In spite of this promising beginning, however, Italian tragedy did not develop as that of the neighboring countries did. Among the numberless writers of tragedy in the sixteenth and seventeenth centuries scarcely one deserves mention. In the early part of the eighteenth century one name became famous, Scipio Maffei (1675-1755; the immediate predecessor of Alfieri), whose "Merope" was vastly popular throughout all Europe.

Yet Italy could not boast of a truly national drama before .the appearance of Vittorio Alfieri (1749-1803), who gave her an honorable rank in this department of the world's literature. The story of his life, as told by himself in his autobiography, is exceedingly interesting. Born in Asti, near Turin, of a noble family, after a youth spent in idleness, ignorance, and selfish pleasure, at the age of twenty-six he "found himself," and being fired with ambition to become a poet, began a long period of self-education. He made especial efforts to master the Italian language, which he, born in Piedmont, and long absent abroad, only half understood. The rest of his life was spent in this study and in the writing of his dramas.

In his reform of the Italian drama, Alfieri did not, like Manzoni later, try to introduce Shakesperean methods. He went back to the tragic system of the Greeks, and tried to improve on the

ALFIERI

THE DECADENCE AND REVIVAL

French followers of the latter. He observed the three unities, especially that of action, even more strictly than Corneille or even Racine.

Alfieri undoubtedly drew his literary doctrines from the great French dramatists, although he indignantly denies any close imitation of them. His language is far different from the courtly, refined, and artificial diction of Corneille and Racine. It is extraordinarily brief and sententious, often harsh in its broken exclamations, and in its complete renunciation of the graces and flowers of poetry.

The most striking innovation made by Alfieri was the reduction of tragedy to its ultimate limits of brevity, only one of his plays containing more than fifteen hundred lines. He purposely cut off the *confidants* of the French drama, with their useless repetitions; he reduced the plot to one brief and definite action, which advanced from beginning to end in a straight line. There is no deviation from this line; the characters are for the most part helplessly entangled in the toils of a relentless fate, and are carried along to an inevitable destruction. The atmosphere is dark and sombre, utterly unrelieved by that tender sympathy, — the pity of it all, — which softens the tragic effect of Shakespere's plays. Horror is the keynote of all these dramas; unnatural love, jealousy between father and son, fratricidal hatred, or devotion to the sacred cause of liberty triumphing over the ties of filial and parental love, — these are the themes of Alfieri's tragedies. Death, murder, suicide, is the outcome of every one.

The actors are few, in many plays only four, and each represents a certain passion. They never change, but remain true each to his own character throughout the whole play. The villains are monsters of cruelty and vice, and the innocent and virtuous are invariably their victims and succumb to them at last.

Alfieri's purpose in producing these plays was not to amuse an idle public, but to promulgate those great principles of liberty which inspired his own life. A deep, uncompromising hatred of kings is seen in each of his plays. There is constant declamation against tyranny and slavery. Freedom is portrayed as something dearer than life itself.[1] Alfieri was the first to speak of a fatherland, a united Italy; he practically founded the patriotic school of literature which has lasted down to the present time. Hence he is even more important

[1] It is interesting to note that Alfieri dedicated one of his plays to George Washington.

THE DECADENCE AND REVIVAL

from a political standpoint than from a literary one. He himself looked on his tragedies as a means of inspiring new and higher political ideas in his fellow countrymen, degraded as they had been by the long oppression of Spain. " I wrote," he says, " because the sad conditions of the times did not allow me to act."

In his twenty-two plays, there is a surprising uniformity of excellence, and it is hard to single out any one preëminent. " Saul," " Agamemnon," " Orestes," and " Philip II." however, may be regarded as affording the best illustrations of his tragic power.

We select for quotation the last play, not only because of its intrinsic merit, but because the theme, which has been treated by Schiller in his " Don Carlos," is modern and hence of more interest to the general reader than the classic and Biblical subjects of most of Alfieri's plays.

The subject of Philip II. was peculiarly well fitted to Alfieri's sombre genius. The character of the king, despotic, heartless, full of jealous suspicion, a veritable Tiberius of modern times, is admirably drawn, while the nobler characters of Don Carlos and Isabella stand out in sharp contrast against the gloomy personage of Philip.

THE GREAT POETS OF ITALY

The story of the plot is well known. Don Carlos, the son of Philip II., is to marry Isabella, princess of France, but for political reasons Philip breaks off the marriage and marries her himself. The result is inevitable. The two young people cannot forget their love at the command of the king. In the first scene Isabella, lamenting her hapless lot, confesses her inability to banish the image of Carlos from her heart.

> *Isa.* Love, apprehension, and each wicked hope,
> Leave ye my breast! I, Philip's faithless wife,
> Dare I behold with fondness Philip's son?
> Yet who beholds that son, and loves him not?
> A heart, though bold, humane; a lofty nature;
> An intellect sublime; and, in a form
> Most fair, a soul of correspondent worth.
> Ah, why did Heav'n and Nature make thee such?
> Alas! why rave I thus? Do I intend,
> By meditating thus on his perfections,
> To tear his image from the deep recesses
> Of my adoring heart? O, if a flame
> So fatal in its consequences, were
> By living man discover'd! O, if he
> Suspected it! He sees me ever sad . . .
> 'T is true, most sad; yet evermore avoiding
> The fascination of his thrilling presence.
> And from Spain's austere palace well he knows
> All joy is banish'd. Who can read my heart?
> O that with other mortals I could vie
> In ignorance! that I could shun myself,

THE DECADENCE AND REVIVAL

> And thus deceive myself, as I can others! . . .
> Unhappy I! My only solace left
> Are tears; and mine, alas, are tears of guilt. —
> But, that with less of risk I may indulge
> My wretchedness, to some interior chamber
> Let me retire in time . . . Ah, who is this?
> Carlos? Ah, let me fly! My ev'ry look,
> My ev'ry word, might now betray me. Hence
> With speed!

Carlos appears, and in a long dialogue, the secret feelings of the two unhappy lovers are revealed in spite of Isabella's efforts to the contrary. The germs of jealous suspicion already exist in Philip. He orders his willing and unscrupulous tool, Gomez, to watch the queen's countenance, while he questions her as to her affection for her stepson, and, later, while he accuses Carlos of treason in her presence. Gomez is only too ready to see evidence of guilt in the queen's behavior, and fans the fire of jealousy which is smoldering in the king's heart. The short scene after the conversation between Philip, Isabella, and Carlos, with its laconic questions and answers, is very characteristic of Alfieri.

> *Phi.* Didst hear?
> *Gom.* I heard.
> *Phi.* Didst see?
> *Gom.* I saw.

THE GREAT POETS OF ITALY

Phi.   O rage!
Suspicion, then . . .
    Gom.   Is certainty.
  Phi.   Is Philip
Still unavenged?
    Gom.   Think . . .
  Phi.   I have thought. — Now follow.

From now on we know that the fate of the two innocent but unfortunate lovers is sealed. No human agency can avert the catastrophe. The jealousy of Philip is as implacable and inevitable as that of Othello, and Alfieri has succeeded almost as effectively as Shakespere in awakening in the spectators those feelings of pity and terror which according to Aristotle it is the chief function of tragedy to produce. A council of state is held in which Carlos is not only accused of heresy and of entering into treasonable correspondence with the enemies of Spain, but is also accused by Philip himself of attempted parricide.

> *Phi.* By an ungrateful son my peace is ruin'd;
> That peace, which each of you, more blest than I,
> Feels in the bosom of his family.
> In vain have I adopted tow'rds my son
> Rigor, with mildness temper'd; vainly tried
> By warm reproof to spur him on to virtue:
> To prayers and to example deaf alike,
> And still more deaf to menaces, he adds

THE DECADENCE AND REVIVAL

One trespass to another; and to these
Impious presumption. So that, at their height,
This day has fill'd the measure of his crimes.
Yes, though I gave to him this day new proofs
Of indiscreet affection, he selects
This very day to give his father's heart
The last proofs of unheard-of wickedness. —
Scarce had the glowing orb that rules the day,
The shining witness of my daily actions,
Retired to cheer my transatlantic realms,
Than with the shades of night, to traitors friendly,
A project horrible and black arose
Within the heart of Carlos. Silently,
Vengeance to take for his forgiven crimes,
He steals with murd'rous footsteps to my chamber.
His right hand with a parricidal sword
He dared to arm: approach'd me unawares;
The weapon lifts; and is about to plunge it
Into my undefended side . . . when, lo!
All unexpectedly, a voice exclaims:
"Philip, be on thy guard!" It was Rodrigo,
Who came to me. At the same time I feel
The stroke, as of a lightly grazing sword
Defeated of its aim. My eager eyes
Glance through the obscure distance. At my feet
A naked sword I see; and in swift flight
Remote, amid the night's uncertain shadows,
Behold my son. I now have told you all.
If there be those among my friends convened,
Who can accuse him of another fault;
If there be those who can of this fault clear him,
Speak without hesitation: and may Heaven
Inspire his words! This is a fearful matter;
My councillors, deliberately weigh it.

The action now hastens to its close. Carlos is thrown into prison. The false-hearted Gomez seeks the queen, feigns to be horror-struck at the king's unnatural hatred of his son, and offers to help Isabella to secure the escape of Don Carlos. She trusts him, visits Carlos in his prison, — is there surprised by the king, and, together with Carlos, dies, the victim of the insane jealousy of the gloomy tyrant.

ACT V.

Scene I.

CARLOS.

Car. What have I now to hope, what fear, but death?
Would I might have it free from infamy! . . .
From cruel Philip, I, alas shall have it
Replete with infamy. — One doubt alone,
Far worse than any death, afflicts my heart.
Perchance he knows my love : Erewhile I saw,
In the fierce glances of his countenance,
I know not what of bitterness, that seem'd,
Spite of himself, his meaning to betray . . .
His conversation with the queen erewhile. . .
My summons ; his observing me . . . What would . . .
(O Heav'ns !) what would her fate be, should his wife
Excite the wrath of his suspicious nature ?
Perchance e'en now the cruel tyrant wreaks
Vengeance on her for an uncertain fault ;
Vengeance that always, when a tyrant rules,
Precedes the crime itself . . . But, if to all,

THE DECADENCE AND REVIVAL

And almost to ourselves, our love's unknown,
Whence should he learn it ? . . . Have my sighs, perchance,
Betray'd my meaning ?   What ?   Shall love's soft sighs
Be by a guilty tyrant understood ? . . .
To make him furious and unnatural,
Could it be needful to a sire like this
To penetrate my love ?   His vengeful hate
Had reach'd its height, and could not brook delay.
The day at length is come, the day is come
When I may satisfy his thirst for blood. —
Ah! treach'rous troops of friends that crowded round me
In my prosperity ! where are ye now ?
I only ask of you a sword ; a sword,
By means of which to 'scape from infamy,
Not one of you will bring me . . . whence that noise ? . . .
The iron gate grates on its hinges!   Ah !
What next may I expect ? . . . Who comes there ?   Ho !

SCENE II.

ISABELLA, CARLOS.

  Car.   Queen, is it thou ?   Who was thy guide ?   What cause
Hither conducted thee ?   Love, duty, pity ?
How didst thou gain admission ?
  Isa.   Wretched prince,
Thou know'st not yet the horrors of thy fate :
Thou as a parricide art stigmatized :
Thy sire himself accuses thee : to death
A mercenary council hath condemn'd thee ;
Nothing is wanting to complete the sentence
But the assent of Philip.
  Car.   If that's all,
That soon will follow.

THE GREAT POETS OF ITALY

Isa. Art thou not o'erwhelm'd?
Car. 'T is long since nought but death has been **my choice**:
Thou know'st it well, of whom I nothing ask'd,
But **leave** to breathe my last where thou dost dwell.
'T is hard, yes, hard, the **horrible aspersion**;
Not unexpected. I 'm compelled to die:
And can I shudder if thou bring the tidings?
Isa. Ah! if thou love me, do not talk of **death**.
Yield, for a short time, to the pressing need . . .
Car. Yield? now I see that thou hast **undertaken**
The cruel office to degrade my nature.
My vengeful father hath deputed thee . . .
Isa. And canst thou think it, prince, that I am then
The minister of Philip's cruelty? . . .
Car. He may to this constrain thee, p'rhaps **deceive thee**.
But wherefore, then, has he permitted thee
To see me in this dungeon?
Isa. Thinkest thou
That Philip knows it? That indeed were death! . . .
Car. What say'st thou? Nothing can escape his **knowledge**.
Who dares to violate his fierce commands? . . .
Isa. Gomez.
Car. Alas! what is it that **I hear**?
What an abominable, fatal name
Hast thou pronounced! . . .
Isa. He 's not thy enemy,
As thou dost think . . .
Car. O Heav'ns, if I believed
He were my friend, my countenance would burn
With shame, more than with anger.
Isa. He alone
Feels pity for thy fate. To me confess'd he
Philip's atrocious plot.

THE DECADENCE AND REVIVAL

Car.   Incautious queen!
Thou art too credulous! what hast thou done?
Why didst thou trust to such a feign'd compassion?
Of the base king the basest minister,
If he spoke truth, 't was with the truth to cheat thee.

Isa. What could it profit him? Of his compassion
Undoubted proofs I quickly can display,
If thou wilt yield to my entreaties. He
By stealth conducted me to this recess;
Prepares the means of thy escape: 't was I
That influenced him. No longer tarry; fly!
Fly from thy father, fly from death and me!

Car. While thou hast time, ah, hasten from my presence;
Gomez no pity feign'd without good reason.
Into what snare thou 'rt fallen! Now, O queen,
Indeed I shudder! Now, what doubt remains?
The secret of our love is fully known
By Philip now . . .

Isa.   Ah, no! Not long ago
Philip I saw, when, from his presence, thou
By dint of force wert dragg'd: he burn'd with rage:
Trembling I listen'd to him, not exempt
From fears like thine. But when in solitude
His converse I recall'd, I felt secure,
That, rather than of this, his fury tax'd thee
With ev'ry other crime . . . I now remember,
He charged thee with intriguing 'gainst my life,
As well as 'gainst his own.

Car.   'T would be a toil
That made me vile as he; yea, e'en more vile,
The dark perplexities to penetrate
Of guilt's inextricable labyrinth;
But, sure I am, that this thy embassy
Conceals some bad design: that which till now

THE GREAT POETS OF ITALY

He but suspected, he would now make clear.
But, be it what it may, depart at once
From this disastrous place. Thy hope is vain,
Vain thy belief that Gomez wills to serve me,
Or, if he will'd it, that I should consent.

 Isa. And must I, then, drag on my wretched days
Midst beings such as these ?
 Car.   'T is too, too true ! —
Delay not now a moment: leave me ; save me
From agonies insufferably keen . . .
Thy pity wounds, if for thyself it feels not.
Go, if thou hold life dear . . .
 Isa.   Life dear to me ? . . .
 Car. My honour, then, remember, and thy fame.
 Isa. And in such danger must I quit thee thus ?
 Car. Ah, what avails it to expose thyself ?
Thyself thou ruinest, and sav'st not me.
Virtue is spotted even by suspicion.
Ah ! from the tyrant snatch the hellish joy
Of casting imputation on thy name.
Go : dry thy tears ; and still thy heaving bosom.
With a dry eye, and an intrepid brow,
Hear of my death. To virtue's cause devote
The mournful days in which thou shalt outlive me . . .
And if among so many guilty creatures
Thou seekest consolation, one remains :
Perez, thou know'st him well, clandestinely
Will weep with thee ; — To him sometimes speak of me . . .
But go — depart ; . . . Ah, tempt me not to weep . . .
Little by little rend not thus my heart !
Take now thy last farewell, . . . and leave me ; . . . go !
I 've need to summon all my fortitude,
Now that the fatal hour of death approaches . . .

THE DECADENCE AND REVIVAL

SCENE III.

PHILIP, ISABELLA, CARLOS.

Phi. Perfidious one, that hour of death is come:
I bring it to thee.
　　Isa.　　　　Are we thus betray'd? . . .
　　Car. I am prepared for death. Give it at once.
　　Phi. Wretch, thou shalt die: but first, ye impious pair,
My fulminating accents hear, and tremble. —
Ye vile ones! long, yes, long, I've known it all.
That horrid flame that burns in you with love,
In me with fury, long has fix'd its torment,
And long been all discover'd. O what pangs
Of rage repress'd! O what resentment smother'd! . . .
At last ye both are fallen in my power.
Should I lament? or utter vain regrets?
I vow'd revenge; and I will have it soon;
Revenge full, unexampled. — On your shame
Meanwhile I feast my eyes. Flagitious woman,
Think not I ever bore thee any love,
Nor that a jealous thought within my heart
E'er woke a pang. Philip could never deign
On a degraded bosom, such as thine,
To fix the love of his exalted nature;
Nor could a woman who deserved betray it.
Thou hast in me thy king offended, then,
And not thy lover. Thou, unworthily,
Hast now my consort's name, that sacred name,
Basely contaminated. I ne'er prized
Thy love; but such inviolable duty
Thou should'st have felt towards thy lord and king,
As should have made thee e'en at a frail thought
Shudder with horror. — Thou, seducer vile; . . .

THE GREAT POETS OF ITALY

To thee I speak not. Guilt becomes thy nature:
The deed was worthy of its impious author. —
Undoubted proofs to me (too much so!) were,
Although conceal'd, your guilty sighs, your silence,
Your gestures, and the sorrow which I saw,
And still can see, your wicked bosoms filling
With equal force. — Now, what more shall I say?
Equal in crime, your torments shall be equal.

   Car. What do I hear? In her there is no fault:
No fault? not e'en the shadow of a fault!
Pure is her heart; with such flagitious flame
It never burn'd, I swear: she scarcely knew
My love; the trespass then . . .
   Phi.   To what extent
Ye, each of you, are criminal, I know;
I know that to thy father's bed, as yet,
Thou hast not raised thy bold and impious thoughts.
Had it been otherwise, would'st thou now live? . . .
But from thy impure mouth there issued accents,
Flagitious accents, of a dreadful love;
She heard them; that suffices.
   Car.   I alone
Offended thee; I seek not to conceal it:
A rapid flash of hope athwart my sight
Shot: but her virtue instantly dispell'd it;
She heard me, but 't was only to my shame;
Only to root entirely from my bosom
The passion illegitimate it foster'd . . .
Yes, now, alas! too illegitimate . . .
Yet it was once a lawful, noble passion:
She was my spouse betroth'd — my spouse, thou know'st;
Thou gav'st her to me; and the gift was lawful,
But 't was not lawful in thee to resume it . . .
Yes, I am criminal in ev'ry shape:

THE DECADENCE AND REVIVAL

I love her; thou hast made that love a crime; . . .
What canst thou now take from me? In my blood
Satiate thy wrath; and gratify in me
The bitter madness of thy jealous pride;
Spare her; for she is wholly innocent . . .
    Phi. She? Not to thee in guilt she yields, but boldness. —
Be silent, madam, of thine own accord,
That silence doth sufficiently betray thee:
'T is useless to deny it, thou dost cherish
A passion illegitimate. Thou show'dst it,
Enough, too much didst show it, when I spoke,
With artful purposes, of him to thee:
Why, then, didst thou so pertinaciously
Remind me that he was my son? O traitress,
Thou didst not dare to say he was thy lover.
And hast thou less than he, within thy heart,
Betray'd thy duty, honor, and the laws?
    Isa. . . . My silence from my fear doth not arise;
But from the stupor that benumbs my senses,
At the incredible duplicity
Of thy bloodthirsty, rabid heart. — At length
My scatter'd senses I once more recover . . .
'T is time, 't is time, that for the heinous fault
I should atone, of being wife to thee. —
Till now I've not offended thee: till now,
In God's sight, in the prince's, I am guiltless.
Although within my breast . . .
    Car.   Pity for me
Inspires her words: ah, hear her not . . .
    Isa.   In vain
Thou seek'st to save me. Ev'ry word of thine
Is as a puncture, which exasperates
The wounds of his proud breast. The time is past
For palliatives. To shun his hated sight,

THE GREAT POETS OF ITALY

The torment of whose presence nought can equal,
Is now my only refuge. — Were it given
To one that is a tyrant e'er to feel
The pow'r of love, I would remind thee, king,
That thou at first didst form our mutual ties :
That from my earliest years, my fondest thoughts,
My dearest hopes were centred all in him ;
With him I trusted to live bless'd and blessing.
To love him then, at once, in me was virtue,
And to thy will submission. Who but thou
Made what was virtue guilt ? Thou didst the deed.
Ties the most holy thou didst burst asunder, —
An easy task to one that 's absolute.
But does the heart change thus ? His image lay
Deeply engraven there : but instantly
That I became thy wife, the flame was smother'd.
And I depended afterwards on time,
And on my virtue, and, perchance, on thee,
Wholly to root it out . . .
 Phi.   I will then now,
What neither years, nor virtue have perform'd,
Do instantly : yes, in thy faithless blood
I 'll quench the impure flame . . .
 Isa.   Yes, blood to spill,
And, when that blood is spilt, to spill more blood,
Is thy most choice prerogative : but, O !
Is it by a prerogative like this
Thou hopest to win me from him to thee ?
To thee, as utterly unlike thy son,
As is, to virtue, vice ? — Thou hast been wont
To see me tremble ; but I fear no more ;
As yet, my wicked passion, for as such
I deem'd my passion, I have kept conceal'd :

THE DECADENCE AND REVIVAL

Now shall it be without disguise proclaim'd,
Since thy dark crimes have made it seem like virtue.
  Phi. He's worthy of thee; thou of him art worthy. —
It now remains to prove, if, as in words,
Ye will be bold in death . . .

SCENE IV.

GOMEZ, PHILIP, ISABELLA, CARLOS.

  Phi.   Hast thou, O Gomez,
All my commands fulfill'd? What I enjoin'd thee
Dost thou now bring?
  Gom.   Perez has breathed his last:
Behold the sword, that with his smoking blood
Yet reeks.
  Car.   O sight!
  Phi.   With him is not extinguish'd
The race of traitors . . . Be thou witness now
How I take vengeance on this impious pair.
  Car. Before I die, alas! how many deaths
I'm destined to behold. Thou, Perez, too? . . .
O infamy! now, now I follow thee.
Where is the sword to which my breast is fated?
Quick, bring it to me. May my blood alone
The burning thirst of this fell tiger slake!
  Isa. O would that I alone could satisfy
His murd'rous appetite!
  Phi.   Cease your vile contest.
This dagger, and this cup await your choice.
Thou, proud contemner as thou art, of death,
Choose first.
  Car.   O weapon of deliverance! . . .

THE GREAT POETS OF ITALY

With guiltless blood yet reeking, thee I choose ! —
O luckless lady, thou hast said too much :
For thee no refuge now remains but death :
But, ah ! the poison choose, for this will be
Most easy . . . Of my inauspicious love
The last advice is this : collect at once
All, all thy fortitude : — and look on me. . . [*He stabs himself.*]
I die . . . do thou now follow my example . . .
Bring, bring the fatal cup . . . do not delay . . .

  Isa. Ah, yes ; I follow thee. O Death, to me
Thou art most welcome ; in thee . . .
    Phi.   Thou shalt live ;
Spite of thyself, shalt live.
    Isa.   Ah, let me . . . O
Fierce torture ! see, he dies : and I ?
    Phi.   Yes, thou,
Sever'd from him, shalt live ; live days of woe :
Thy ling'ring grief will be a joy to me.
And when at last, recover'd from thy love,
Thou wishest to live on, I, then, will kill thee.

  Isa. Live in thy presence ? . . . I support thy sight ?
No, that shall never be . . . My doom is fix'd . . .
The cup refused, thy dagger may replace it. . . [*She darts most rapidly towards the dagger of Philip, and stabs herself with it.*]
    Phi. Stop !
    Isa.   Now I die . . .
    Phi.   Heav'ns, what do I behold ?
  Isa. Thou see'st thy wife . . . thy son . . . both innocent . . .
And both by thy hands slain . . . — I follow thee,
Loved Carlos . . .
    Phi.   What a stream of blood runs here,
And of what blood ! . . . Behold, I have at least
Obtained an ample, and a horrid vengeance . . .

THE DECADENCE AND REVIVAL

But am I happy ? . . . — Gomez, do thou hide
The dire catastrophe from all the world. —
By silence, thou wilt save my fame, thy life.[1]

[1] The above passages are taken from the translation of Alfieri's tragedies by Charles Lloyd, published in Bohn's Library.

IX

THE NINETEENTH CENTURY

In the history of Italy as a whole, the nineteenth century stands forth as perhaps the most important epoch since the downfall of Rome. For fourteen hundred years the devoted land had been the battle-field of the nations. The vast hordes of Goths, Huns, Lombards, Saracens and Normans had in turn swept like a devastating flood over its fertile plains and valleys. Then, when a new nation seemed about to rise from the ruins of the ancient Roman people, the century-long contest between the Pope and Emperor divided not only the country at large into the warring factions of Guelphs and Ghibellines, but filled even the very cities with discord and bloody feuds. Later, the centuries following the Renaissance saw the still sadder spectacle of Italy lying idle and helpless while the mighty ambitions of Spain and France struggled for her possession, a struggle the result of which, as we have already seen, left Italy the slave, bound hand and foot, of Spanish tyranny, superstition and oppression.

THE NINETEENTH CENTURY

During all this long period, there was practically no patriotism in the larger sense of the word, no general desire for a united country. Only the voice of the sad-browed Florentine poet was heard through the long centuries, uttering that song, which in the patriotic revival of the early nineteenth century,

> The voices of the city and the sea
> The voices of the mountains and the pines

repeated, till the familiar lines became

> footpaths for the thought of Italy.

This voice of Dante, finding an echo in the hearts of such men as Alfieri, Foscolo and Mazzini, did more than anything else to bring about the wonderful consummation of Italian unity, one of the most significant phenomena of a century destined to be known in history as the century of science and political progress.

The story of the Risorgimento in Italy, with its indomitable energy, its inability to acknowledge defeat, its untiring devotion to the sacred cause of a United Fatherland, is full of inspiration. The heroism of men like the Bandiera brothers, the genius and unselfish sacrifices of Mazzini, the legendary exploits of Garibaldi, the providential events that prepared the House of Savoy to take the leadership in the upbuilding of a new nation, all the epic vicissitudes of that long struggle, up to the fateful 20th of September, 1870, when the walls of Porta Pia were broken to admit the victorious army of Victor Emmanuel, — all these things form a story at once fascinating and uplifting.

The literature of the first seven decades of the nineteenth century is deeply impressed with this patriotic and national character. The mighty impulse given to it by the dramas of Alfieri, with their fierce hatred of tyranny and their virile proclamation of liberty, was carried on by his successors. It is true that one of the greatest of the early poets of the century, Vincenzo Monti (1754–1828), can hardly be called a patriot, in the stern unbending sense in which Alfieri used that word. Amiable though he was, he was fickle, having the principles of a Mr. Worldly Wiseman in real life, seeking for personal advantage in the troubled waters of Italian politics at the end of the eighteenth and the beginning of the nineteenth century. Living before, during and after the French Revolution, his poetry follows with flexible versatility all the vicissitudes of his country during his own lifetime. In the "Bassvilliana,"[1] his most famous poem, he scourged

[1] So called from Hugo Bassville, a French diplomat, who was

THE NINETEENTH CENTURY

the excesses of the French Revolution, only to recant later and turn his words of blame into praise. When Napoleon was in the ascendant in Italy, Monti dedicated to his glory a number of poems; but when the " great wheel " of Napoleon's prosperity began to roll down hill, Monti let go for fear his own career should be involved in the ruin of the great Corsican.

Almost every other writer, however, of the early nineteenth century contributed his share to the upbuilding of the national character and to the preparation for that unity of Italy which was to come so many years later. Thus in the drama, we have the " Carmagnola " and " Adelchi " of Alessandro Manzoni, and the " Arnold of Brescia " of Giovanni Battista Niccolini; in satire the genial verses of Giuseppe Giusti; and in the novel, the " Battle of Benevento " of Francesco Domenico Guerrazzi, the " Niccolò de' Lapi " of Massimo d' Azeglio, the " Jacopo Ortis " of Ugo Foscolo, and especially the famous " Promessi Sposi " (the Betrothed) of Manzoni, — all filled with intense indignation at the degraded state of Italy, and a

killed by a mob in Rome. In Monti's poem, his spirit is allowed to enter Paradise only after having witnessed all the horrors committed by the French Revolution.

burning passion for a free and united country. The same end was sought by the political writings of Giuseppe Mazzini, the pure-minded patriot and founder of the famous society of Young Italy, — by Vincenzo Gioberti, whose "Moral and Civil Primacy of the Italian People" stirred the whole country with the hope of a Utopian republic under the presidency of the Pope; by Carlo Botta in his historical writings; by Silvio Pellico in his pathetic journal of his experiences as a political prisoner; and even by Gabriele Rossetti in his anti-papal commentary on Dante's "Divine Comedy."

The various phases of the Romantic movement, which in other countries was purely literary, here took on a peculiar national stamp. The treatment of mediæval subjects, the new view of nature and man, in the hands of such writers as Mazzini, Foscolo, and Niccolini, were all made subservient to the patriotic function of Italian literature. This is especially true of melancholy, that "Weltschmerz" so characteristic of the whole Romantic school, and which in Italy had more than a sentimental cause in the condition of the land.

The two greatest writers of the first half of the century were Alessandro Manzoni (1785–1873), and Giacomo Leopardi (1798–1837). The former

THE NINETEENTH CENTURY

exerted a vast influence on the patriotic literature of the times, both by his dramas, already referred to, and especially by his famous historical novel "I Promessi Sposi," — one of the greatest novels of any time or country. Through this book, which described with the effectiveness of a truly creative genius the wretched state of Italy under Spanish rule, Manzoni became the most popular writer in his own country, and enjoyed a widespread fame throughout all Europe. As a lyrical poet he was scarcely less famous. His ode entitled the "Fifth of May," written on the death of Napoleon, was universally hailed as the noblest poem of the times, and was translated into all European tongues.

Still greater than Manzoni, though less fortunate in reaping the rewards of greatness, was the poet, philosopher, and classical scholar Leopardi. He was born in the small town of Recanati, situated among the Abruzzi Mountains, where his father, Count Monaldo Leopardi, lived in a gloomy chateau. The young Leopardi came into the world endowed with a sickly body and a morbid sensitiveness of disposition. His home life was wretched, utterly lacking in those "little, nameless, unremembered acts of kindness and of love" which make the childhood of most men the happiest period of their lives. His

THE GREAT POETS OF ITALY

father was stern and set in his ways, and hated the new French doctrines of Church and State, which, making their way into Italy, soon became the object of passionate devotion on the part of Giacomo. His mother was a narrow bigot, without any apparent love or sympathy for her sickly child. Shut out from all society by his rank and by the dearth of congenial companions in the dull, provincial town of Recanati, the young boy plunged with all his heart and soul into the study of Greek, Latin, Hebrew, French, and German, finding the necessary books in his father's library. The results of all this passion for study were on the one hand marvelous, on the other hand disastrous. At the age of seventeen he had become deeply versed in Greek, and certain dissertations of his on Plotinus caused Niebuhr to declare that he was the foremost, nay the only Greek scholar in Italy.

But this severe study, accompanied as it was by an utter neglect of the rules of hygiene, by lack of cheerful companions and sympathy at home, ruined his health. From now on to the end of his life, his existence was one long agony, interrupted by periods of feverish study, by restless wandering, or by the composition of those wonderful poems which have given him a place in the literature of

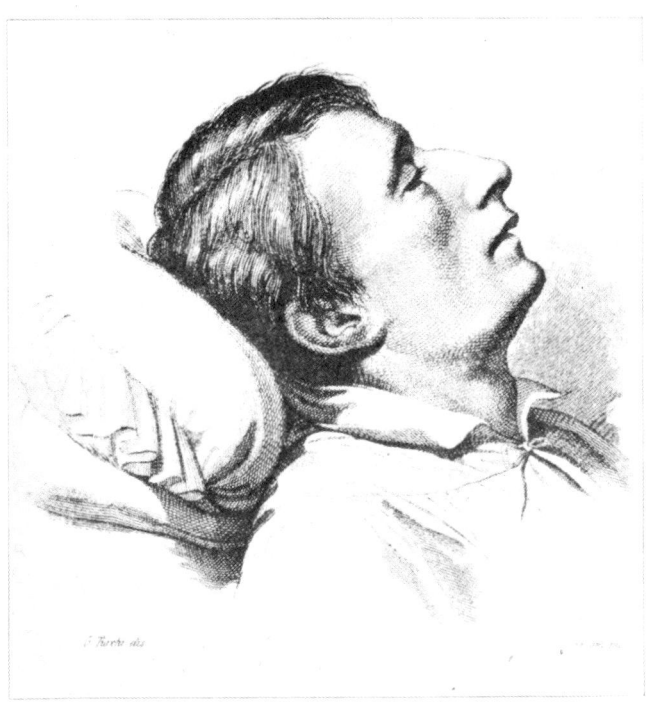

LEOPARDI

THE NINETEENTH CENTURY

Italy, close to the great quadrumvirate of Dante, Petrarch, Ariosto, and Tasso. Life for him became a weary pilgrimage, unrelieved either by present pleasure or by the hope of future happiness. The spirit of pessimism, which was part of his nature, now became his constant companion, "flesh of his flesh, and bone of his bone." He remained at home, almost a prisoner, until in 1822 he found it impossible to live there longer and went to Rome, where, however, he soon became disgusted with the frivolous social life. Later we find him in Milan, where he wrote his commentary on Petrarch's Sonnets. Thence he went to Florence, but soon returned to Recanati, which in turn he again left to resume his wanderings through the cities of Italy, always struggling with poverty and ill health, and, worst of all, the prey of his ever-increasing spirit of pessimism.

In 1833 his health became so broken that it was evident that the end was not far off. Accompanied by his friend Antonio Ranieri, he went to Naples, where he died June 14, 1837, fifteen days before his thirty-ninth birthday.

In spite of this brief career, with its many periods of enforced idleness caused by sickness, Leopardi has won for himself a high rank among the most

THE GREAT POETS OF ITALY

distinguished men of his native land. It is the common opinion, not only of Italian critics, but of the world at large, that he is the greatest poet of modern Italy. Sainte-Beuve called him the " noblest, calmest, most austere of poets," Matthew Arnold says he is worthy to be " named with Milton and Dante," while Gladstone declared that he was " one of the most extraordinary men whom this century has produced, one who in almost every branch of mental exertion had capacity for attaining the highest excellence."

His literary activity manifested itself in the field of classical philology, in philosophy and in poetry. The keynote to his philosophy is pessimism, in which during his whole life he lived and moved and had his being. The pessimism of Leopardi, unlike the " Weltschmerz " of Chateaubriand, Lamartine, or Byron,—which always seems more than half affected, and is largely due to a certain fashion in literature at the beginning of the nineteenth century,—is sincere, profound, and crushing. Undoubtedly, he had a natural tendency to melancholy; and the excessive study of his early years, his morbid sensitiveness, the lack of sympathy and love, his poverty and pecuniary embarrassments, the wretched state of Italy, loved by him so

THE NINETEENTH CENTURY

deeply, — all these added to the dark cloud of melancholy which in his youth shut out the sunshine from his world, and which grew ever thicker and blacker as his life drew to its end.

At first his pessimism was merely personal, but soon he extended it to all modern society, as distinguished from the happy days of early Greece and Rome. Last of all he made pessimism the corner-stone of his philosophy of life. Not only is the world in misery now, but it always has been so and is destined to be so to the end of time. Happiness, virtue, love, the beauty of nature, even patriotism, are but illusions, iridescent bubbles that please the eye of inexperienced youth, but inevitably passing away into thin air.

Sadness is the prevailing note in the poetry of Leopardi, even when he writes on political subjects. He was a patriot, not virile, hopeful, ever fighting as Mazzini, but passive and despairing, pouring out his love for his native land in lamentations for her misery.

> My native land, I see the walls and arches,
> The columns and the statues, and the lonely
> Towers of our ancestors,
> But not their glory, not
> The laurel and the steel that of old time
> Our great forefathers bore. Disarmèd now,

THE GREAT POETS OF ITALY

Naked thou showest thy forehead and thy breast!
O me, how many wounds,
What bruises and what blood! How do I see thee,
Thou loveliest Lady! Unto Heaven I cry,
And to the world: "Say, say,
Who brought her unto this?" To this and worse,
For both her arms are loaded down with chains,
So that, unveiled and with disheveled hair,
She crouches all forgotten and forlorn,
Hiding her beautiful face
Between her knees, and weeps.
Weep, weep, for well thou may'st, my Italy!
Born, as thou wert, to conquest,
Alike in evil and in prosperous sort!
   If thy sweet eyes were each a living stream,
Thou could'st not weep enough
For all thy sorrow and for all thy shame.
For thou wast queen, and now thou art a slave.
Who speaks of thee or writes,
That thinking on thy glory in the past
But says, "She was great once, but is no more."
Wherefore, oh wherefore? Where is the ancient strength,
The valor and the arms, the constancy?
Who rent the sword from thee?
Who hath betrayed thee? What art, or what toil,
Or what o'erwhelming force,
Hath stripped thy robe and golden wreath from thee?
How didst thou fall, and when,
From such height unto a depth so low?
Doth no one fight for thee, no one defend thee,
None of thy own? Arms, arms! For I alone
Will fight and fall for thee.
Grant me, O Heaven, my blood
Shall be as fire unto Italian hearts!

THE NINETEENTH CENTURY

> Where are thy sons ? I hear the sound of arms,
> Of wheels, of voices, and of drums;
> In foreign fields afar
> Thy children fight and fall.
> Wait, Italy, wait! I see, or seem to see,
> A tumult as of infantry and horse,
> And smoke and dust, and the swift flash of swords
> Like lightning among clouds.
> Wilt thou not hope ? Wilt thou not lift and turn
> Thy trembling eyes upon the doubtful close ?
> For what, in yonder fields,
> Combats Italian youth ? O gods, ye gods,
> Oh, misery for him who dies in war,
> Not for his native shores and his beloved,
> His wife and children dear,
> But by the foes of others
> For others' cause, and cannot dying say
> " Dear land of mine,
> The life thou gavest me I give thee back." [1]

Besides his patriotic poems, Leopardi's poetry is mainly autobiographical, or rather it is the analysis of the hopes, disappointments and despair of his own soul. From his early youth he had a yearning for love, and at the same time a feeling that for such as he woman's love was not to be. Two women especially seem to have been the object of his affection, one of whom he knew in early life;

---

[1] This translation is taken from *Modern Italian Poets*, by William Dean Howells, published by Harper & Brothers.

THE GREAT POETS OF ITALY

and to whom he addressed his poem entitled "Silvia."

> Silvia, dost thou still
> That time remember of thy days on earth,
> When beauty in thine eyes, that flash'd at will
> Smiles of a roguish mirth,
> Shone radiant, and the girl,
> Joyous at whiles, at whiles of pensive mood,
> Was blossoming into lovelier womanhood.
>
> From out thy quiet room,
> The neighboring street along,
> Thy voice was heard, still breaking into song,
> When thou, upon thy woman's work intent,
> Didst sit, the long day through,
> Thy thoughts serenely bent
> On what the days to come for thee might do.
> 'T was May, with all its fragrance and its flowers,
> And so thine hours flow'd onward — happy hours.
>
> Throwing my studies for awhile aside,
> My books and all the lore,
> That 't was my joy and pride
> From my first youth to ponder o'er and o'er,
> I hurried from my room,
> And from a casement high
> Of my paternal home, at sound
> Of that dear voice, would strain
> My ears to catch
> Its every tone, and watch
> The nimble hand that plied
> The shuttle of the overwearied loom.

THE NINETEENTH CENTURY

Above me was the sky, a cloudless blue,
Then caught my eye
The gardens down below, the lanes ablaze
With golden leafage, then the distant sea,
And after that the mountain towering nigh.
No tongue of man can say,
What rapturous feelings then my breast did sway.

Oh, what sweet thoughts, what hopes, my Silvia,
Were ours, what songs with ecstasy elate!
And what to our glad eyes
Seem'd human life and fate!
When I remember all
That promised then so fair,
I sink disconsolate,
My thoughts are turned to gall,
And lamentation of my hapless state.
O Nature! Nature! Why,
Why not fulfill for us
What thou didst promise then? Oh why
Befool thy children thus?

Ere Winter chill had yet embrown'd the land,
By strange disease attacked and overcome,
Thou, darling, wert cut off. Thou didst not see
Thy budding years to perfect flower expand,
Nor ever throbb'd thy heart, to hear the praise
Of thy dark hair, or see love-lighted eyes
Bent upon thine with fond admiring gaze,
Nor ever did thy mates discourse to thee
Of love on festal days.

So, too, for me
Sweet hope was slain. So also to my years
The Fates denied a Springtime. How, ah how,

THE GREAT POETS OF ITALY

> Hast thou pass'd utterly away from me,
> Thou dear companion of my manhood's dawn,
> My hope, for ever to be mourned with tears!
> Is this the world our fancy drew? Are these
> The joys, the love, the deeds, the scenes to be,
> Whereof so oft in happy hours we spoke?
> Is this of all of mortal kind the doom?
> When first the woful truth upon us broke,
> Thou, hapless one, wast stricken to the heart,
> And unto thee from far with beckoning hand
> It show'd chill death, and a dark empty tomb.[1]

Leopardi had a deep love for nature, of which he has reproduced many phases in verse of exquisite beauty. He, however, was not attracted to its bright and cheerful aspects, but by evening scenes, by moonlight, and lonely landscapes, such as harmonize with his own melancholy and afford a figure of man's unhappy state. Thus, in the "Setting of the Moon," his mind is drawn by the scene before him to thoughts of the passing away of life's illusions: —

> The shadows melt away in air,
> Mountain and vale and all around
> Are with a sombre pall embrown'd,
> And night is left forlorn and bare:
> And with a song of doleful strain
> The waggoner is fain
> To hail the last departing gleam

[1] Translated by Sir Theodore Martin.

THE NINETEENTH CENTURY

>Of what has been the guide all night
>To him and to his team;
>So doth youth disappear,
>And quit this mortal sphere!
>Away they fleet,
>Like phantoms of a dream,
>All the illusions that were late so sweet,
>And the far-reaching hopes,
>That are man's chiefest stay,
>Grow fainter day by day;
>Life is in darkness wrapt, profound,
>Black, desolate, and drear,
>And if into its maze he tries to peer,
>The 'wildered wayfarer descries
>Nor plan nor purpose, goal or bound,
>In the long vista that before him lies,
>And sees himself, in sooth, a stranger and alone,
>In a strange world, to him till then unknown.[1]

The following lines on the Infinite reveal not only the habitual sadness of the poet's mind, but likewise the power of his imagination: —

>This lonely knoll was ever dear to me,
>This hedgerow, too, that hides from view so large
>A portion of the far horizon's verge.
>But as I sit and gaze, thoughts rise in me
>Of spaces limitless that lie beyond,
>Of superhuman silences, and depths
>Of quietude profound. So by degrees
>Awe troubles not my heart. And as I hear
>The wind that rustles through the brake hard by,

[1] Martin.

THE GREAT POETS OF ITALY

> That fitful sound with these vast silences
> I set me to compare, and so recall
> Eternity, and the roll of ages dead,
> And the live present, with its mad turmoil.
> Thus thought is founder'd in immensity,
> And shipwreck in that ocean's sweet to me.[1]

In the "Night Chant of a Nomad Asiatic Shepherd," the lonely beauty of night leads him to melancholy reflections on the mystery of human life.

> What doest thou, O moon, there in the skies?
> Tell me, thou silent moon, what doest thou?
> As night falls, thou dost rise
> And go upon thy way,
> These lonely deserts ever in thy view,
> Then sinkest down to rest.
>
> Art thou not weary yet
> Of traversing again, and yet again,
> One everlasting round?
> Art thou not sick at best,
> Or dost thou still delight,
> In gazing on these valleys mountain-bound?
> This shepherd's life of mine
> Is very like to thine.
>
> At break of day he rises, leads his flock
> Across the plains, on, onward, ever on;
> Cattle he sees, spring-heads, and grass, and then
> At eve he lays him down to rest again:
> No hope for anything beyond has he.

[1] Martin.

THE NINETEENTH CENTURY

Tell me, O moon, of what avail ?
Tell me whereto they tend,
My sojourn here, that soon must have an end,
And thy immortal course, that ne'er can fail ?

Grown old, white-haired, and frail
In limb, half-clad, his shoulders bent
Beneath a heavy load,
O'er hill and dale he hies him on his road,
O'er cutting rocks, deep sands, through brake and brier,
Battered by wind and storm, now scorched with heat,
Now shrivell'd up by cold and stung by sleet ;
For breath he pants, yet still he hurries on
Through torrent, marsh, and mire,
Stumbles, gets up, and, quickening his pace,
Stays not for food or rest ;
Tattered and torn, with bare and bleeding feet,
He struggles on — and all to reach at last
The goal, for which that weary road was trod,
For which that heavy toil was undergone,
Into that vast abhorr'd abyss to fall
Headlong and find therein
Oblivion of all !
Such, maiden moon, as this
The life of mortals is.

For trouble man is born,
And birth but the assurance is of death ;
The first things that he knows are grief and pain,
And even while yet he draws his earliest breath,
Mother and father strain
To console their child for being born.
Then, as in years he older grows,
They give him help, and early both and late,
Study by word and deed

THE GREAT POETS OF ITALY

To put heart into him, and make amends
For what he must endure as being man.
Nor for their offspring can
Parents do service to more gracious ends, —
But why have brought them into sunlight ? Why
This life through lengthening days uphold,
That, as the years go by,
Perforce must for its being be consoled ?
And why, if life be sad beyond relief,
Should we thus lengthen out its tale of grief ?
And such, O thou inviolate moon, as this
The life of mortals is.
But mortal thou art not, and so
May'st be indifferent to my tale of woe.

And yet thou lone, eternal pilgrim, thou,
That art so pensive, may'st perchance
Know what they mean, this life of ours on earth,
Our sufferings, our sorrows, and couldst tell
This dying, what it means, and what this cold
Uncoloring of the countenance,
This passing from the earth, and all
Familiar things and the companionship
Of those that hold us dear;
And of a surety, thou dost know full well
The Why of things, and canst perceive
What fruit is born of morning and of eve,
And of time's silent, everlasting flow.
Thou knowest surely too for whom the Spring
The treasure of its loving smiles unveils,
To whom the scorching sunbeams are a boon,
Whom Winter profits by its snows and ice ;
Thousands of things thou knowest, and thousands canst divine,
That are from me, a simple shepherd, hid.

THE NINETEENTH CENTURY

Full often when I gaze on thee
Standing so still above these desert wastes,
Whose far circumference borders on the sky,
Or, as my flock moves with me, following on,
By slow and silent steps, along the heavens;
Or when I see on high the stars aflame,
Strange thoughts arise within me, and I say,
These myriad torches, why are they alight?
Unto what end that infinite of air,
Those infinite depths of azure sky serene?
What does this solitude so vast import,
And what am I?

Thus with myself I reason; questioning
Whereto this boundless glorious universe,
And living things innumerable there?
Then of the ceaseless toil I think, the mighty powers,
That move all things on earth, all things in heaven,
Revolving without pause unceasingly,
To come back evermore to whence they sprang.
Not in all this can I divine
Or use or profit; but most sure it is,
That thou, immortal maid, dost know it all.
As for myself, this do I know and feel,
That from these constant circlings to and fro,
And this so fragile entity of mine,
Whate'er perchance they may of woe or weal
To others bring,
To me life sadness is and suffering.

Oh, my dear flock, that resteth there so still,
How happy you, that, as I do believe,
Have no forebodings of your hapless doom!
How do I envy you!

THE GREAT POETS OF ITALY

Not only for that ye
From care art wellnigh free,
That heat, or hurt, or toilsome road,
Or even the wildest scare
By you so quickly are forgot;
But, rather, that you ne'er
Have felt the pressure of life's irksome load.
Laid on the grass to rest, beneath the shade,
Ye are at peace and utterly content.
For months and months such is thy state;
By 'noyance of no kind are ye perplexed.
I sit me down beneath the welcome shade,
Upon the grass, and straight
My mind is cumbered with a leaden weight
Of dull despondency, and thoughts that sting
And smite as with a goad.
So, sitting there, still further off am I
From finding comfort and tranquillity;
And yet I lack for nought,
And know no reason why I should be sad.
What makes your happiness, or small or great,
I cannot tell, but ye are fortunate,
And I, my flock, have little joy the while;
Nor 't is for only this I make my moan.

If ye could speak, my question would be this:
Tell me why every animal, that lies
Couch'd in some pleasant spot, and takes its rest,
Should have a sense of bliss,
But, when I lay me down to rest, a sense
Of sadness and disgust takes hold of me.

Perchance if I had wings,
Above the clouds to fly,

THE NINETEENTH CENTURY

And one by one to number all the stars;
Or could like lightning dart from peak to peak,
I should be happier, my belovèd flock,
And thou be happier, too, thou pale, white moon:
And yet my thoughts, mayhap, are far astray,
Of what the lot of other lives may be.
Mayhap, whate'er their form, whate'er their state, —
In kindly homestead or in savage lair, —
To everything that breathes its natal day
A day is of disaster and dismay.[1]

Leopardi wrote no more beautiful or touching expression of his own despair than in the poem entitled "Sappho's Last Song," which may be regarded as the classic poem of pessimism in general: —

Night, restful night, and the declining moon's
Wan bashful rays, and thou, that gleamest through
The fringe of silent woodland on the cliff,
Day's harbinger! how very sweet and dear
These sights were to my eyes, while yet to me
Fate and dread Erinnyes were unknown!
Now gentle sounds and sights to my despair,
Lovelorn, bring no delight. I feel a joy,
A joy, that never heretofore I felt
When, wild careering through the liquid air,
And o'er the quaking plains, the South wind blast
Sweeps storms of blinding dust, and when the car,
The ponderous car of Jove, loud thundering,
High o'er our heads, rends the sky's murky pall;
It gives me joy, 'mong storm-tost clouds to float

[1] Martin.

THE GREAT POETS OF ITALY

O'er headlands grim, and chasms immersed in gloom,
To see the panic flight of herds, and hear
The torrent smite its banks with sounding thud,
And the triumphant rage of the resistless flood.
  Fair is thy vesture, O thou sky divine,
And fair, O dewy earth, art thou! Alas!
No share of all this beauty have the Gods
And cruel fate to luckless Sappho given.
To thy proud realms, to all thy beauteous forms,
O nature, I, an outcast, vile, despised
By him I love, my heart and pleading eyes
Turn all in vain. Joy there is none for me
In sunny meads, or in the maiden flush
Of dawn forth issuing from the gates of heaven;
Me not the song of plumaged birds delights,
Nor the soft murmuring of the beech-tree leaves;
And where the shimmering stream beneath the shade
Of willows drooping to receive her kiss
Unbares her spotless bosom, from my foot
Her winding current she withdraws in scorn,
Flies through her fragrant banks, and leaves me all forlorn.
  What deadly fault, what infamy profane
Polluted me ere I was born, that heaven
And fortune both should frown upon me thus?
How sinn'd I as a child, sinn'd at a time
When life is ignorant of all misdeed,
That the fair scheme and blossoms of my youth
Should thus be blighted, that my iron thread
Round the relentless Parca's spindle should
Be whirled in such sad wise? Rashly the words
Fell from my lips! Mysterious counsels sway
The destinies of things. 'T is mystery all,
All save our sorrows here. A race unblest
We are, to affliction born; and wherefore so

THE NINETEENTH CENTURY

Lies in the lap of the Celestials.
Ah me! the longings, aspirations, hopes,
Of days when we were young! The all-ruling Sire,
The Powers Eternal dower'd mankind with all
The dreams, the illusions that appeared so fair.
A man in manly enterprise may shine,
Be rich in storied verse, divine in song,
Yet, poorly clad, will pass unnoted by the throng.
   Then let me die. Its veil ignoble doff'd,
The naked soul to Dis will wing its flight,
And mend the cruel blunder of the blind
Dispenser of events. And thou, to whom
Long bootless love, unswerving constancy,
And the vain frenzy of unslaked desire
Bound me, live happily! Me Jove did not
With the sweet juice besprinkle from the vase
That of its balm is niggard, when the dreams
And fond delusions of my girlish days
Died out. The first to flee away are all
The days that are the brightest of our life;
Then come disease, old age, and icy death's
Dark shadow, and to hope's triumphant dreams,
And cherished fancies, Tartarus succeeds;
And genius, erst so vaunting, sinks, the prey
Of her that over Hades reigns supreme,
Of black unending night, and Acheron's silent stream![1]

This world-weariness of Sappho, the yearning for the rest of the grave, finds more personal expression in the most pathetic of all of Leopardi's poems, that to Himself: —

[1] Martin.

THE GREAT POETS OF ITALY

Now thou shalt rest forever,
O weary heart! The last deceit is ended,
For I believed myself immortal. Cherished
Hopes, and beloved delusions,
And longings to be deluded, — all are perished!
Rest thee forever! Oh, greatly,
Heart, hast thou palpitated. There is nothing
Worthy to move thee more, nor is earth worthy
Thy sighs. For life is only
A heap of dust. So rest thee!
Despair for the last time. To our race Fortune
Never gave any gift but death. Disdain, then,
Thyself and Nature and the Power
Occultly reigning to the common ruin:
Scorn, heart, the infinite emptiness of all things![1]

During the whole of the patriotic period of Italian literature, there was a plenitude of poets; yet the vast majority of them have lived their life on the stage, have reaped their meed of praise or blame and are now rapidly passing into oblivion. The more important names of the early part of the century we have already mentioned. Among those who flourished toward the middle of the century, and who deserve mention even in this brief sketch, are Francesco dall' Ongaro (1808–1873), whose patriotic songs give a life-like picture of the sufferings and aspirations of the people in the war for liberty; the sentimental and romantic Giovanni

[1] Howells.

THE NINETEENTH CENTURY

Prati (1815-1884); and Aleardo Aleardi (1812-1878), whose contemplative poetry and feeling for nature remind us of Lamartine. The number of contemporary poets is likewise large, including such names as Luigi Capuana, Edmondo de Amicis, Guido Mazzoni, Enrico Panzacchi, Giovanni Pascoli, and Lorenzo Stecchetti (pen-name for Olindo Guerrini). For one reason or another we select among these contemporary names five as worthy of especial mention: Giosuè Carducci, Arturo Graf, Antonio Fogazzaro, Ada Negri and Gabriele d' Annunzio.

Greatest of all these and undoubtedly the greatest of modern Italian poets since the time of Leopardi, is Giosuè Carducci. Born in 1836, in Valdicastello, in the province of Tuscany, where his father was a physician, he received an excellent education, and devoting himself to the life of a teacher and scholar, became at the early age of twenty-four years professor in the University of Bologna, where he has remained until this day, revered by his colleagues and pupils. When, a few years ago, the thirty-fifth anniversary of his first lecture as professor was celebrated, all Italy streamed to Bologna to do him honor, while royalty itself sent him messages of love and congratulation. A writer at the time says:

THE GREAT POETS OF ITALY

"Seldom if ever since Petrarch has any living poet received such overwhelming tokens of love and reverence." No happier lot can be conceived than that of Carducci at the present time. An honored scholar, a great poet, the intimate friend of Queen Margarita, the idol of the cultured youth of Italy, and one of the few survivors of the past generation of lofty, high-minded patriots, he reaps to an unusual degree the fruits of a life of singular probity, faithfulness to duty and unwearied struggle for the independence and unity of his native land.

The whole course of Carducci's life is closely connected with the history of the Risorgimento. His poetry reflects all phases of that epic struggle, and future generations will study his works for the spirit, as they will turn the pages of history for the outward facts of the movement. Carducci is not merely a poet, but a literary critic and scholar of the first class. Few men have done more than he has in recent years toward the interpretation and illustration of the great poets of Italy, especially Dante, Petrarch and Leopardi. His significance for us, however, lies not in his literary criticism, but in his poetry. Here we see plainly reflected the sentiments, ideas and feelings of his soul in the presence of nature, history and the many-sided

CARDUCCI

THE NINETEENTH CENTURY

drama of modern life, all expressed in a style compact, terse, yet marked by classic elegance and grace.

For Carducci is the leader of the reaction against Romanticism in Italy, and the founder of a new school of classic art. When his " Odi Barbare " was published, a violent contest took place over the form of many of his poems, which were an attempt to introduce into modern Italian the metrical effects of Horace and other classic writers. His influence has been deep and lasting on the outer form of poetry, which under the exaggerations of Romanticism had lost much of that classic simplicity and good taste so natural to the Italian artistic mind. Carducci is not a popular poet, in the general acceptation of that word, and has often been accused even by his own countrymen of being obscure. This difficulty of being understood, however, does not come from real obscurity, either of thought or expression, but from the compactness of style, and the wealth of allusions, in which he resembles Horace more, perhaps, than any other modern writer.

Among the many phases of Carducci's character, as reflected in his poetry, we find a deep and earnest love for nature, of which he is fond of catching and describing every phase, almost always adding to it some touch of personal experience, joy, sorrow or loss of faith. He loves the bright sunlight of Italy, shining on the streets of the busy city — thus, says he, love shines on the heart, scattering the clouds of melancholy which surround it : —

> Fleecy and white into the western space
> Hurry the clouds; the wet sky laughs
> Over the market and streets; and the labour of man
>   Is hailed by the sun, benign, triumphal.
>
> High in the rosy light lifts the cathedral
> Its thousand pinnacles white and its saints of gold
> Flashing forth its hosannas; while all around
>   Flutter the wings and the notes of the brown-plumed choir.
>
> So 't is when love and its sweet smile dispel
> The clouds which had so sorely me oppressed;
> The sun again arises in my soul
>   With all life's holiest ideals renewed
>
> And multiplied, the while each thought becomes
>   A harmony and every sense a song.[1]

Not only is he attracted by the picturesque beauty of inanimate nature, but by animal life as well, even in its humbler forms. He does not sing of the lion and tiger, as his contemporary Leconte de Lisle has done, but of the horse, the ox, and even the patient ass. His sonnet on the ox is one

---

[1] The following translations (unless otherwise specified) are from *Poems of Giosuè Carducci*, translated by Frank Sewall, published by Dodd, Mead & Co.

THE NINETEENTH CENTURY

of his best productions, distinguished as it is by a sort of statuesque beauty of style : —

> I love thee, pious ox; a gentle feeling
> Of vigour and of peace thou givest my heart.
> How solemn, like a monument, thou art!
> Over wide fertile fields thy calm gaze stealing,
> Unto the yoke with grave contentment kneeling,
> To man's quick work thou dost thy strength impart,
> He shouts and goads, and answering thy smart,
> Thou turn'st on him thy patient eyes appealing.
>
> From thy broad nostrils, black and wet, arise
> Thy breath's soft fumes; and on the still air swells,
> Like happy hymn, thy lowing's mellow strain.
> In the grave sweetness of thy tranquil eyes
> Of emerald, broad and still, reflected dwells
> All the divine green silence of the plain.

Standing in the graveyard of the Certosa at Bologna, he thinks of the dead, not as at rest after life's fitful fever, not as among the innumerable company of just men made perfect in the presence of God and the angels, but lying in the cold and darkness of the mouldering earth, shut out forever from the beauty of nature, giving voice to their envy of those happy mortals still lingering in the *dolce vita* above : —

> The dead are saying: "Blessed are ye who walk along the hillsides
> Flooded with the warm rays of the golden sun.

THE GREAT POETS OF ITALY

" Cool murmur thé waters through flowery slopes descending,
Singing are the birds to the verdure, singing the leaves to the wind.

" For you are smiling the flowers ever new on the earth ;
For you smile the stars, the flowers eternal of heaven."

The dead are saying : " Gather the flowers, for they too pass away ;
Adore the stars, for they pass never away.

" Rotted away are the garlands that lay around our damp skulls.
Roses place ye around the tresses golden and black.

" Down here it is cold. We are alone. Oh, love ye the sun !
Shine, constant star of Love, on the life which passes away ! "

So, too, in " Ruit Hora," he describes the hour of twilight, the *heure exquise* of Paul Verlaine, that time of day so beautifully described by Dante in the eighth canto of the " Purgatorio." In this poem there is an evident reminiscence of Horace, yet with a touch of sadness that Horace never knew:—

O now so long-desired, thou verdurous solitude,
Far from all rumour of mankind !
Hither we come companioned by two friends divine,
By wine and love, O Lydia.

Ah, see how laughs in sparkling goblets crystalline
Lyæus, god eternal-young !
How in thy dazzling eyes, resplendent Lydia,
Love triumphs and unbinds himself !

THE NINETEENTH CENTURY

Low down the sun peeps in beneath the trellised vine,
And rosily reflected, gleams
Within my glass; golden it shines, and tremulous,
Among thy tresses, Lydia.

Among thy raven tresses, O white Lydia,
One pale-hued rose is languishing;
Softly upon my heart a sudden sadness falls,
Falls to restrain Love's rising fires.

Tell me, wherefore beneath the flaming sunset-sky
Mysterious lamentations moan
Up from the sea below? Lydia, what songs are they
Yon pines unto each other sing?

See with what deep desire yon darkening hills outstretch
Their summits to the sinking sun:
The shadow grows, and wraps them round; they seem to ask
The last sweet kiss, O Lydia.

I seek thy kisses when the shade envelops me,
Lyæus, thou who givest joy;
I seek thy loving eyes, resplendent Lydia,
When Great Hyperion falls.

Now falls, now falls the imminent hour. O roseate lips,
Unclose: O blossom of the soul,
O flower of all desire, open thy petals wide:
Beloved arms, unclose yourselves.[1]

Likewise Horatian in sentiment as well as in

[1] Translated by Greene, in his *Italian Lyrists of To-day*. Published by John Lane.

THE GREAT POETS OF ITALY

form, and with a still deeper tinge of sadness, which, in spite of his hatred of Romanticism and of sentimental religion, he cannot shake off, is the beautiful poem on "Monte Mario:" —

> Cypresses solemn stand on Monte Mario;
> Luminous, quiet is the air around them:
> They watch the Tiber through the misty meadows
> Wandering voiceless.
>
> They gaze beneath them where, a silent city,
> Rome lies extended; like a giant shepherd,
> O'er flocks unnumbered, vigilant and watchful,
> Rises St. Peter's.
>
> Friends, on the summit of the sunlit mountain
> Mix we the white wine, scintillating brightly
> In mirrored sunshine; smile, O lovely maidens;
> Death comes to-morrow.
>
> Lalage, touch not in the scented copses
> The boasted laurel that is called eternal,
> Lest it should lose there, in thy chestnut tresses,
> Half of its splendour.
>
> Between the verses pensively arising,
> Mine be the laughter of the joyous vintage,
> And mine the rosebuds fugitive, in winter
> Flowering to perish.
>
> We die to-morrow, as the lost and loved ones
> Yesterday perished; out of all men's mem'ries
> And all men's loving, shadow-like and fleeting
> We too shall vanish.

THE NINETEENTH CENTURY

Yes, we must die, friends; and the earth, unceasing
Still in its labour, round the sun revolving,
Shall ev'ry instant send out lives in thousands,
Sparks evanescent;

Lives which in new loves passionate shall quiver,
Lives which in new wars conquering shall triumph,
And unto gods new sing in grander chorus
Hymns of the future.

Nations unborn yet! in whose hands the beacon
Shall blaze resplendent, which from ours has fallen,
Ye too shall vanish, luminous battalions,
Into the endless.

Farewell, thou mother, Earth, of my brief musings,
And of my spirit fugitive! How much thou,
Æons-long whirling, round the sun shalt carry
Glory and sorrow!

Till the day comes, when, on the chilled equator,
Following vainly heat that is expiring,
Of Man's exhausted race survive one only
Man, and one woman,

Who stand forsaken on the ruined mountains,
Mid the dead forests, pale, with glassy eyeballs,
Watching the sun's orb o'er the fearful icefields
Sink for the last time.[1]

Equal to his love for the natural beauty of Italy, her sun, her blue skies, her rugged hills, is Carducci's love for the history and the literature of

[1] Greene.

THE GREAT POETS OF ITALY

his native land. Of the large number of poems devoted to patriotic themes, — elegies on martyrs and patriots, contempt for priestcraft and the temporal power of the Pope, hymns of praise to the House of Savoy, — we have only room to quote one, — his famous sonnet on Rome: —

> Give to the wind thy locks; all glittering
> Thy sea-blue eyes, and thy white bosom bared,
> Mount to thy chariots, while in speechless roaring
> Terror and Force before thee clear the way!
>
> The shadow of thy helmet like the flashing
> Of brazen star strikes through the trembling air.
> The dust of broken empires, cloud-like rising,
> Follows the awful rumbling of thy wheels.
>
> So once, O Rome, beheld the conquered nations
> Thy image, object of their ancient dread.
> To-day a mitre they would place upon
>
> Thy head, and fold a rosary between
> Thy hands. O name! again to terrors old
> Awake the tired ages and the world!

Carducci's work as professor of literature has led him to deep and profound study of the great poets both of classic Greece and Rome and of modern Italy. He is, however, no mere mechanical investigator, burying himself in the dust of bygone years, but is filled with living, passionate love for all that is great in literature. The results of his long years

THE NINETEENTH CENTURY

of critical work, both in regard to the subject and form of poetry, is enough to fill a number of volumes. Not only in his prose writings, however, do we find the influence of his studies, but in all his poetry, both in the reform of outward expression (shown especially in the effort to engraft upon Italian poetry the metrical forms of the classics) and in constant reference or allusion to the great poets of all times and nations. This union of form and subject is well seen in the following sonnet on the Sonnet, worthy to be classed with the similar productions by Wordsworth and Keats: —

> From Dante's lips the Sonnet soared divine
> On angel's wings through azure air and gold;
> On Petrarch's 't was the speech of hearts that pine,
> A stream from heaven in murmuring verse outrolled;
>
> The Mantuan nectar and the Venusine,
> To Tibur granted by the muse of old,
> Torquato gave; a dart, a fiery sign,
> Alfieri hurled it 'gainst the tyrant's hold;
>
> The nightingale in Ugo's[1] sweetest lays
> Beneath the Ionian cypress made it ring,
> Acanthus-blossomed, o'er his native bays;
>
> And I, not sixth, but last, as joy I bring,
> Tears, perfume, wrath, and Art, in lonely days
> Its fame recall, as to the tombs I sing.[2]

[1] Ugo Foscolo.   [2] Greene.

THE GREAT POETS OF ITALY

Carducci's love for Vergil finds frequent expression in his poetry; never was a more beautiful tribute paid to the "wielder of the stateliest measure ever moulded by the lips of man," than in the following sonnet:—

> As when above the heated fields the moon
>   Hovers to spread its veil of summer frost,
>   The brook between its narrow banks half lost
> Glitters in pale light, murmuring its low tune;
>
> The nightingale pours forth her secret boon
>   Whose strains the lonely traveller accost;
>   He sees his dear one's golden tresses tossed,
> And time forgets in love's entrancing swoon;
>
> And the orphaned mother who has grieved in vain
> Upon the tomb looks to the silent skies
> And feels their white light on her sorrow shine;
>
> Meanwhile the mountains laugh, and the far-off main,
> And through the lofty trees a fresh wind sighs:
> Such is thy verse to me, Poet divine!

But the especial object of Carducci's love and reverence is the great poet and patriot, Dante Alighieri, whose extraordinary revival in the early part of the nineteenth century was one of the most powerful factors in the movement of the Risorgimento. Not only does he address him in a number of poems, not only does he refer to him again and

THE NINETEENTH CENTURY

again, but the influence of Dante on his thoughts, feelings, and even his diction is seen in nearly everything he wrote. No better brief account of the meaning of Dante's work can be found than in Carducci's lecture on the "Opera di Dante," which he delivered in Rome January 7, 1888. The same subject is beautifully treated in the sonnet in which Carducci declares his unchangeable love for the Divine Poet, in spite of the fact that he, the ardent patriot of a United Italy and disbeliever in the Roman Church, cannot accept Dante's theory either of church or state: —

> O Dante, why it is that I adoring
>   Still lift my songs and vows to thy stern face,
>   And sunset to the morning grey gives place
> To find me still thy restless verse exploring?
>
> Lucia prays not for my poor soul's resting;
>   For me Matilda tends no sacred fount;
>   For me in vain the sacred lovers mount,
> O'er star and star to the eternal soaring.
>
> I hate the Holy Empire, and the crown
> And sword alike relentless would have riven
> From thy good Frederic on Olona's plains.
>
> Empire and Church to ruin have gone down,
> And yet for them thy songs did scale high heaven.
> Great Jove is dead. Only the song remains.

THE GREAT POETS OF ITALY

Indeed, there is no more characteristic feature of Carducci than his revolt against not only the Roman Church, with its superstitions, its mass of meaningless forms and its claim of temporal power, but also against the whole system and influence of Christianity. He repudiates the Christian virtues as something foreign to the great Latin race to which he belongs. He glorifies the old classic pagan spirit, its objectivity as opposed to the gloomy subjectivity of Christianity, its love of beauty and its joy in the sunshine and glory of this world, while he dismisses thoughts of the other world, as beyond our ken. The most audacious of all his poems is the "Hymn to Satan," published in 1865, which aroused fierce controversy. Less violent, yet showing equally his antipathy to what he would call the "cunningly devised" fable of Christianity, are the following two poems. In the first, entitled "Pantheism," it is not the spirit of God which permeates nature, but the spirit of sensuous love, the *ewig weibliche*, that "spell of femininity which is in the blood of all mankind:" —

> I told it not, O vigilant stars, to you;
> To thee, all-seeing sun, I made no moan;
> Her name, the flower of all things fair and true,
> Was echoed in my silent heart alone.

THE NINETEENTH CENTURY

Yet now my secret star tells unto star,
Through the brown night, to some vague sphery tune;
The great sun smiles at it, when, sinking far,
He whispers love to the white and rising moon.

On shadowy hills, on shores where life is gay,
Each bush repeats it to each flower that blows;
The flitting birds sing, 'Poet grim and grey,
At last Love's honeyed dreams thy spirit knows.'

I told it not, yet heaven and earth repeat
The name beloved in sounds divine that swell,
And mid the acacia-blossom's perfume sweet
Murmurs the Spirit of All — 'She loves thee well.'[1]

So also in the poem entitled "In a Gothic Church," the poet seeks the cool interior of the church not to worship that God whom he repudiates, but to meet the lady of his choice: —

> They rise aloft, marching in awful file,
> The polished shafts immense of marble grey,
> And in the sacred darkness seem to be
>   An army of giants
>
> Who wage a war with the invisible;
> The silent arches soar and spring apart
> In distant flight, then re-embrace again
>   And droop on high.
>
> So in the discord of unhappy men,
> From out their barbarous tumult there go up

[1] Greene.

THE GREAT POETS OF ITALY

    To God the sighs of solitary souls
        In Him united.

    Of you I ask no God, ye marble shafts,
    Ye airy vaults! I tremble — but I watch
    To hear a dainty well-known footstep waken
        The solemn echoes.

    'T is Lidia, and she turns, and, slowly turning,
    Her tresses full of light reveal themselves,
    And love is shining from a pale shy face
        Behind the veil.

No better indication can be given of the spirit of Carducci, his strength, his manly courage amid the conflicts of life, than is summed up in the following beautiful sonnet, which somehow recalls Browning's last song : —

    My lonely bark beneath the seagull's screaming
      Pursues her way across the stormy sea;
      Around her mingle, in tumultuous glee,
    The roar of waters and the lightning's gleaming.

    And memory, down whose face the tears are streaming,
      Looks for the shore it can no longer see;
      While hope, that struggled long and wearily
    With broken oar, at last gives up its dreaming.

    Still at the helm erect my spirit stands,
      Gazing at sea and sky, and bravely crying
    Amid the howling winds and groaning strands:
      Sail on, sail on, O crew, all fates defying,

THE NINETEENTH CENTURY

> Till at the gate of dark oblivion's lands
> We see afar the white shores of the dying.[1]

Carducci is a link between the older and newer generation. So long has he been before the public that we can hardly feel like numbering him among the contemporary poets. Out of the large number of these latter, three or four merit mention here, either from their own greatness, or from the fortuitous circumstances which have given them worldwide notoriety.

One of the strangest literary phenomena of modern Italy is Arturo Graf, who, the son of a German father and of an Italian mother, was born in Greece, and is to-day one of the foremost literary men of Italy. The one unchanging note of his poetry is pessimism, darker even than that of Leopardi. This singular gloom, so out of place in

[1] This sonnet is based upon the following song of Heine's which Carducci also translated more literally elsewhere: —

> Mit schwarzen Segeln segelt mein Schiff
> Wohl über das wilde Meer;
> Du weisst, wie sehr ich traurig bin,
> Und kränkst mich doch so sehr.
>
> Dein Herz ist treulos wie der Wind
> Und flattert hin und her;
> Mit schwarzen Segeln segelt mein Schiff
> Wohl über das wilde Meer.

THE GREAT POETS OF ITALY

sunny Italy, is well seen in the sonnet entitled
"The Depth and the End:" —

>Upon my poisoned lips all vain delight
>Has died forever: hopes that might have been,
>And pious falsehoods flourishing unseen
>Within my heart, have killed my heart outright.
>
>In vain the rose takes fire on branches green,
>In vain a sweet face beams with love and light,
>In vain o'er conquered skies the sun is bright;
>The depth and end of all things I have seen.
>
>The end and depth, the Never and For Ever;
>And in my bitter cup, O sacred Death,
>Living, I drank the drops that souls dissever.
>
>The fall of worlds in ruined space I see;
>I hear the bells of Time with failing breath
>Ring hours and years through void eternity.[1]

In the "Mors Regina" we have a literary pendant to the famous picture of the Todten-Insel by Böcklin : —

>Foam-girt amid the ocean's thunderous call,
>A mountain measureless is heaped on high,
>Black in the whiteness of the dazzling sky,
>And built of fallen cities, wall o'er wall.
>
>On the steep summit where the sunbeams fall,
>A glorious fane doth to the Sun reply
>From dome of opal where the eagles fly;
>And adamantine columns gird the hall.

[1] Greene.

THE NINETEENTH CENTURY

> Round is the Temple, each way open wide ;
> And in the midst a lofty Throne designed,
> With gloomy purple hung on every side.
>
> There on the throne, aloft in splendid space,
> Sits Death, a crownèd queen: while all mankind
> Lie prone around and watch her changeless face.

Among the best known of the younger poets of to-day is Ada Negri, who, born (1870) and raised in poverty, sings the song of the submerged classes in her volume of verse, "Fatalità," which, published in 1892, at once took the world by storm. It was the most popular volume of poems which had been published in Italy for years, was translated into German, and won the enthusiastic commendations of the veteran poet and novelist, Paul Heyse.

Far better known to the world of letters and to the stage in Europe and America than any of the above, not even excepting Carducci, is the strange, erratic genius known as Gabriele d' Annunzio. The taking of this name, " Gabriel of the Annunciation " (his real name is said to be Gaetano Rapagnetta), shows at once the colossal vanity of this young man, who apparently thinks he is the herald of a new era of Renaissance, destined to restore Italy to her hegemony in the world of art and literature.

THE GREAT POETS OF ITALY

D' Annunzio's career is a remarkably precocious one. Born at Pescara, on the Adriatic Sea, in 1863, he was hailed as a genius at the age of fifteen, and became the "spoiled darling" of the Italians. From that time down to the present, scarcely a year has passed that he has not startled, if not shocked the world with some remarkable production. He began as a poet, and showed in his earliest years a singular combination of gorgeous style and morbid fancy. The following sonnet, however, is not only beautiful but free from any taint of immorality: —

> Beneath the white full-moon the murmuring seas
> Send songs of love across the pine-tree glade;
> The moonlight, filtering through the dome-topped trees,
> Fills with weird life the vast and secret shade;
> A fresh salt perfume on the Illyrian breeze
> From seaweeds on the rocks is hither swayed,
> While my sad heart, worn out and ill at ease,
> A wild poetic longing doth invade.
>
> But now more joyous still the love-songs flow
> O'er waves of silver sea; from pine to pine
> A sweet name echoes in the winds that blow,
> And hovering through yon spaces diamantine,
> A phantom fair with silent flight and slow
> Smiles on me from its great-orbed eyes divine.[1]

[1] Greene.

THE NINETEENTH CENTURY

The next two sonnets reveal his remarkable power of descriptive imagination, as well as his tendency to be influenced by other writers: —

I.

At times, exhausted by the pains austere
Of long night-labors with success uncrowned,
I lean upon my books, and hear
The sea that bellows through the night profound;
And in the northern wind a sudden fear
Destroys each fairest dream my heart has found,
When all my sweetest visions disappear,
And doubt and cold and the void have hemmed me round:

Then think I often of a great ship lost,
With shattered keel, in the whirlwind's storm and stress,
Alone 'twixt sea and heaven, from land afar:

I think of the shipwrecked men that, tempest-tossed,
Helpless and hopeless in their last distress,
Despairing cling to the last remaining spar.

II.

Again! again! on the remaining mast
Like a living bunch of fruit on the tempest swayed,
The shipwrecked men upon the whirlwind cast
Utter their desperate cries and shout for aid.
In vain! in vain! The black hull sinks at last,
A horrid bier, by vain hopes undelayed,
Deep in the roaring waves where, dense and vast,
A bank of seaweed lurks in silent shade.

The cuttlefish shall watch with hungry eyes,
With horrible eyes, with yellowish eyes and grim,
That tragic agony of life that dies:

THE GREAT POETS OF ITALY

> Then, in a play of shadows strange and dim,
> Entwined around men's bodies serpent-wise,
> Long tentacles shall seize each human limb.[1]

The sonnet entitled the "Prelude" reveals with cynical self-knowledge his predilection for foul and slimy things in art: —

> As from corrupted flesh the over-bold
> Young vines in dense luxuriance rankly grow,
> And strange weird plants their horrid buds unfold
> O'er the foul rotting of a corpse below;
>
> As spreading crimson flowers with centered gold
> Like the fresh blood of recent wounds o'erflow,
> Where vile enormous chrysalids are rolled
> In the young leaves, and cruel blossoms blow:
>
> E'en so within my heart malignant flowers
> Of verse swell forth: the leaves in fearful gloom
> Exhale a sinister scent of human breath.
>
> Lured by the radiance of the blood-red bowers,
> The unconscious hand is stretched to pluck the bloom,
> And the sharp poison fills the veins with death.[2]

D'Annunzio next devoted himself to the novel, and produced in rapid succession "The Innocent," "Triumph of Death," the "Virgin of the Rocks,"

---

[1] Greene. The influence of a famous scene in Victor Hugo's *Toilers of the Sea* is apparent in these last lines.

[2] Greene. Here D'Annunzio is influenced by Baudelaire's *Fleurs du Mal.*

THE NINETEENTH CENTURY

and " Fire," — books marked by wonderful descriptions, slender plots, skillful adaptation of language and thoughts borrowed from the writers of Italy, Germany, France, and even Russia, and stained (with the exception of the " Virgin of the Rocks ") with a morbid fondness for scenes of obscenity and vice. In reading these books we hardly know which of our feelings is greater, admiration for the author's extraordinary gift of style, or disgust at his corrupt imagination.

Much the same things may be said of D' Annunzio's dramas, which occupy his later period, and which, through the incomparable acting of Eleonora Duse, has made D' Annunzio's name known the world over. Among the dramas the two which are best known are the " Dead City " and " Francesca da Rimini." The former, full of a gloomy magnificence of description of the desert, is a strange introduction into modern drama of the fatality of the Greek tragedy, and is vitiated both morally and as a work of art by the far-fetched device by means of which ancient horrors are made to do service on the modern stage.

The best of all his dramas and perhaps his best work in general is the " Francesca da Rimini," in which the story told so beautifully and with such

THE GREAT POETS OF ITALY

incomparable conciseness and delicate reserve by Dante in the fifth canto of the "Inferno" is retold in detail, clothed in a wealth of description and local color, and steeped in an atmosphere of blood, treachery, and lust.

Francesca thinks she has wed Paolo Malatesta, handsome and courtly, but discovers that he has only been the proxy for his brother, and that her real husband is Gianciotto, Lord of Ravenna, a fierce, cruel and tyrannical cripple. Her love, however, has been given to Paolo, and she cannot take it back. The inevitable tragedy of illicit love and of jealous rage follows. The younger brother of Paolo and Gianciotto also loves his sister-in-law, and being repulsed by her as a silly boy becomes mad with jealousy and reveals the truth to Gianciotto, who watches the lovers, discovers their guilt and slays them. This is about all there is to the brief plot, the rest of the play being padded with long descriptions, reminiscences, and dialogues, together with many episodes in which soldiers, troubadours, merchants, ladies, and knights, a whole Canterbury Pilgrimage of figures, crowd the stage; all destined to reproduce the local color of the thirteenth century in Italy, with its strange contrasts of poetry and cruelty.

THE NINETEENTH CENTURY

Some of the passages are strangely beautiful, such as that in which Francesca and her sister Samaritana, about to separate, recall the days of their innocent childhood: —

> *Samaritana.*   O, sister, sister,
> Listen to me : stay with me still ! O stay
> With me ! we were born here,
> Do not forsake me ! do not go away,
> Let me still keep my bed
> Beside your bed, and let me still at night
> Feel you beside me.
>   *Francesca.* He has come.
>   *Samaritana.*   Who ? Who has come
> To take you from me ?
>   *Francesca.*   Sister, he has come.
>   *Samaritana.* He has no name, he has no countenance,
> And we have never seen him.
>   *Francesca.*   It may be
> That I have seen him.
>   *Samaritana.* I have never been apart
> From you and from your breath ;
> My life has never seen but with your eyes;
> O, where can you have seen him, and not I
> Seen him as well ?
>   *Francesca.*   Where you
> Can never come, sweetheart, in a far place
> And in a lonely place
> Where a great flame of fire
> Burns, and none feed that flame.
>   *Samaritana.* You speak to me in riddles,
> And there is like a veil over your face.
> Ah, and it seems as if you had gone away,

And from afar off
Turned and looked back; and your voice sounds
As out of a great wind.
  Francesca.   Peace, peace, dear soul,
My little dove. Why are you troubled? Peace;
You also, and ere long,
Shall see your day of days,
And leave our nest as I have left it; then
Your little bed shall stand
Empty beside my bed; and I no more
Shall hear through dreams at dawn
Your little naked feet run to the window,
And no more see you, white and barefooted,
Run to the window, O my little dove,
And no more hear you say to me: "Francesca,
Francesca, now the morning-star is born,
And it has chased away the Pleiades."
  Samaritana. So we will live, ah me,
So we will live forever;
And time shall flee away,
Flee away always!
  Francesca. And you will no more say to me at morn:
"What was it in your bed that made it creak
Like reeds in the wind?" Nor shall I answer you:
"I turned about to sleep,
To sleep and dream, and saw,
As I was sleeping, in the dream I dreamed . . ."
Ah, I shall no more tell you what is seen
In dreams. And we will die,
So we will die forever;
And time shall flee away,
Flee away always!
  Samaritana. O Francesca, O Francesca, you hurt my
   heart,

THE NINETEENTH CENTURY

    And see, Francesca,
    You make me tremble all over.[1]

Still another poetical scene is that in which Paolo returns from Florence, whither he had gone as Captain of the People, and finds himself drawn irresistibly to the presence of Francesca, where both yield to the sweet spell of love: —

    Francesca.   Paolo, give me peace!
    It is so sweet a thing to live forgetting,
    But one hour only, and be no more tossed,
    Out of the tempest.
    Do not call back, I pray,
    The shadow of that time in this fresh light
    That slakes my thirst at last
    Like that long draught
    That at the ford I drank,
    Out of the living water.
    And now, I desire now
    To think my soul has left
    That shore to come into this sheltering shore,
    Where music and where hope are sisters; so
    To forget all the sorrow that has been
    Yesterday, and shall be
    To-morrow, and so let
    All of my life, and all the veins of it,
    And all the days of it,
    And all old things in it, far-away things,
    But for one hour, one hour,
    Slip away quietly, a quiet tide,

[1] From Arthur Symons's translation, published by Frederick A. Stokes Company, New York.

Unto that sea,
Even these eyes might behold smilingly,
Were it not hidden by the tears that tremble
And do not fall. O peace, peace in that sea
That was so wild with waves
Yesterday, and to-day is like a pearl.
Give me peace!

Paolo. It is the voice of spring
I hear, and from your lips the music runs
Over the world, that I have seemed to hear,
Riding against the wind,
Sing in the voice of the wind,
At every turn of the way,
At every glade, and high
On the hilltops, and on the edges of the woods,
And under them the streams,
When my desire bent back,
Burning with breath, the mane of my wild horse,
Over the saddle-bow, and the soul lived,
In the swiftness of that flight,
On swiftness,
Like a torch carried in the wind, and all
The thoughts of all my soul, save one, save one,
Were blown backward, spent
Like sparks behind me.

The last scene, the consummation of the tragedy, is told with genuine dramatic skill. Gianciotto, who is about to set out for Pesaro, of which he has been named Podestà, has been told by Malatestino of the intended visit of Paolo to Francesca. He feigns to carry out his planned journey, but returns

THE NINETEENTH CENTURY

in the middle of the night. In the meantime, Paolo comes to Francesca's room, and the lovers, in fancied security, repeat to each other once more the " old, old story : " —

    Francesca.   It says
Here in the book, here where you have not read :
" We have been one life ; it were a seemly thing
That we be also one death."
    Paolo.   Let the book
Be closed !
        [*He rises, closes the book on the reading desk, and blows out the taper.*
                And read in it no more. Not there
Our destiny is written, but in the stars,
That palpitate above
As your throat palpitates,
Your wrists, your brow,
Perhaps because they were your garland once,
Your necklet when you went
Burningly through the ways of heaven : From what
Vineyard of earth were these grapes gathered in ?
They have the smell
Of drunkenness and honey.
They are like veins, they are swollen with delight,
Fruits of the night! The flaming feet of Love
Shall tread them in the winepress. Give me your mouth
Again ! Again !
        [*Francesca lies back on the cushions, forgetful of everything. All at once, in the dead silence, a violent shock is heard on the door, as if some one hurled himself against it. The lovers start up in terror, and rise to their feet.*
    The Voice of Gianciotto. Francesca, open ! Francesca!
        [*The woman is petrified with terror. Paolo looks around the*

room, *putting his hand to his dagger. He catches sight of the bolt of the trap-door.*

Paolo (in a low voice.) Take heart! take heart, Francesca!
I will get down
By way of the trap-door.
Go, go, and open to him.
But do not tremble.

[*He lifts the trap-door. The door seems to quiver at the repeated blows.*

The Voice of Gianciotto. Open, Francesca, open!

Paolo. Open to him! Go now.
I wait beneath. If he but touches you
Cry out and I am with you.
Go boldly, do not tremble!

[*He begins to go down, while the woman, in obedience to him, goes to open the door, tottering.*

The Voice of Gianciotto. Open! upon your life, Francesca, open!

[*The door being opened, Gianciotto, armed and covered with dust, rushes furiously into the room, looking for his brother in every direction. Suddenly he catches sight of Paolo, standing head and shoulders above the level of the floor, struggling to free himself from the bolt of the trap-door, which has caught in a corner of his cloak. Francesca utters a piercing cry, while Gianciotto falls upon his brother, seizing him by the hair, and forcing him to come up.*

Gianciotto. So, you are caught in a trap,
Traitor! They are good to have you by the hair,
Your ringlets!

Francesca. Let him go! Me, take me!

[*The husband loosens his hold. Paolo springs up on the other side of the trap-door, and unsheathes his dagger. Gianciotto, drawing back, bares his sword, and rushes upon him with terrible force. Francesca throws herself between the two men;*

THE NINETEENTH CENTURY

but as her husband has leant all his weight on the blow, and is unable to draw back, her breast is pierced by the sword, she staggers, turns on herself, towards Paolo, who lets fall his dagger, and catches her in his arms.

Francesca (dying). Ah, Paolo!

[*Gianciotto pauses for an instant. He sees the woman clasped in the arms of her lover, who seals her expiring life with his lips. Mad with rage and sorrow, he pierces his brother's side with another deadly thrust. The two bodies sway to and fro, for an instant, without a sound. Then, still linked together, they fall at full length on the pavement. Gianciotto stoops in silence, bends his knee with a painful effort, and, across the knee, breaks his blood-stained sword.*

If we were to close this book with Gabriele d' Annunzio, we should perhaps leave the reader with too gloomy a view of the present tendencies of Italian literature. D' Annunzio does not represent the whole literary spirit of Italy, and a large number of his countrymen repudiate his morbid immorality and his extravagance. Indeed, he is more popular in France than in his own country. The better spirit of Italy finds expression in the man who, both as a poet and novelist, is the real leader of Italian literature to-day. Antonio Fogazzaro is a man of genius, of genuine Christian character, of a tender and romantic love for nature, and for all that is " pure and of good report " in life. He is most widely known as a novelist, his best books

THE GREAT POETS OF ITALY

being "Daniele Cortis," "Il Piccolo Mondo Antico," and "Il Piccolo Mondo Moderno." Yet he began as a poet. The spirit which animates all his work, and has made him the favorite of the best classes in Italy, is well illustrated in the following poems, the first being a "Sonnet on the Cathedral of St. Mark at Venice:" —

> Cold is my soul like thee, O glorious fane!
> And thy mosaics' mingled shadow and gold
> Are like the shapes that I in fancy mould
> Mid tomb-like silence of my heart's domain,
>
> Where love lies buried, love that shone in vain,
> Like thy gemmed treasure, useless and untold;
> And to the hoped ideal, the Faith I hold,
> One lamp lifts up a light that ne'er shall wane.
>
> Yet sometimes thro' thy gate that moaning opes
> Sunlight comes in, whiffs o' the salt lagoon,
> Sad silent forms that linger for awhile;
>
> And so to me, at times, come sunlit hopes,
> Quick fever-fits of life that vanish soon,
> Or a sweet, tender face that stays to smile.

In the beautiful poem entitled "A Sera" (Evening), of which we can only give an extract here, Fogazzaro reproduces with singular felicity the tender, half-melancholy impressions made on the mind of a deeply religious man, one who has reflected much on the meaning of life, and who,

FOGAZZARO

THE NINETEENTH CENTURY

standing at eventide in the Alpine landscape of his native land,[1] listens to the bells as they call to one another from mountain and valley: —

The Bells of Oria.

Westward the sky o'ergloometh,
The hour of darkness cometh.
From spirits of Evil,
From Death and the Devil,
Keep us, O Lord, night and day!
Come, let us pray.

The Bells of Òsteno.

O'er waters waste we too must sound,
From lonely shores where echoes bound,
Our voice profound.
From Spirits of Evil,
From Death and the Devil,
Keep us, O Lord, night and day!
Come, let us pray.

The Bells of Puria.

We, too, remote and high,
From the dark mountains cry:
Hear us, O Lord!
From Spirits of Evil,
From Death and the Devil,
Keep us, O Lord, night and day!
Come, let us pray!

Echoes from the Valley.

Come, let us pray!

[1] Fogazzaro was born (1842) in Vicenza, but for many years has lived in Oria (Valsolda) on Lake Lugano.

THE GREAT POETS OF ITALY

All the Bells.

The light is born and dies,
    Enduring never;
Sunset follows sunrise
    Forever;
All things, O Lord, all-wise!
    Save thine Eternity,
    Are vanity.

Echoes from the Valley.

Vanity!

All the Bells.

Come, let us pray and weep,
From the heights and from the deep,
For the living, for them that sleep,
For so much sin unknown, and so much pain,
    Have mercy, Lord!
All suffering and pain,
That does not pray to Thee;
All error that in vain
Does not give way to Thee;
All love that must complain,
Yet yields no sway to Thee,
    Pardon, O Holy One!

Echoes from the Valley.

O Holy One! [1]

---

[1] Greene. Three very good books on modern Italian poetry have been published in recent years, — namely, Howells' *Italian Poets of To-day;* Greene's *Italian Lyrists of To-day,* and Sewall's *Poems of Giosuè Carducci.*

INDEX

INDEX

ACQUASPARTA, Cardinal, mission to Florence, 36.
Addison, influence on Italian literature, 259.
Adone, poem by Marini, discussion of, 255-6; influence of, 256; quotation from, 256-7.
Adrian, Pope, 96.
Æneas, 59.
Æneid, 195, 223.
Aix-la-Chapelle, Treaty of, 259.
Alberico, Vision of, 56.
Albert, Emperor, murder of, 40.
Alberti, Leon Battista, 169-70.
Albigenses, Crusade against, 12.
Aleardi, Aleardo, 309.
Alfieri, Vittorio, 215, 262, 286; founder of Italian tragedy, 263; life, 264; as writer of tragedies, 264 ff.; style of, 265; character of his tragedies, 265-6; his reform of Italian tragedy, 265-6; object in writing his tragedies, 266; founder of patriotism in Italian literature, 266-7; *Philip II.*, 267 ff.; and Italian Unity, 285.
Alighieri, origin of name, 30.
Alighieri, Antonia, daughter (?) of Dante, 33.
Alighieri, Beatrice, daughter of Dante, 33.
Alighieri, Dante; see Dante.

Alighieri, Jacopo, son of Dante, 33.
Alighieri, Pietro, son of Dante, 33.
Ambrogini, Angelo; see Politian.
Amicis, Edmondo de, 309.
Aminta, of Tasso, 217, 223.
Angelica, in Boiardo's *Orlando Innamorato*, 191; in Ariosto's *Orlando Furioso*, 196; falls in love with Medoro, 203, 204 ff.
Annunzio, Gabriele d', 309; discussion of, 327 ff.; sonnets by, 328-330; *Prelude*, 330; novels, 330, 331; dramas, 331 ff.; *Francesca da Rimini*, 331 ff.
Anselm, 9.
Antepurgatory, those punished in, 87.
Antoniano, Inquisitor, 219.
Apennines, 18.
Aquinas; see St. Thomas Aquinas.
Arabs, 7; in Sicily, 13.
Aretino; see Bruni, Leonardo.
Arezzo, 120, 165.
Argyropoulos, 173.
Ariosto, Ludovico, 26, 182, 188, 189, 190, 215, 217, 223, 261, 291; life of, 192, 193; his Satires, 193-4; his *Orlando Furioso*, 194 ff.; character of,

INDEX

193; death of, 193; relation of his poem to that of Boiardo, 194; his reflections on life, 213; his humor, 213.
Aristophanes, 261.
Aristotle, 14, 117, 270.
Armida, enchantress in *Jerusalem Delivered*, 236; carries off Rinaldo, 247 ff.
Arnaut, Daniel, 16.
Arnold, Matthew, 108; Sonnet on *Austerity of Poetry* (Jacopone da Todi), 24 (note); on Leopardi, 292.
Arnold of Brescia, 2.
Arthur, King, and his Round Table, 19.
Arthurian Romances, 190, 191.
A Sera, poem by Fogazzaro, 340 ff.
Augustus, age of, 182.
Avignon, 147; Petrarch settles at, 121; Papacy at, 121.
Azeglio, Massimo d', novels, 287.

BANDELLO, Matteo, 183.
Bandiera brothers, 285.
Bannerman, Anne, translator, 141.
Banquet, of Dante, 37, 43, 86 (note), 145.
Bassvilliana, of Monti, 286, 287.
Bassville, Hugon de, 286 (note).
Baudelaire, influence on Gabriele d' Annunzio, 330.
Beatrice Portinari, 17, 44 ff., 72, 128; love of Dante for, 33; death of, 51; sends Vergil to guide Dante, 59; meets Dante in "Earthly Paradise," 106; compared with Laura, 127.

Belcari, 171.
Bembo, Pietro, 184.
Beneventum, Battle of, 34, 87.
Benivieni, 171, 172.
Berni, Francesco, 183.
Bertrand de Born, seen by Dante in Hell, 73.
Biondo, Flavio, 166.
"Blacks," party in Florence, 35.
Boccaccio, Giovanni, 168, 169, 182, 183, 251; on Dante's education, 31; founder of Italian prose and of the modern novel, 146, 150; life, 145 ff.; becomes acquainted with Petrarch, 147; learns Greek, 147; admirer of Dante, 147, 148; lectures on *Divine Comedy*, 148; life of Dante and commentaries on *Divine Comedy*, 148; character of, 148 ff.; religious conversion, 149, 150; death of, 150; Latin works, 150; *Decameron*, 150 ff.; prose style, 152; his Italian poetry, 153 ff.; his popularity, 153; his influence, 153.
Böcklin, Arnold, 326.
Boëthius, 65 (note).
Bohn Library, 26 (note), 145 (note), 250 (note), 283 (note).
Boiardo, Matteo, 26, 182, 189 ff., 194, 217, 223; *Orlando Innamorato*, 183; 190 ff.
Boileau, *Le Lutrin*, 260.
Bologna, 18, 21, 27, 126; visited by Dante in exile, 39.
Bologna, University of, visited by Dante, 32; Petrarch at, 121; Tasso at, 216; Carducci at, 309.

346

INDEX

Boniface VIII., 60; claims Tuscany as heir of Countess Matilda, 36.
Botta, Carlo, historian, 288.
Bourbon, House of, in Italy, 252, 254.
Bracciolini, Poggio, 165, 166.
Browning, Robert, 113, 324; *Sordello*, 13; quotation from (*One Word More*), 51.
Brunetto Latini; see Latini, Brunetto.
Bruni, Leonardo, 165.
Buonconte da Montefeltro, post-mortem fate of body, 87 ff.
Butler, A. J., 115 (note).
Byron, 292; translator, 214 (note), 258.

CACCIAGUIDA, great-great-grandfather of Dante, 30; speaks of his ancestors, 31; prophesies Dante's exile, 37, 38, 39; seen by Dante in Paradise,109.
Cæsar, 93.
Calvo, Bonifacio, 13.
Campaldino, Battle of, 87; Dante present at, 32.
Caprona, Dante present at surrender of, 32.
Capet, Hugh, King of France, 96.
Capua, 6.
Capuana, Luigi, 309.
Carducci, Giosuè, quoted, 114; discussion of, 309 ff.; education, 309; as a professor, 309, 310,318; popularity in Italian literature, 310; as a critic, 310, 319; as a poet, 310 ff.; and Romanticism, 310, 314; difficulty of style, 311; character of, 310, 311; influence on Italian poetry, 311; likeness to Horace, 311; love for Nature, 311, 312; poem on *Sunlight and Love*, 312; *Sonnet to the Ox*, 313; poem on the *Certosa at Bologna*, 313, 314; *Ruit Hora*, 314; *Monte Mario*, 316, 317; *Sonnet on Rome*, 318; and House of Savoy, 318; as an investigator, 318; prose writings, 319; *Sonnet on the Sonnet*, 319; *Sonnet on Vergil*, 320; love for Dante, 320; *Sonnet on Dante*, 321; and United Italy, 321; Neo-Paganism of, 322; antipathy to Christianity, 322; *Pantheism*, 322, 323; *In a Gothic Church*, 323, 324; *My Lonely Bark*, 324.
Cariteo, 254.
Carlovingian romances, 188, 191.
Carlyle, Thomas, 113; *Essay on Dante* 116.
Cary, H. F., translator, 28; translation of the *Divine Comedy*, 116.
Casella, met by Dante in Purgatory, 82 ff.
Castiglione, Baldasarre, 183.
Cato, guardian of Purgatory, 81.
Cavalcanti, Guido, 27; sonnet to, by Dante, 28; answer to Dante's sonnet, 28; father of, seen by Dante, 69.
Celestine V., 60.
Cellini, Benvenuto, 183.
Cerchi, family of, 36.
Certaldo, Boccaccio dies at, 150.

INDEX

Certosa at Bologna, poem on, by Carducci, 313.
Cervantes, 213.
Chansons de Geste, influence on Italy, 25, 26; development of, in Italy, 189 ff.
Charlemagne, crowned Emperor, 7; hero of *Chansons de Geste*, 25; in *Orlando Innamarato*, 191; in *Orlando Furioso*, 195.
Charles of Anjou, 252; called to Italy by Pope Urban IV., 34; restores the Guelphs to power in Florence, 35.
Charles of Valois, called to Florence to pacify the city, 36.
Charles VI., Emperor, 122.
Charles VIII., of France, 252.
Charpentras, 121.
Chateaubriand, 292.
Chaucer, 153, 165.
Chiabrera, Gabriello, 257, 258.
Childe Harold, 258.
Chrysoloras, Johannes, 166.
Church, Dean, *Essay on Dante*, 116.
Church of Christ, symbolized in " Earthly Paradise," 106.
Ciani, Gioachino, 149.
Cicero, 4, 121.
Cimabue, 95, 117.
Cino da Pistoia, 27.
Cinzio, Cardinal, 222.
Cinzio, Giraldo, 183.
Cloridan and Medoro, episode in *Orlando Furioso*, 196 ff.
Clorinda, heroine of Tasso's *Jerusalem Delivered*, 231, 233; and Tancred, 234, 235, 241 ff.
Colonna family, 122.

Colonna, friend of Petrarch, 124.
Colonna, Vittoria, 184; Michael Angelo's sonnets on, 185–6.
Comedy, in Italy, 261.
Conrad, Emperor, made Knight of Cacciaguida, 30.
Conradin, death of, 34, 35.
Constantinople, 6, 166.
Convivio, of Dante (see *Banquet*), 43, 44.
Copernicus, 56.
Corneille, 263; influence on Italian Drama, 259; influence on Alfieri, 265.
" Counter Reformation," 253.
Countess Matilda, 36.
Crusades, 9.

DACRE, translator, 135, 136.
Dante, 7, 13, 14, 16, 17, 18, 25, 126, 145, 147, 173, 180, 186, 213, 215, 248, 251, 255, 291, 292, 310, 314, 332; influenced by Guinicelli, 21; and religious revivals, 23; sonnet to Guido Cavalcanti and Lapo, 28; sadness of his life, 29; ancestry, 30; early life, 30; family, 31; education, 31; marriage, 32; children, 33; politics and public life, 33; enters public life, 34; joins guild of physicians, 35; exiled, 37; decrees against, 37; story of his exile, 37–9; refuses amnesty, 39; letter to a friend in Florence, 39; hopes in Henry VII. of Luxemburg, 40; last refuge, 40; last days and death, 41; legends of his exile, 41; his character, 42,

INDEX

43; *Banquet*, 43; *De Monarchia*, 43, 44; *New Life*, discussion of, 44 ff.; first meeting with Beatrice, 45; sonnet on Beatrice, 47; sonnet to pilgrims after death of Beatrice, 51; *Divine Comedy*, discussion of, 54 ff.; influence on Boccaccio, 148; sonnets by Boccaccio on, 155, 156; quoted, 162; compared with Tasso, 216; and Italian Unity, 285; Carducci's love for, 320; sonnet on, by Carducci, 321.

Dante da Majano, 27.

Decameron of Boccaccio, discussion of, 150 ff.

De Monarchia of Dante, 43, 44.

Didactic poetry in North Italy, 22.

Dies Irae, 22.

Dis, City of, described, 67, 68.

Divine Comedy, 14, 17, 147, 148, 169, 213, 215; date of composition, 40; discussion of, 54 ff.; symmetrical arrangement of, 54; symbolism and allegory of, 55; outline of, 58 ff.; story of Francesca da Rimini, 63 ff.; Dante meets Brunetto Latini, 71, 72; story of Ulysses' last voyage, 74 ff.; story of Ugolino, 77 ff.; Dante meets Sordello, 89 ff.; description of "Valley of Princes," 89 ff.; description of "Earthly Paradise," 102 ff.; meeting with Beatrice, 106; ascent to Paradise, 108 ff.; characteristics of its greatness, 113, 114, 115.

"Dolce stil nuovo," 18.

Donati, Corso, 36, 108.

Donati, Gemma, marries Dante, 32, 33.

Donati, Piccarda, seen by Dante in Paradise, 108.

Don Carlos of Schiller, 267.

Don Quixote, 213.

Drama, Italian, 215; sketch of, in Italy, 261.

Dryden, 153.

Duse, Eleonora, 331.

"EARTHLY PARADISE" described, 102 ff.

Elizabeth, Queen, age of, 182.

Encyclopedias, mediæval, 10.

England visited by Dante (?), 39; influence of, on Italy, 259.

Enzo, son of Frederick II., lyric poet, 14.

Erminia, in love with Tancred, episode in *Jerusalem Delivered*, 236 ff.

Este, House of, 190, 193, 212, 258.

Este, Cardinal, 192.

Este, Duke of, 192.

Euphuism, 256.

Fabliaux, 151.

Facetiae of Poggio Bracciolini, 160.

Fairfax, translation of *Jerusalem Delivered*, mentioned, 250.

Farinata degli Uberti, seen by Dante in Hell, 69.

Fasani, 23.

Ferraro, Humanists at, 159; Boiardo at, 190; Ariosto at, 192; Tasso at, 216.

INDEX

Fiammetta, sonnets of Boccaccio on, 154.
Ficino, Marsiglio, 167, 173.
Filelfo, Francesco, 166, 167.
Filicaja, Vincenzo, sonnet on Italy, 258-9.
Firenzuola, 183.
"Flagellants," 23, 24.
Flanders, visited by Dante, 39.
Florence, becomes centre of new school, 21; early poets of, 27; building activity in, 34; political condition of, 34; Dante's love for, 39; and Petrarch, 122; Boccaccio at, 146 ff.; Humanists at, 159; Renaissance at, 163, 164 ff.; centre of Humanist movement, 163.
Fogazzaro, Antonio, 309, 339 ff.; as a novelist, 339, 340; *A Sera*, 340 ff.; *Sonnet on St. Mark's Cathedral in Venice*, 340.
Foscolo, Ugo, 285, 287, 319 (note).
France, influence on Italy, 252, 259, 284.
Francesca da Rimini, 40; story of, 63 ff.
Francesca da Rimini, drama by d' Annunzio, 331 ff.
Francis; see St. Francis.
Franco-Italian Epic, 26.
Franks, 3, 5.
Frederick II., 13, 15, 16, 34, 70, 87; as a poet, 14.
Frederick Barbarossa, 34.
Free cities, rise of, 7; increased power of, 9.
French language, origin of, 5.
French Revolution, in Italy, 286, 287.

French romances, influence on Italian literature, 25, 26.

GAMBARA, VERONICA, 184.
Garibaldi, 254, 285.
Garnett, *History of Italian Literature*, 180.
Gaspary, 26 (note).
Gaul, 5.
Geibel, Emanuel, 263.
Genoa, 7, 13; Renaissance at, 163.
German emperors, contest with popes, 9.
Germany, 7; visited by Dante, 39; influence on Italy, 259.
Ghibellines, 33, 35, 284.
Gian della Bella, decree of, 35.
Gioberti, Vincenzo, 288.
Giotto, 95, 117.
Giusti, Giuseppe, satirist, 287.
Giustiniani, Lionardo, 171.
Gladstone, W. E., 32, 113, 292.
Goethe, 77, 190; influence on Italian literature, 259.
Goldoni, Carlo, 215, 259, 261, 262.
Gongorism, 256.
Gonzaga, Margaret, marries the Duke of Este, 221.
Gonzaga, Prince Vincenzo, 221.
Gothic Church, In a, poem by Carducci, 323, 324.
Goths, 2, 6, 284.
Graf, Arturo, 309, 325 ff.; *The Depth and the End*, 326; *Mors Regina*, 326, 327.
Gray, influence on Italian literature, 259.
Greek, Boccaccio and the study of, 147.

INDEX

Greene, translator, 315, 317, 320, 326, 328, 330; *Italian Lyrists of To-day*, 342 (note).
Gregory VII., 8, 9, 94.
Guarini, 182; *Pastor Fido*, 153.
Guelphs, 33, 284.
Guerrazzi, Francesco Domenico, novels, 287.
Guerrini, Olindo, 309.
Guicciardini, 183.
Guinicelli, Guido, 27, 45, 126; poem on *Love and the Gentle Heart*, 19, 20; life and works, 18; follower of Guittone d' Arrezzo, 18; and new conception of love, 18; influence on Dante, 21; makes love spiritual, 21; seen by Dante in Purgatory, 97.
Guittone d' Arrezzo, 18; literary ancestor of Dante, 16; leader of early Tuscan School, 16; life and works, 16, 17; *Sonnet to the Virgin Mary*, 17.

HAPSBURG, House of, in Italy, 252, 254.
Heine, 325.
Hell, location and shape of, 57.
Henry III. of England, 90.
Henry VII. of Luxemburg, 54; comes to Italy, 40; Dante's hopes in, 40; death of, 40.
Hermaphroditus, of Panormita, 160.
Heyse, Paul, 327.
Hohenstauffens, 15, 34.
Holy Roman Empire, 158.
Homer, quoted by Dante, 45; in Limbo, 61; Boccaccio and, 147.

Horace, Dante's knowledge of, 32; influence on Carducci, 311, 314.
Howells, William D., translator, 295, 308; *Italian Poets of To-day*, 342 (note).
Hugo, Victor, influence on Gabriele d' Annunzio, 330.
Humanism, definition of, 157, 158, 160; at Rome, 163; at Florence, 163.
Humanists, 158, 159, 160, 171; moral and religious character of, 160, 161; and Latin language, 169.
Huns, 6, 8, 284.
Hunt, Leigh, translator, 133; *Stories from the Italian Poets*, 214 (note).

ILARIO, FRA, 41.
Iliad, 195, 223.
Innocent VI., Pope, 147.
Inquisition, 253.
I Promessi Sposi of Manzoni, 289.
Italian language, earliest examples of, 5, 6.
Italian literature, origins of, 1 ff.; recent origin of, 1; lack of originality, 11; Provençal influence on, 11; condition of, in the 17th and 18th centuries, 254 ff.
Italian nation, origin of, 3, 4.
Italy, sonnet on, by Filicaja, 258; troubadours in, 12; history of, in 16th and 17th centuries, 252 ff.; condition of, under Spanish rule, 253; unity of, 285; poem on, by Leopardi,

INDEX

293, 294, 295; Carducci's love for, 317, 318.

JACOBS, JOSEPH, *Stories from the Decameron*, 153 (note).
Jacopone da Todi, story of his conversion, 24.
Jeremiah, quotation from, 51.
Jerusalem Delivered, 182, 195, 219, 223; story of, 224 ff.; Sophronia and Olindo, 226 ff.; Erminia, 236 ff.; Tancred and Clorinda, 234, 235, 241 ff.; Armida and Rinaldo, 247 ff.
Jesuits, 253, 254, 259; teachers of Tasso, 216, 219.
John, King of France, 122.
Julius II., Pope, and the Renaissance. 163.

KEATS, JOHN, 153, 319.
Klopstock, influence on Italian literature, 259.
Knights of St. Mary, 16.
Kraus, F. X., 113.

LAMARTINE, ALPHONSE DE, 292, 309.
Lanfranc, 9.
Lapo Gianni, 27; sonnet to, by Dante, 28.
Latin language, two forms of, 4; long continuance of, in Italy, 6; language of the Church, 9.
Latin literature, in Italy during Middle Ages, 9, 10, 11; in 15th century, 168, 169.
Latin races, origin of, 3.
Latini, Brunetto, his *Tresor*, 31; met by Dante in Hell, 71.

Laudi, 23, 24, 25, 171, 172.
Launcelot, 65.
Laura de Noves, 186; dies, 124; treatment of, in Petrarch's poetry, 127; life of, 128; sonnets on, by Petrarch, 129 ff.
Laurentian Library, Florence, 165.
Leo III., Pope, crowns Charlemagne emperor, 7.
Leo X., Pope, and Renaissance, 163.
Leontius Pilatus, professor of Greek at Florence, 147.
Leopardi, Giacomo, 288, 310, 325; discussion of, 285 ff.; life, 289 ff.; ill health, 289 ff.; as a classical scholar, 290; wanderings of, 291; death, 291; philosophy of, 292; pessimism of, 292 ff.; as a poet, 293 ff.; poem on *Italy*, 293–5; desire for love, 295 ff.; poem on *Silvia*, 296 ff.; love for Nature, 298; poem on the *Setting of the Moon*, 298 ff.; poem on the *Infinite*, 299, 300; *Night Chant of a Nomad Asiatic Shepherd*, 300 ff.; *Sappho's Last Song*, 305 ff.; poem to *Himself*, 308.
Leopardi, Count Monaldo, father of Giacomo, 289.
Limbo, kind of souls in, 61.
Lisle, Leconte de, 312.
Livy, 119.
Lloyd, Charles, translator, 283.
Lofft, Capel, translator, 129.
Lombards, 2, 3, 6, 7, 284.
Lombardy, 3.
Longfellow, H. W., 113, 153,

INDEX

250; quotations from, 29, 41; translator, 116, 187.
Louis XIV., age of, 182.
Love, conventional conception of, in Provençal and Sicilian poetry, 14; new conception of, in Italian poetry, 17, 18; becomes spiritualized in Guinicelli, 21.
Lowell, J. R., 113; quoted, 114; *Essay on Dante*, 116.
Lucan, in Limbo, 61.
Lucia, 92.
Lucifer, 57, 80, 95.
Ludovico il Moro, 252.
Lunigiana, visited by Dante in exile, 39.

MACAULAY, LORD, 258.
Macgregor, translator, 130, 131, 134, 137, 138, 145.
Machiavelli, Niccolò, 183; *Mandragora* of, 261.
Maffei, Scipio, his *Merope*, 264.
"Malebolge," 73.
Manfred, 34; death of, 87.
Manzoni, Alessandro, 264; *I Promessi Sposi*, 287; dramas, 287; discussion of, 288, 289.
Margarita, Queen of Italy, friend of Carducci, 310.
Marini, Giovanni Battista, 255 ff.
Marinism, 256.
Marsigli, Luigi, 164, 165.
Martin, Sir Theodore, translator, 289, 299, 300, 305, 307.
Matilda, 107.
Mazzini, Giuseppe, 285, 288, 293.
Medici family, 188.
Medici, Cosimo de', 165, 167, 179.

Medici, Giuliano de', 175.
Medici, Lorenzo de', 170, 171, 173, 189, 252; life, 179; as a poet, 180, 182.
Medici, Piero de', 179.
Medoro; see Cloridan and Medora.
Medoro, wins the love of Angelica, 203, 204.
Merope, of Maffei, 264.
Metastasio, Pietro, 262, 263; his musical dramas, 262, 263.
Metellus, 93.
Michael Angelo, 184 ff.
Middle Ages, difference between, and the modern world, 117, 118.
Milton, John, 57, 292; influence on Italian literature, 259.
Minos, judge in Hell, 63.
Molière, 261; influence on Goldoni, 259, 262.
Monnier, *Le Quattrocento*, 255 (note).
Montaperti, battle of, 35, 69; poem on, by Guittone d' Arezzo, 16.
Montecassino, 109.
Monte Corvo, 41.
Monte Mario, poem by Carducci, 316, 317.
Montepulciano, birth-place of Politian, 173.
Monti, Vincenzo, 286, 287.
Montpellier, University of, Petrarch at, 121.
Morgante, poem by Pulci, 189.
Murrone, Peter; see Celestine V.

NAPLES, Boccaccio at, 146; Renaissance at, 163, 164; Uni-

353

INDEX

versity of, founded by Frederick II., 14.
Napoleon, Vincenzo Monti and, 287; ode on his death by Monti, 289.
Nardi, 183.
Negri, Ada, 309, 327.
Neo-Paganism, of Carducci, 322.
New Learning, 147.
New Life, of Dante, 14, 28, 42, 55, 145; story of, 44 ff.; final words of, 52.
Niccoli, Niccolò, 165.
Niccolini, Giovanni Battista, 287.
Nicholas V., Pope, 163, 166.
Niebuhr, on Leopardi, 290.
Night Chant of a Nomad Asiatic Shepherd, poem by Leopardi, 300 ff.
Niobe, 95.
Normans, 2, 3, 6, 284.
Northern France, troubadours in, 12.
Northern Italy, share in indigenous lyric poetry, 21; religious and didactic poetry, 22.
Norton, C. E., translator of *Divine Comedy*, 116.
Nott, translator, 140, 142.
Novellino, 151.
Noves; see Laura.
Noves, Audebert de, father of Petrarch's Laura, 128.

ODERISI of Adubbio, 95.
Odi Barbare of Carducci, Contest over, 311.
Old French, 1.
Ongaro, Francesco dall', 308.
Orfeo, of Politian, 175.

Orlando Furioso, of Ariosto, 215; analysis of, 195; episode of Cloridan and Medoro, 196 ff.; madness of Orlando, 204 ff.; death of Zerbino, 208 ff.; charm of, 212, 213; represents Renaissance, 213; style of, 213.
Orlando Innamorato, of Boiardo, discussion of, 190 ff.
Ossian, influence on Italian literature, 259.
Ostrogoths, 3.
Othello, 270.
Ovid, 119; *Ars Amatoria*, symbolical interpretation of, 11.
Ox, Sonnet on, by Carducci, 313.
Oxford, visited by Dante (?), 32.

PADUA, University of, visited by Dante, 32, 39; Tasso at, 216.
Panormita, 164.
Pantheism, poem by Carducci, 322, 323.
Paradise, location and description of, 107 ff.
Paradise Lost, 195.
Parini, Giuseppe, 260, 261.
Paris, visited by Dante (?), 32, 39; and Petrarch, 123; Boccaccio born in, 146.
Patriotism, lack of, in Italy, 8; in Italian literature, 286, 287, 288.
Pellico, Silvio, 288.
Pescara, birth-place of d' Annunzio, 328.
Pest, described in *Decameron*, 151; Laura dies of, 128.
Peter of Aragon, 90.

INDEX

Peter Damian, 9, 109.
Peter Lombard, 9.
Petrarch, Francesco, 168, 169, 173, 180, 182, 184, 186, 193, 222, 251, 254, 255, 291, 310; begins movement of Renaissance, 119; life of, 120 ff.; education, 121; Latin works of, 125, 126; friends, 122; crowned poet at Rome, 123; happy life, 123; melancholy, 123; strange contrast in character, 124, 137; death of, 125; *Africa*, 125; lyrical poetry of, 126 ff.; Italian poetry, 127 ff.; sonnets to Laura in life, 129 ff.; sonnets to Laura in death, 138 ff.; Latin letters, translation of, 145 (note); indifferent to Dante, 147; followers of, 164.
Petrarchism, 184.
Petroni, Pietro de', Carthusian monk, 149.
Philip II. of Alfieri, discussed, 267, 268; quoted, 268 ff.
Philip III. of France, 90.
Pico della Mirandola, 167.
Pier delle Vigne, 14; seen by Dante in Hell, 70.
Pierre Vidal, troubadour, in Italy, 12.
Pistoia, the "Whites" and the "Blacks" emigrate from, 35, 36.
Pius II., Pope, 166.
Plautus, 261.
Plotinus, 290.
Polenta, Guido da, visited by Dante, 40.
Politian, 169, 170, 171, 180; as a scholar, 167, 168; as a poet, 173; life, 173; *Dance Song*, 174, 175.
Political poetry, in Tuscan School, 16.
Pontano, 164.
Pope, Alexander, *Rape of the Lock*, 260; influence on Italian literature, 259.
Pope, temporal power of, and Carducci, 318.
Portinari; see Beatrice.
Portinari, Folco, 44.
Porto, Luigi da, 183.
Prati, Giovanni, 309.
Preciosity, 256.
Provençal, 1, 2, 11-15, 25.
Provence, 11; destruction of its prosperity, 12.
Ptolemaic system, 56, 117.
Pulci, Luigi, 26, 188, 189, 214.
Purgatory, 13, 16; location and shape, 57, 80.

QUADRIVIUM, 32.

RACINE, influence on Italian drama, 259; influence on Alfieri, 265.
Rambaud de Vaqueiras, in Italy, 12.
Rapagnetta, Gaetano; see Annunzio, G. d'.
Raphael, 188.
Ravenna, 33, 102 (note), 147.
Reformation, 158, 252.
Religious literature in northern Italy, 22.
Religious revivals in Italy, 22, 23.
Renaissance, 157 ff., 182; begun

INDEX

by Petrarch, 119; Petrarch's influence on, 126; definition of, 157; difference between, and the spirit of the Middle Ages, 160 ff.; accomplishment of, in 15th century, 168; reaches its climax in 16th century, 188; reflected in Ariosto, 213; decline of, 251, 252; moral character of, 252.

Revival of Learning, 157; definition of, 158.

Rienzi, Cola di, 2, 124.

Rinaldo of Tasso, 223.

Rinaldo and Armida, story of, in *Jerusalem Delivered*, 247 ff.

Risorgimento, 285, 286; Carducci and, 310.

Robert, King of Naples, 122.

Romagna, Province of, 18.

Romance languages, 13; origin of, 4, 5.

Roman Church, and Carducci, 322.

Roman civilization, degradation of, 8.

Romanticism, in Italy, 288; opposed by Carducci, 311; hatred of, by Carducci, 316.

Rome, downfall of, 3; Petrarch crowned poet at, 123; Petrarch makes pilgrimage to, 136; Renaissance at, 163, 164; sonnet on, by Carducci, 318.

Roscoe, Thomas, translator, 179, 257.

Rose, translator of Ariosto, 197 ff.

Rossetti, Dante G., translator, 17, 19, 154; *Dante and His Circle*, 26 (note); translation of *New Life*, 116.

Rossetti, Gabriel, commentary on *Divine Comedy*, 288.

Rossetti, Maria, *A Shadow of Dante*, 115.

Rudolph, Emperor of Germany, 90.

Ruit Hora, poem by Carducci, 314.

Ruskin, John, 113; quoted, 87.

SACHETTI, FRANCO, 183 (note).

"Sacred Representations," 171.

Sade, Ugo de, husband of Petrarch's Laura, 128.

Sainte-Beuve, on Leopardi, 292.

Salutato, Coluccio, 164, 165.

Sannazaro, 182; *Arcadia*, 153; influence of, 254.

Santa Croce, church of, in Florence, 34; monastery of, 41.

Santo Spirito, church of, in Florence, 164.

Santo Stephano, church of, in Florence, 148.

Sappho's Last Song, poem by Leopardi, 305 ff.

Saracens, 6, 8, 284.

Savoy, House of, 285, 318.

Scala, Bartolommeo della, 39.

Scartazzini, *Companion to Dante*, 115.

Schiller, *Don Carlos*, 267.

Scipio Africanus, 125.

Serafino, 255 (note).

Setting of the Moon, poem by Leopardi, 298 ff.

Seven Wise Men, 151.

Sewall, Frank, translator, 312; *Poems of Giosuè Carducci*, 342.

INDEX

Sforza, Galeazzo, 175.
Shelley, 220; translator of sonnet to Cavalcanti, 28.
Shakespeare, 153, 255, 270.
Sicilian dialect, 5, 15; poets, first to write in Italian, 14; poetry, 14, 24; school of poetry, 15, 17, 18, 271.
Sicily, 3, 4, 7, 126; civilization under Frederick, 13.
Sidney, Sir Philip, 183.
Silvia, poem by Leopardi, 296 ff.
Selve, poem by Lorenzo de' Medici, 180–182.
Sismondi, *Literature of the South of Europe*, 179 (note), 257 (note).
Sofonisba, drama by Trissino, 263.
Sonnet, sonnet on, by Carducci, 319.
Sophronia and Olindo, episode in *JerusalemDelivered*, 226 ff.
Sordello, 13; met by Dante in Purgatory, 89 ff.
Sorrento, Tasso born at, 216; Tasso returns to, 220; attacked by Turks, 223.
Spain, 3; troubadours in, 12; end of rule of, in Italy, 259.
Spaniards in Italy, 252, 253, 284.
Speculum Majus, 10.
Spenser, Edmund, 183.
Stabat Mater, 25.
Stampa, Gaspara, 184.
Stanzas of Politian, 175, 179.
Statius, 119; seen by Dante in Purgatory, 96 ff.
St. Anna, Asylum of, Tasso in, 221.
St. Benedict, 109.

St. Bernard, quoted, 161.
St. Bonaventura, 10; seen by Dante in Paradise, 109.
St. Brandon, Voyage of, 56.
St. Clement, church of, 6.
St. Dominic, story of, 109.
Stecchetti, Lorenzo; see Guerrini, Olindo.
St. Francis of Assisi, 22, 108.
St. James, 112.
St. John, 112.
St. Mark's Cathedral, Venice, sonnet on, by Fogazzaro, 340.
St. Onofrio, monastery of, Tasso dies in, 222.
St. Paul, 59, 124.
St. Peter, 112.
St. Thomas Aquinas, 10, 117; seen by Dante in Paradise, 108.
Sunlight and Love, poem by Carducci, 312.
Swabia, House of, 34.
Symbolism in literature, 10, 11.
Symonds, J. A., *Introduction to Dante*, 115 (note); translator, 170, 172, 175, 182; on the Renaissance, 187; quoted, 254.
Symons, Arthur, translator, 335.

TANCRED and Clorinda, episode in *Jerusalem Delivered*, 234, 235, 241 ff.
Tasso, Torquato, 182, 190, 251, 291; life of, 216 ff.; education, 216; insanity of, 217 ff.; legend of his love for Leonora d' Este, 218, 219; wanderings of, 220 ff.; in Rome, 222; death of, 222; works, 222 ff.; *Aminta*, 153, 217, 223; *Torris-*

INDEX

mondo, 223; *Jerusalem Delivered*, story of, 223 ff.
Taylor, J. B., translator, 130, 186.
Tebaldeo, 255.
Tennyson, Lord, 113, 153; quoted, 42.
Terence, 261.
Testi, Fulvio, 258.
Thackeray, W. M., 214.
Theodoric, 3.
Tholuck, 113.
Thomas of Celano, follower of St. Francis, 22.
Torrismondo of Tasso, 223.
Tragedy, in Italy, 263 ff.
Trajan, story of his justice, 94 ff.
Trissino, *Sofonisba*, 263.
Triumphs of Petrarch, 128.
Trivium, 32.
Troubadours, 11, 12, 21, 27, 126; imitated by North Italian poets, 12; influence in Sicily, 14; conception of love, 18; Italian, 13; spiritual, of St. Francis, 22.
Tugdale, Vision of, 56.
Tuscan dialect, 5, 15; poetry, 24; school of poets, 15, 16.
Tuscany, becomes centre of early Italian poetry, 15; disorders of, in Dante's time, 33.

UGOLINO DELLA GHERARDESCA, story of, 77 ff.
Ulysses, 248; story of his last voyage, 74 ff.
Umbria, home of St. Francis, 22.
Urban II., Pope, buried at Sorrento, 224.

Urban VI., Pope, 122; calls Charles of Anjou to Italy, 34.

VALDICASTELLO, birth-place of Carducci, 309.
Valla, Lorenzo, 164, 169.
"Valley of Princes," scene in, 89 ff.
Vandals, 3.
Varchi, 183.
Vasari, Giorgio, 183.
Vaucluse, 125, 141; Petrarch at, 122.
Venetian dialect, 5.
Venice, 7, 13; Dante's embassy to, 41; and Petrarch, 122; Renaissance at, 163.
Vergil, 4, 11, 32, 119, 121; sent by Beatrice to guide Dante, 59; sonnet on, by Carducci, 320.
Verlaine, Paul, 314.
Verona, first place visited by Dante in exile, 39.
Victor Emanuel, 286.
Villani, on Dante's education, 31.
Vincent of Beauvais, 10.
Visigoths, 3.
Volkspoesie, Italian, in 15th century, 170.
Voltaire, 261, 263; influence on Italian drama, 259.
"Vulgar Latin," 4, 5.

WASHINGTON, GEORGE, 266 (note).
Weimar, 190.
"Weltschmerz," 127, 288, 292.
"Whites," party of Florence, 35; banished, 36, 37.

INDEX

Wiffen, translator of *Jerusalem Delivered*, 224 ff.
Witte, 113.
Wollaston, translator, 142.
" Wood of Suicides," 70.
Woodhouselee, translator, 141.
Wordsworth, 319; quoted, 159.
Wrangham, translator, 136, 139, 140.

Wrottesley, translator, 132.

YOUNG, influence on Italian literature, 259.
"Young Italy," 288.

ZERBINO, death of, episode in *Orlando Furioso*, 208 ff.
Zorzi, Bartolomeo, 13.